T0281721

Python for SAS Users

A SAS-Oriented Introduction to Python

Randy Betancourt
Sarah Chen

Apress®

Python for SAS Users: A SAS-Oriented Introduction to Python

Randy Betancourt
Chadds Ford, PA, USA

Sarah Chen
Livingston, NJ, USA

ISBN-13 (pbk): 978-1-4842-5000-6
https://doi.org/10.1007/978-1-4842-5001-3

ISBN-13 (electronic): 978-1-4842-5001-3

Managing Director, Apress Media LLC: Welmoed Spahr
Acquisitions Editor: Susan McDermott
Development Editor: Laura Berendson
Coordinating Editor: Rita Fernando

Cover designed by eStudioCalamar

Cover image designed by Freepik (www.freepik.com)

Distributed to the book trade worldwide by Springer Science+Business Media New York, 233 Spring Street, 6th Floor, New York, NY 10013. Phone 1-800-SPRINGER, fax (201) 348-4505, e-mail orders-ny@springer-sbm.com, or visit www.springeronline.com. Apress Media, LLC is a California LLC and the sole member (owner) is Springer Science + Business Media Finance Inc (SSBM Finance Inc). SSBM Finance Inc is a **Delaware** corporation.

For information on translations, please e-mail rights@apress.com, or visit http://www.apress.com/rights-permissions.

Apress titles may be purchased in bulk for academic, corporate, or promotional use. eBook versions and licenses are also available for most titles. For more information, reference our Print and eBook Bulk Sales web page at http://www.apress.com/bulk-sales.

Any source code or other supplementary material referenced by the author in this book is available to readers on GitHub via the book's product page, located at www.apress.com/9781484250006. For more detailed information, please visit http://www.apress.com/source-code.

Printed on acid-free paper

Table of Contents

About the Authors

Randy Betancourt's professional career has been in and around data analysis. His journey began by managing a technical support group supporting over 2000 technical research analysts and scientists from the US Environmental Protection Agency at one of the largest mainframe complexes run by the federal government. He moved to Duke University, working for the administration, to analyze staff resource utilization and costs. There, he was introduced to the politics of data access as the medical school had most of the data and computer resources.

He spent the majority of his career at SAS Institute Inc. in numerous roles, starting in marketing and later moving into field enablement and product management. He subsequently developed the role for Office of the CTO consultant.

Randy traveled the globe meeting with IT and business leaders discussing the impact of data analysis to drive their business. And they also discussed challenges they faced. At the same time, he talked to end users, wanting to hear their perspective. Together, these experiences shaped his understanding of trade-offs that businesses make allocating scarce resources to data collection, analysis, and deployment of models.

More recently, he has worked as independent consultant for firms including the International Institute for Analytics, Microsoft's SQL Server Group, and Accenture's Applied Intelligence Platform.

Sarah Chen has 12 years of analytics experience in banking and insurance, including personal auto pricing, compliance, surveillance, and fraud analytics, sales analytics, credit risk modeling for business, and regulatory stress testing. She is a Fellow of both the Casualty Actuarial Society and the Society of Actuaries (FCAS, FSA), an actuary, data scientist, and innovator.

Sarah's career began with five and a half years at Verisk Analytics in the Personal Auto Actuarial division, building predictive models for various ISO products. At Verisk she learned and honed core skills in data analysis and data management.

Her skills and domain expertise were broadened when she moved to KPMG, working with leading insurers, banks, and large online platforms on diverse business and risk management problems.

From 2014 to present, Sarah has been working at HSBC bank on wholesale credit risk models. She has experiences in PD, LGD, and EAD models in commercial real estate, commercial and industrial banks, and non-bank financial institution portfolios. She has been active in innovations within the organization.

Over the years, she has used many analytics tools including R and SAS and Python.

Sarah graduated summa cum laude with BA in Mathematics from Columbia University in 2007. She is the founder of Magic Math Mandarin, a school that emphasizes values and tomorrow's skills for children.

About the Technical Reviewers

Ferrell Drewry wrote his first SAS program in 1977 and has continued to use SAS software throughout his 30-year career in the pharmaceutical industry that includes experience managing data management, programming, biostatistics, and information technology departments. Today, Ferrell works as a SAS programmer and manager (in that order) on phase II/III clinical trials.

Ferrell holds a BS in Accounting from the University of Northern Colorado and an MS in Business Administration with a concentration in Management Information Sciences from Colorado State University.

Ferrell lives on the southeastern North Carolina coast where he enjoys being close to his grandchildren, surfing, fishing, and tinkering with his Raspberry Pi (almost in that order).

Travis E. Oliphant is the Founder and CEO/CTO of Quansight, an innovation incubation company that builds and connects companies with open source communities to help gain actionable, quantitative insight from their data. Travis previously co-founded Anaconda, Inc. and is still a Director. Since 1997, he has worked in the Python ecosystem, notably as the primary creator of the NumPy package and as a founding contributor of the SciPy package. Travis also started the Numba project and organized and led the teams that built Conda, Dask, Bokeh, and XND. Travis holds a PhD from the Mayo Clinic and BS and MS in Mathematics and Electrical Engineering from Brigham Young University.

Acknowledgments

As this project developed, there are a number of individuals whose contributions and insights were invaluable. Alan Churchill provided many suggestions used to form the introduction and provided sound advice on how to effectively write the SAS and Python examples. Soon Tan, CEO of Ermas, and Kit Chaksuvej, Senior Technical Consultant at Ermas, provided ideas for improving the source code examples. Tom Weber provided detailed feedback on Chapter 8, "SASPy Module." Tom has been with SAS Institute's R&D for 31 years and recently co-authored "SASPy, a Python interface to Base SAS," available on GitHub.

We were fortunate to have Randy's former boss at SAS Institute, Ferrell Drewry, generously agree to review all of the SAS code and related content. He is an outstanding SAS programmer. Ferrell's meticulous attention to detail helped us tremendously.

And in another piece of good fortune, we received a great deal of benefit by having Travis Oliphant as a technical reviewer for the Python sections of the book. Not only was he generous with his time by providing detailed input, Travis' experiences with Python gave us insights into how the language is constructed. His commitment to the open source development community is a genuine inspiration.

We also want to acknowledge the great support from the Apress Media team we collaborated with. Susan McDermott, Senior Editor, helped us by navigating us through the process of book writing. We sincerely appreciate Susan's enthusiasm and encouragements, and Rita Fernando, coordinating editor, whose steady guidance helped to keep us on track and was always available to offer us assistance when we needed it.

Finally, a personal acknowledgment from Randy to his wife Jacqueline and sons Ethan and Adrian who were enthusiastic supporters from the very beginning of this project.

Introduction

For decades, Base SAS software has been the "gold standard" for data manipulation and analysis. The software can read any data source and is superb at transforming and shaping data for analysis. It has been the beneficiary of enormous resource investments over its lifetime. The company has one of the industry's most innovative R&D staff, and its products are well supported by an outstanding technical support and well documented by very capable technical writers. SAS Institute Inc. has remained focused on gathering customer input and building desired features. All of these characteristics help explain its popularity.

Since the beginning of this millennium, the accelerated growth of open source software has produced outstanding projects offering data scientists enormous capabilities to tackle problems that were previously considered outside the realm of feasibility. Chief among these is Python. Python has its heritage in scientific and technical computing domains and has a very compact syntax. It is a full-featured language that is relatively easy to learn and is able to scale offering good performance with large data volumes. This is one of the reasons why firms like Netflix[1] use it so extensively.

By nature, SAS users are intrepid and are constantly trying to find new ways to expand the use of the software in pursuit of meeting business objectives. And given the extensive role of SAS within organizations, it only makes sense to find ways to combine the capabilities of these two languages to complement one another.

We have four main goals for our readers. The first is to provide a quick start to learning Python for users already familiar with the SAS language.

Both languages have advantages and disadvantages when it comes to a particular task. And since they are programming languages, their designers had to make certain trade-offs which can manifest themselves as features or quirks, depending on one's perspective. This is our second goal: help readers compare and contrast common tasks taking into account differences in their default behaviors. For example, SAS names are

---

[1]Python at Netflix, at https://medium.com/netflix-techblog/python-at-netflix-bba45dae649e

INTRODUCTION

case-insensitive, while Python names are case-sensitive. Or the default sort sequence for the pandas library is the opposite of SAS' default sort sequence and so on.

Rather than attempting to promote one language over the other, our third goal is to point out the integration points between the two languages. The choice of which tool to utilize for a given task typically comes down to a combination of what you as a user are familiar with and the context of the problem being solved. Knowing both languages enlarges the set of tools you can apply for the task at hand.

And finally, our fourth goal is to develop working examples for all of the topics in both Python and SAS which allows you the opportunity to "try out" the examples by not just executing them but by extending them to suit your own needs.

We assume you already have some basic knowledge of Python, for example, you already know how to import modules and execute Python scripts. If you don't, then you will want to spend more time with Chapter 1, "Introduction," covering topics such as Python installation, executing Python in a Windows environment, and executing Python in a Linux environment.

In Chapter 2, "Python Types and Formatting," we cover topics related to the Python Standard Library such as data types, Booleans with a focus on truth testing, numerical and string manipulations, and basic formatting. If you are new to Python, then it is worthwhile to spend time on this chapter practicing execution of the Python and SAS examples.

If you have a solid grasp of Python Standard Library, you can skip to Chapter 3, "pandas Library." Beyond introducing you to DataFrames, we deal with the missing data problem endemic to any analysis task. The understanding of the pandas library underpins the remainder of the book.

Chapter 4, "Indexing and Grouping," extends your knowledge of the pandas library by focusing on DataFrame indexing and GroupBy operations. A detailed understanding of these operations is essential for shaping data. We end this chapter by introducing techniques you can use for report production.

Data manipulation such as merging, concatenation, subsetting, updating, appending, sorting, finding duplicates, drawing samples, and transposing are covered in Chapter 5. We have developed scores of examples in both Python and SAS to address and illustrate the range of problems you commonly face in preparing data for analysis.

In Chapter 6, "pandas Readers," we cover many of the popular readers and writers used to read and write data from a range of different sources including Excel, .csv files, relational databases, JSON, web APIs, and more. And while we offer detailed explanations, it is the numerous working examples you can use in your own work that make this chapter so valuable.

Working with date, datetime, time, and time zone is the focus in Chapter 7. In this increasingly instrumented world we live in, we are faced with processing time-based data from literally trillions of sensors. Forming and appropriately handling time Series data is no longer just the domain for time-based forecasting. Once again, we rely on the breadth of the provided examples to help you improve your skills.

In our last chapter, we introduce and discuss SASPy, the open source library from SAS Institute used to expose a Python interface to Base SAS software. The provided examples focus on building useful pipelines where the strengths of both languages come together in a single program to accomplish common data analysis tasks. This integration point between SAS and Python offers an enormous range of possibilities limited only by your imagination.

We hope you enjoy this book as much as we enjoyed putting it together!

Feedback

We would love to receive your feedback. Tell us what you liked, what you didn't like, and provide suggestions for improvements. You can go to our web site, `www.pythonforsasusers.com`, where you can find all of the examples from this book, get updated examples, and provide us feedback.

CHAPTER 1

Why Python?

There are plenty of substantive open source software projects out there for data scientists, so why Python?[1] After all, there is the R language. R is a robust and well-supported language written initially by statistician for statisticians. Our view is not to promote one language over the other. The goal is to illustrate how the addition of Python to the SAS user's toolkit is a means for valuable skills augmentation. Besides, Bob Muenchen has already written *R for SAS and SPSS Users.*[2]

Python is used in a wide range of computing applications from web and internet development to scientific and numerical analysis. Its pedigree from the realm of scientific and technical computing domains gives the language a natural affinity for data analysis. This is one of the reasons why Google uses it so extensively and has developed an outstanding tutorial for programmers.[3]

Perhaps the best answer as to why Python is best expressed in the *Zen of Python*, written by Tim Peters.[4] While these are design principles used to influence the development of a language like Python, they apply (mostly) to our own efforts. These aphorisms are worth bookmarking and re-reading periodically.

---

[1]Python is an open source language promoted, protected, and advanced by the Python Software Foundation: `https://www.python.org/psf/`. It is currently developed on GitHub

[2]Muenchen, Robert A, (2011). R for SAS and SPSS Users, 2nd Edition.

[3]Google's Python Class at `https://developers.google.com/edu/python/`

[4]PEP 20—The Zen of Python at `www.python.org/dev/peps/pep-0020/`

© Randy Betancourt, Sarah Chen 2019
R. Betancourt and S. Chen, *Python for SAS Users*, https://doi.org/10.1007/978-1-4842-5001-3_1

Setting Up a Python Environment

One of the first questions a new Python user is confronted with is which version to use, Python 2 or Python 3. For this writing we used Python 3.6.4 (Version 3.6, Maintenance 4). The current release of Python is 3.7.2, released on December 24, 2018. Python release 3.8.0 is expected in November 2019. As with any language, minor changes in syntax occur as the developers make feature improvements and Python is no exception. We have chosen Python 3.6 since this was the latest release as time of writing and the release of 3.7 has not impacted any of the chapters. You can read more about the differences between Python 2 and Python 3.[5]

An attractive feature for Python is the availability of community-contributed modules. Python comes with a base library or core set of modules, referred to as the Standard Library. Due to Python's design, individuals and organizations contribute to the creation of thousands of additional modules which are mostly written in Python. Interested in astronomical calculations used to predict any planet's location in space? Then the kplr package is what you need.[6] Closer to home, we will utilize the Python-dateutil 2.7.3 package to extend Python's base capabilities for handling datetime arithmetic.[7]

Just as you can configure your SAS development environment in numerous ways, the same is true for Python. And while there are various implementations of Python, such as Jython, IronPython, and PyPy to make life simpler, organizations package distributions for you so you can avoid having to understand dependencies or using build scripts to assemble a custom environment. At the time of this writing, we are using the Anaconda distribution 5.2.0 for Windows 10 located at Anaconda's distribution page at `www.anaconda.com/download/`.

The Anaconda distribution of Python also supports OSX and Linux. They conveniently take care of all the details for you by providing familiar tools for installing, uninstalling, upgrading, determining package dependencies, and so on. But they do much more than just make a convenient distribution. They provide detailed documentation, support a community of enthusiastic users, and offer a supported enterprise product around the free distribution.

---

[5]Should I use Python 2 or Python 3 for my development activity? at `https://wiki.python.org/moin/Python2orPython3`

[6]kplr: A Python interface to the Kepler data at `http://dfm.io/kplr/`

[7]Python-dateutil 2.7.3 at `https://pypi.org/project/python-dateutil/`

Anaconda3 Install Process for Windows

The following text describes the steps for installing a new version of Python 3.6. If you have an existing version already installed, you can either uninstall the older version or follow the instructions for managing multiple Python installs at `https://conda.io/docs/user-guide/tasks/manage-python.html`.

1. From `www.anaconda.com/download/` download the Anaconda3-5.2.0 for Windows Installer for Python 3.6. Select the 32-bit or 64-bit installer (depending on your Windows machine architecture).

2. From this download location on your machine, you should see the file Anaconda3-5.2.0-Windows-x86-64.exe (assuming your Windows machine is 64-bit) for launching the Windows Installer.

3. Launch the Windows Installer (see Figure 1-1).

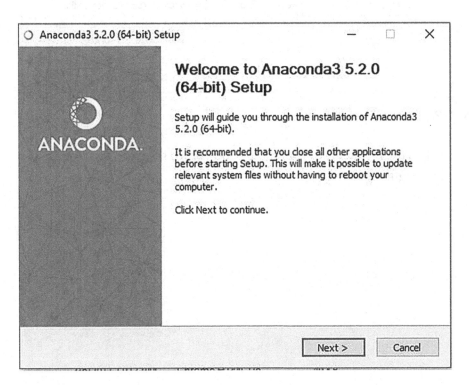

Figure 1-1. *Windows Installer*

4.   Click Next to review the license agreement and click the "I Agree" button (see Figure 1-2).

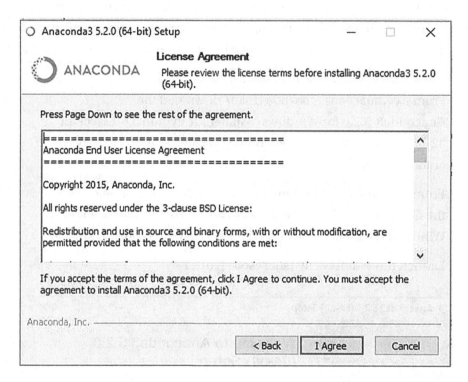

Figure 1-2. *License Agreement*

5.   Select the installation type, stand-alone or multi-user (see Figure 1-3).

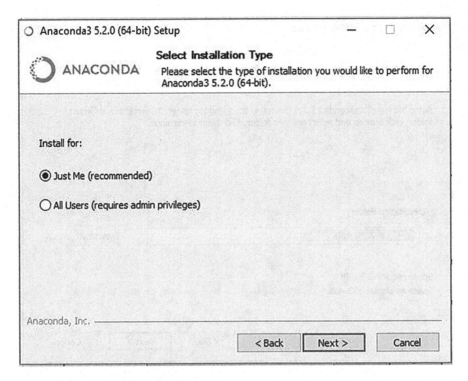

Figure 1-3. *Select Installation Type*

6.   Select the installation location (see Figure 1-4).

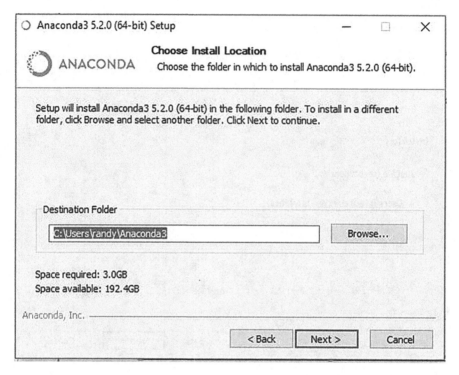

Figure 1-4. *Select Installation Location*

7. Register Anaconda as the default Python 3.6 installation by ensuring the "Register Anaconda as my default Python 3.6" box is checked. Press the "Install" button (see Figure 1-5).

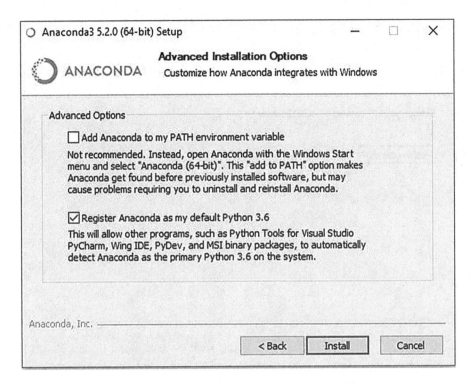

Figure 1-5. *Advanced Installation Options*

8. Start the installation process (see Figure 1-6). You may be asked
    if you would like to install Microsoft's Visual Studio Code. Visual
    Studio provides a visual interface for constructing and debugging
    Python scripts. It is an optional component and is not used in
    this book.

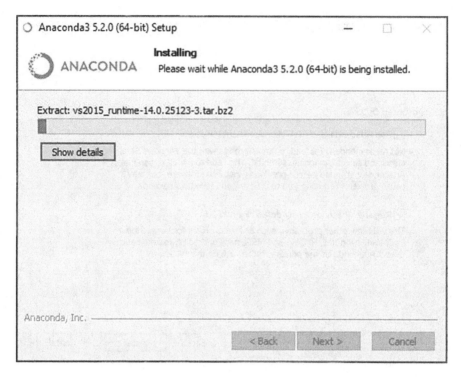

Figure 1-6. *Start Installation*

9. Validate the install by opening a Windows Command Prompt
    window and enter (after the > symbol prompt):

    > python

Assuming the installation worked correctly, the output should look similar to
Listing 1-1.

Listing 1-1. Python Command for Windows

```
C:\Users\randy>python
Python 3.6.5 |Anaconda, Inc.| (default, Mar 29 2018, 13:32:41) [MSC v.1900
64 bit (AMD64)] on win32
Type "help", "copyright", "credits" or "license" for more information.
>>>
```

This is an indication that the installation is complete including modifications made
to Windows environment variable PATH.

Troubleshooting Python Installation for Windows

If you receive the error message, 'Python' is not recognized as an internal or external command then ensure the Windows PATH environment variable has been updated to include the location of the Python installation directory.

1. On Windows 10, open File Explorer and select "Properties" for "This PC" (see Figure 1-7).

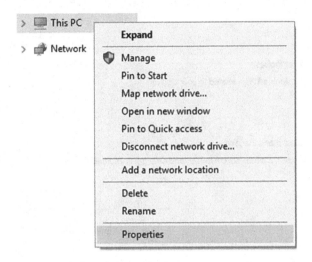

Figure 1-7. *PC Properties*

2. Right-click the "Properties" dialog to open the Control Panel for the System (see Figure 1-8).

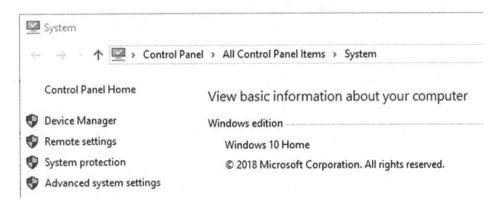

Figure 1-8. *PC Control Panel*

3. Select "Advanced" tab for System Properties and press the Environment Variables... button (see Figure 1-9).

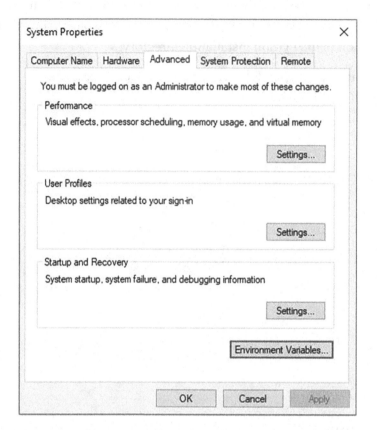

Figure 1-9. *Advanced System Properties*

4. Highlight the "Path" Environment Variables (see Figure 1-10).

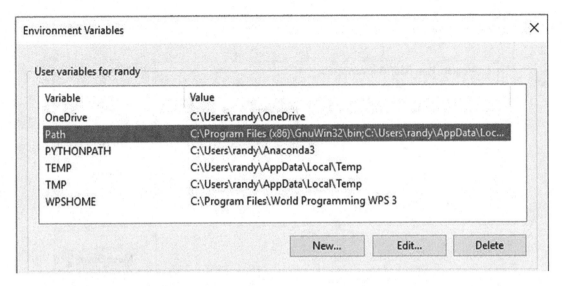

Figure 1-10. *Environment Variables*

5. Edit the Path Environment Variables by clicking the "New" button (see Figure 1-11).

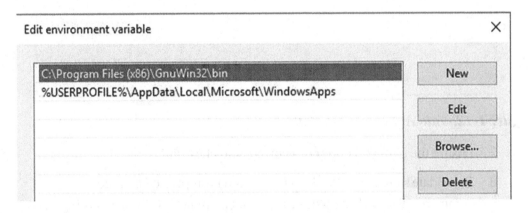

Figure 1-11. *Edit Environment Variables*

6. Add the Anaconda Python installation path specified in step 6 from the Anaconda3 Install Process for Windows as seen earlier (see Figure 1-12).

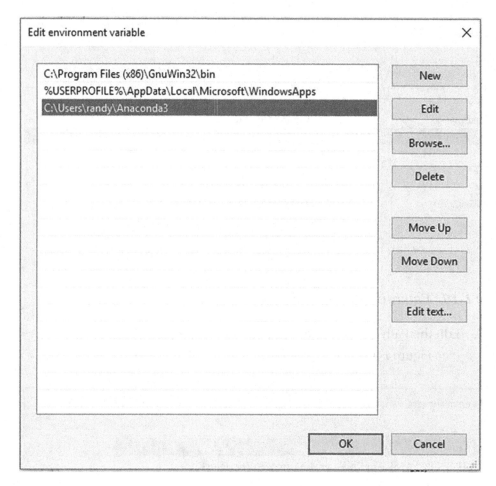

Figure 1-12. *Add Anaconda3 to Path*

7.   Ensure the path you entered is correct and click "OK".

8.   To validate start a new Windows Command Prompt and enter the command "Python". The output should look similar to the one in Listing 1-2.

Listing 1-2. Validate Python for Windows

```
C:\Users\randy>python
Python 3.6.5 |Anaconda, Inc.| (default, Mar 29 2018, 13:32:41) [MSC v.1900
64 bit (AMD64)] on win32
Type "help", "copyright", "credits" or "license" for more information.
>>>
```

The three angle brackets (>>>) is the default prompt for Python 3.

Anaconda3 Install Process for Linux

The following are the steps to install Python 3.6 in a Linux environment.

1. From www.anaconda.com/download/ download the
    Anaconda3-5.2.0 for Linux Installer for Python 3.6. This is actually
    a script file. Select the 32-bit or 64-bit installer (depending on
    your machine architecture). Select "Save File" and click "OK"
    (see Figure 1-13).

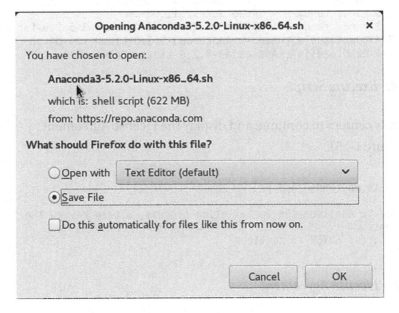

Figure 1-13. *Execute Linux Install*

2. Open a Linux terminal window and navigate to the location for the
    default directory /<userhome>/Downloads.

    ```
    $ cd /home/randy/Downloads
    ```

3. Change the permission to allow the script to execute with chmod
    command.

    ```
    $ chmod +x Anaconda3-5.2.0-Linux-x86_64.sh
    ```

4. If you are using a Bash shell, you can execute the shell script with ./ preceding the script filename (see Figure 1-14).

```
$ ./Anaconda3-5.2.0-Linux-x86_64.sh
```

Alternatively, you can execute the script with the following (Figure 1-14):

```
$ sh Anaconda3-5.1.0-Linux-x86_64.sh
```

```
drwxr-xr-x.  2 randy randy        45 Jul 17 11:21 .
drwx------. 15 randy randy      4096 Jul 17 11:00 ..
-rw-rw-r--.  1 randy randy 651745206 Jul 17 11:22 Anaconda3-5.2.0-Linux-x86_64.sh
[randy@rhel7-4 Downloads]$ chmod +x Anaconda3-5.2.0-Linux-x86_64.sh
[randy@rhel7-4 Downloads]$ ./Anaconda3-5.2.0-Linux-x86_64.sh
```

Figure 1-14. *Execute Script*

5. Press <enter> to continue and display the License Agreement (Figure 1-15).

```
Welcome to Anaconda3 5.2.0

In order to continue the installation process, please review the license
agreement.
Please, press ENTER to continue
>>>
```

Figure 1-15. *License Agreement*

6. Accept the license term by entering "yes" and pressing <enter> (Figure 1-16).

```
Do you accept the license terms? [yes|no]
[no] >>> yes
```

Figure 1-16. *Accept License Terms*

7. Confirm the Anaconda3 installation directory and press <enter> (Figure 1-17).

```
Anaconda3 will now be installed into this location:
/home/randy/anaconda3

  - Press ENTER to confirm the location
  - Press CTRL-C to abort the installation
  - Or specify a different location below

[/home/randy/anaconda3] >>> ▊
```

Figure 1-17. *Confirm Install Location*

8. Append the Anaconda3 installation directory to the $PATH
    environment variable by entering "yes" and pressing <enter>
    (Figure 1-18).

```
installation finished.
Do you wish the installer to prepend the Anaconda3 install location
to PATH in your /home/randy/.bashrc ? [yes|no]
[no] >>> yes▊
```

Figure 1-18. *Append to $PATH Variable*

You may be asked if you would like to install Microsoft's Visual
Studio. Visual Studio provides a visual interface for constructing and
debugging Python scripts. It is an optional component and is not
used in this book.

9. Confirm the installation by closing the terminal window used
    to execute the installation script and opening a new terminal
    window. This action will execute the .bashrc file in your home
    directory and "pick up" the updated $PATH environment variable
    that includes the Anaconda3 installation directory (Figure 1-19).

```
[randy@rhel7-4 ~]$ python
Python 3.6.5 |Anaconda, Inc.| (default, Apr 29 2018, 16:14:56)
[GCC 7.2.0] on linux
Type "help", "copyright", "credits" or "license" for more information.
>>> ▊
```

Figure 1-19. *Confirm Installation*

Executing a Python Script on Windows

Now that you have a working version of Python 3, we can begin. Consider the Python program in Listing 1-3. It is a simple script illustrating a Python for loop. The set of numbers contained inside the square brackets [ ] make up the elements of a Python list. In Python, a list is a data structure that holds an arbitrary collection of items. The variable i is used as the index into the loop. The variable product holds the integer value from the arithmetic assignment of product * i. And finally, the print function displays the output.

Listing 1-3. loop.py Program

```
# First Python program using a for loop

numbers = [2, 4, 6, 8, 11]
product = 1
for i in numbers:
    product = product * i
print('The product is:', product)
```

Notice there appears to be no symbols used to end a program statement. The end-of-line character is used to end a Python statement. This also helps to enforce legibility by keeping each statement on a separate physical line.

Coincidently, like SAS, Python honors a semi-colon as an end-of-statement terminator. However, you rarely see this. That's because multiple statements on the same physical line are considered an affront to program legibility.

The pound sign (#) on the first line indicates the statement is a comment. The same program logic is written in SAS and shown in Listing 1-4. It uses a NULL DATA Step with a DO/END loop and the PUT statement to write its output to the SAS log. All of the SAS code examples in this book are executed using SAS release 9.4M5.

Listing 1-4. Equivalent of loop.py Written in SAS

```
data _null_;
    array numbers {5} _TEMPORARY_ (2,4,6,8,11);
    product=1;
```

```
   do i=1 to dim(numbers);
      product=product*numbers{i};
   end;
put 'The product is: ' product;
run;
```

Follow these steps to execute the `loop.py` example on Windows:

1. Using your favorite text editor, copy the loop.py script from Listing 1-3. It is recommended you not use Windows Notepad since it is unlikely to preserve the indentations the Python script requires. An alternative editor for Windows is Notepad++ shown in Figure 1-20.

```
1    # First Python program using a for loop
2
3    numbers = [2, 4, 6, 8, 11]
4    product = 1
5    for i in numbers:
6        product = product * i
7    print('The product is:', product)
```

Figure 1-20. *Notepad++ Editor Version of loop.py*

2. Open a Windows Command window and navigate to the directory where you saved the `loop.py` Python script.

3. Execute the `loop.py` script from the Windows Command window by entering

   ```
   > python loop.py
   ```

This style of executing a Python script is the equivalent of executing a SAS program in non-interactive mode. Similar to the behavior of SAS, any output or errors generated from the Python script's execution is displayed in the Windows Command window as shown in Listing 1-5.

Listing 1-5. Output from loop.py

```
C:\Users\randy\source\python> python loop.py
The product is: 4224
```

If you received an error executing this script, it is likely that you misspelled the path or filename for the loop.py script resulting in a "No Such File or Directory" error message shown in Listing 1-6.

Listing 1-6. No Such File or Directory

```
C:\Users\randy\source\python> python for_loop.py
python: can't open file 'for_loop.py': [Errno 2] No such file or directory
```

As a means to ensure Python code is legible, there are strict rules on indentation. The Python program in Listing 1-7 is the same as the loop.py script from Listing 1-3 except all the statements are left aligned. Notice how the modified loop.py script when executed raises the IndentationError shown in Listing 1-8.

Listing 1-7. Modified loop.py with No Indentation

```
# First Python program using a for loop

numbers = [2, 4, 6, 8, 11]
product = 1
for i in numbers:
product = product * i
print('The product is:', product)
```

When the modified loop.py script is executed, the lack of indentation raises the error shown in Listing 1-8.

Listing 1-8. Expected an Indented Block Error

```
C:\Users\randy\source\python> python loop1.py
  File "loop1.py", line 6
    product = product * i
        ^
IndentationError: expected an indented block
```

Once you get over the shock of how Python imposes the indentation requirements, you will come to see this as an important feature for creating and maintaining legible, easy-to-understand code. The standard coding practice is to have four whitespaces rather than using <TAB>'s. In the section "Integrated Development Environment (IDE) for Python," you will see how this and other formatting details are handled for you automatically.

Case Sensitivity

Naturally, the incorrect spelling of language keywords, variables, and object names are sources of errors. Unlike the SAS language, Python names are case-sensitive. Consider the simple two-line Python script in Listing 1-9.

Listing 1-9. Case Sensitivity

```
C:\Users\randy\python> python
Python 3.6.5 |Anaconda, Inc.| (default, Mar 29 2018, 13:32:41) [MSC v.1900
64 bit (AMD64)] on win32
Type "help", "copyright", "credits" or "license" for more information.
>>> Y=201
>>> print(y)
Traceback (most recent call last):
  File "<stdin>", line 1, in <module>
NameError: name 'y' is not defined
```

Python scripts can be executed interactively. In this example, we invoke the Python command. This causes the command line prompts to change to the default Python prompt, >>>. To end an interactive Python session, submit the statement exit().

The variable Y (uppercase) is assigned the integer value of 201. The Python print() function is called for the variable y (lowercase). Since the variable y is not presently defined in the Python namespace, a NameError is raised.

Line Continuation Symbol

Should you find you have a line of code needing to extend past the physical line (i.e., wrap), then use the backslash (\). This causes the Python interpreter to ignore the physical end-of-line terminator for the current line and continues scanning for the next end-of-line terminator. The Python line continuation symbol is shown in Listing 1-10.

Listing 1-10. Line Continuation

```
>>> y = 1 + \
...     2
>>> print(y)
3
```

Finally, a word about name choices. Names should be descriptive because more than likely you will be the one who has to re-read and understand tomorrow the code you write today. As with any language, it is a good practice to avoid language keywords for object names.

A language that makes it hard to write elegant code makes it hard to write good code.

—Eric Raymond, Why Python?[8]

Executing a Python Script on Linux

The steps for executing a Python script on Linux are similar to the ones for executing on Windows described previously.

1. Use an editor such as nano or vi and copy the loop.py Python program from Figure 1-21. Save this file as loop.py. Notice that the .py extension is used to indicate a Python script (Figure 1-21).

```
# First Python program using a for loop

numbers = [2, 4, 6, 8, 11]
product = 1
for i in numbers:
    product = product * i
print('The product is:', product)
```

Figure 1-21. *vi Editor Displaying loop.py*

2. Open a terminal window and navigate to the directory where you saved the loop.py Python script.

3. Execute the loop.py Python script with command

   `$ python loop.py`

The execution of the Python script writes its output and error messages to the terminal window. You should see the output from Figure 1-22.

---

[8]www.linuxjournal.com/article/3882

```
[randy@rhel7-4 python]$ python loop.py
The product is: 4224
[randy@rhel7-4 python]$ ▌
```

Figure 1-22. *Output from loop.py on Linux*

Now that you understand how to execute Python scripts in "non-interactive mode," you are probably wondering about Python's equivalent for SAS Display Manager or the SAS Studio client. This leads us to the next topic, "Integrated Development Environment (IDE) for Python."

Integrated Development Environment (IDE) for Python

In order to improve our Python coding productivity, we need a tool for interactive script development, as opposed to the non-interactive methods we have discussed thus far. We need the equivalent of the SAS Display Manager or SAS Studio.

SAS Display Manager, SAS Enterprise Guide, and SAS Studio are examples of an integrated development environment or IDE for short. Beyond just editing your SAS programs, these IDEs provide a set of services, such as submitting programs for execution, logging execution, rendering output, and managing resources. For example, in the SAS Display Manager, opening the LIBREF window to view assigned SAS Data Libraries is an example of the IDE's ability to provide a non-programming method to visually inspect the properties and members for a SAS LIBNAME statements assigned to the current session.

As you might expect, not all IDEs are created equal. The more sophisticated IDEs permit setting checkpoints to enable a "walk through" of code execution displaying variable values and resource states on a line-at-a-time basis. They also provision methods to store a collection of programs into a coherent set of packages. These packages can then be re-distributed to others for execution. Perhaps the most compelling feature is how an IDE encourages team collaboration by allowing multiple users to work together creating, testing, and documenting a project composed of a collection of these artifacts.

If you are familiar with R and like using RStudio, then you will appreciate the similarities between RStudio and Spyder. Spyder is a component bundled with the Anaconda distribution. Spyder IDE Executing loop.py is illustrated in Figure 1-23.

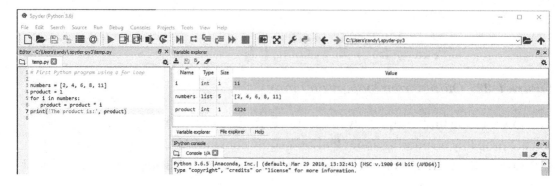

Figure 1-23. *Spyder IDE Executing loop.py*

One of the more interesting IDEs developed specifically for the data scientist community is the Jupyter notebook. It uses a web-based interface to write, execute, test, and document your code. Jupyter notebooks support over 40 languages, including Python, R, Scala, and Julia. It also has an open architecture, so vendors and users can write plug-ins for their own execution engines, or what Jupyter refers to as kernels. SAS Institute supports a bare-bones SAS kernel executing on Linux for Jupyter notebooks.[9]

A compelling feature for Jupyter notebooks is the ability to develop and share them across the Web. All of the Python examples used in this book were developed using the Jupyter notebook. Best of all, the Anaconda distribution of Python comes bundled with the Jupyter notebook IDE.

Jupyter Notebook

Figure 1-24 displays the start page for a Jupyter notebook. Using the Windows Start Menu, you launch the Jupyter notebook by using the following path:

```
Start -> Anaconda3 ->Jupyter Notebook
```

This action launches the Jupyter notebook into the default browser. Alternatively, you can launch the notebook on Windows using the command line command

```
> python -m notebook
```

Another commonly used command is

```
> jupyter notebook
```

---

[9]SAS Jupyter kernel at https://github.com/gaulinmp/sas_kernel

This method is convenient if you wish to change directories to a Window's folder location used to store and retrieve Python scripts. This allows you to change directories before you launch the notebook.

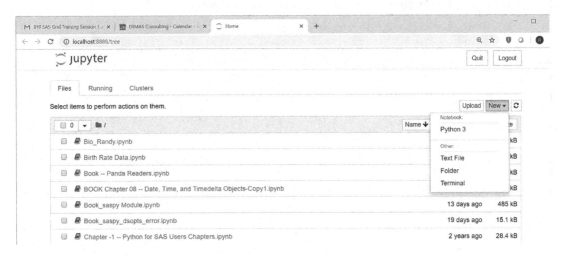

Figure 1-24. *Jupyter Notebook Home Page*

To start a new project

1. On the dashboard (labeled Home page), click the New button on the upper right and then select Python 3 from the drop-down. This launches a new untitled notebook page.

2. Enter the `loop.py` script created earlier into a cell. You can also copy the script you created earlier and paste directly into the notebook cell.

3. Click the "Play" button to execute the code you copied into the cell (Figure 1-25).

The documentation on how to use the Jupyter notebook is concise, and it is worth the effort to read. See `https://jupyter.org/`.

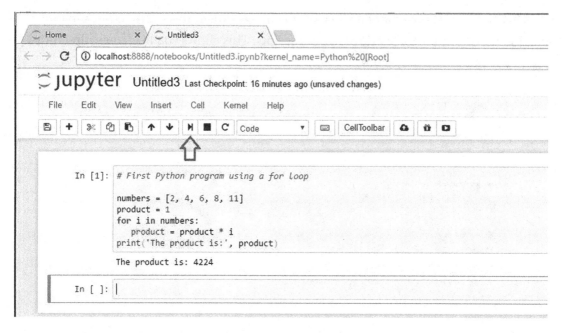

Figure 1-25. *Jupyter Notebook with loop.py Script*

You may have multiple notebooks, each represented by a browser tab, opened at the same time. You may also have multiple instances of Jupyter notebooks opened at the same time (with multiple notebooks open, pay attention to names to avoid accidental overwriting).

Jupyter Notebook for Linux

Open a terminal window and enter the command

```
$ jupyter notebook &
```

On Linux the terminal window remains open while the Jupyter notebook is active.

In some instances, the Linux default browser may not open automatically after the Jupyter notebook command is issued. If that is the case

1. Start a new browser instance.

2. The notebook should launch a browser session. If it does not start the browser, then look for the message in the Linux terminal window:

See Figure 1-26, Launch Jupyter notebook on Linux. Copy/paste this URL into your browser when you connect for the first time to login with a token: `http://localhost:8888/?token=<token string>` and copy the URL into the browser address window.

```
(base) -bash-4.2$ jupyter notebook &
[1] 9871
(base) -bash-4.2$ [I 14:33:44.610 NotebookApp] Writing notebook server cookie secret to /run/user/1000/jupyter/notebook_cookie_secret
[I 14:33:47.077 NotebookApp] Loading IPython parallel extension
[I 14:33:47.226 NotebookApp] JupyterLab extension loaded from /opt/anaconda3/lib/python3.7/site-packages/jupyterlab
[I 14:33:47.226 NotebookApp] JupyterLab application directory is /opt/anaconda3/share/jupyter/lab
[I 14:33:47.249 NotebookApp] Serving notebooks from local directory: /home/trb
[I 14:33:47.249 NotebookApp] The Jupyter Notebook is running at:
[I 14:33:47.249 NotebookApp] http://localhost:8888/?token=9aa13f968665557973c31735c94ff742e29af21c0f58da43
[I 14:33:47.249 NotebookApp] Use Control-C to stop this server and shut down all kernels (twice to skip confirmation).
[C 14:33:47.318 NotebookApp]

    Copy/paste this URL into your browser when you connect for the first time,
    to login with a token:
        http://localhost:8888/?token=9aa13f968665557973c31735c94ff742e29af21c0f58da43
START /usr/bin/firefox "http://localhost:8888/tree?token=6dc56900974f85afdfc994f02fe66802a03a5cf53fc16007"
```

Figure 1-26. *Launching Jupyter notebook on Linux*

Summary

In this chapter we illustrated how to install and configure the Python environment for Windows and Linux. We also introduced basic formatting and syntax rules needed to execute simple Python scripts. And we introduced different methods for executing Python scripts including the use of Jupyter notebooks. With a working Python environment established, we can begin exploring Python as a language to augment SAS for data exploration and analysis.

CHAPTER 2

Python Types and Formatting

In this chapter we discuss Python "types" along with string and numeric formatting. Python has different "types," some of which are built into the language, some of which are added by third parties, and some of which are created by Python code. These types can represent all kinds of data and allow Python to be used as a general-purpose programming language in addition to its use as a data processing language. As a general rule, SAS programmers need not concern themselves with data types. This is because the data model used to store variables in Foundation SAS datasets (.sas7bdat) is a simple one. The data "types" for SAS are either numeric or character. Internally SAS uses floating-point representation for numeric values.

The SAS language handles a tremendous amount of details without user intervention when reading and writing numeric or character data. For example, SAS informats (both SAS-supplied and user-defined ones) provide the mappings for reading various data types for numeric and character data inputs. Similarly, SAS formats provide the mappings needed to write various data types. We will begin by discussing numerics, followed by strings (character variable values in SAS). Further in the chapter, we examine how Python formats both numeric and character data types.

We begin by examining numerics which include Boolean type operators used for truth testing. This is followed by an overview of what Python refers to as strings and SAS refers to as character variables. Finally we will discuss formatting for both numerics and strings.

© Randy Betancourt, Sarah Chen 2019
R. Betancourt and S. Chen, *Python for SAS Users*, https://doi.org/10.1007/978-1-4842-5001-3_2

Numerics

Python has three distinct numeric data types:

1. Integers

2. Floating point

3. Complex numbers

In addition, Booleans are a subtype of integers which is discussed in detail. Complex numbers will not be discussed as they are outside the scope of this book. In Python numbers are either numeric literals or created as the result of built-in operators or functions. Any numeric literal containing an exponent sign or a decimal point is mapped to a floating-point type. Whole numbers including hexadecimals, octal, and binary numbers are mapped as integer types.

Python permits "mixed" arithmetic operations, meaning numerics with different types used in expressions are permitted. In Listing 2-1, the built-in function `type()` is used to return the object's data type. (Throughout this book we will rely on the built-in `type()` function extensively to return information from a Python object.)

Listing 2-1. Mixed Types

```
>>> nl = '\n'
>>>
>>> x = 1
>>> y = 1.5
>>> z = x * y
>>>
>>> print(nl               ,
...        'x type is:' , type(x) , nl,
...        'y type is:' , type(y) , nl,
...        'z type is:' , type(z))

 x type is: <class 'int'>
 y type is: <class 'float'>
 z type is: <class 'float'>
```

In this example, x is an integer, y is a float. The product of x and y, is assigned to z which Python then cast as a float. This illustrates the rule Python uses for mixed arithmetic operations. This example also neatly illustrates the compactness of Python as a language. Similar to the SAS language, there is no need to declare variables and their associated data types as they are inferred from their usage.

In contrast, the Base SAS language does not make a distinction between integers and floats. Newer SAS language implementations such as DS2 and Cloud Analytic Services (CAS) define a range of numeric data types such as integer and floats. These newer language implementations are outside the scope of this book. Listing 2-2 illustrates this same program logic written in SAS. The line numbers from the SAS log have been included.

Listing 2-2. SAS Data Types

```
4    data types;
5        x = 1;
6        y = 1.5;
7        z = x*y;
8
9        Put "x is: " x /
10           "y is: " y/
11           "z is: " z;
12
13 title "SAS Reported 'type' for numeric variables";
14 proc print data=sashelp.vcolumn(where=(libname='WORK' and
15                                 memname='TYPES'));
16     id name;
17     var type;
18 run;
```

OUTPUT:

```
x is: 1
y is: 1.5
z is: 1.5
```

This SAS program creates the temporary SAS dataset WORK.TYPES. With the creation of the SAS dataset, we can search the SAS DICTIONARY table SASHELP.VCOLUMN and return the "type" associated with the SAS variables, x, y, and z. The results from PROC PRINT is displayed in Figure 2-1. It shows variables x, y, and z are defined as num, indicating they are numerics.

SAS Reported 'type' for numeric variables

name	type
x	num
y	num
z	num

Figure 2-1. *SAS Data Types for Numerics*

You are not likely to encounter issues related to data type differences when working with SAS and Python. For the most part, issues related to mapping data types arise when reading data from external environments, particularly with relational databases. We will discuss these issues in detail in Chapter 6, "pandas Readers and Writers."

Python Operators

Similar to SAS the Python interpreter permits a wide range of mathematical expressions and functions to be combined together. Python's expression syntax is very similar to the SAS language using the operators +, –, *, and / for addition, subtraction, multiplication, and division, respectively. And like SAS parentheses (()) are used to group operations for controlling precedence.

Table 2-1 displays the Python floating-point and numeric type operations precedence (excluding complex numbers).

Table 2-1. *Python Arithmetic Operations Precedence*[1]

Precedence	Operation	Results
1	x ** y	x to the power y
2	divmod(x, y)	The pair (x // y, x % y)
3	float(x)	x converted to floating point
4	int(x)	x converted to integer
5	abs(x)	Absolute value of x
6	+x	x unchanged
7	−x	x negated
8	x % y	Remainder of x / y
9	x // y	Floor of x and y
10	x * y	Product of x and y
11	x / y	Quotient x by y
12	x − y	Difference of x and y
13	x + y	Sum of x and y

Boolean

As stated previously Python's Boolean data type is a subtype of integer. Because of its utility in data cleansing tasks and general-purpose testing, we will cover this data type in detail. Python's two Boolean values are True and False with the capitalization as shown. In a numerical context, for example, when used as an argument to arithmetic operations, they behave like integers with values 0 for False and 1 for True. This is illustrated in Listing 2-3.

---

[1]Lutz, Mark (2013). Learning Python, 5th Edition, 141.

Listing 2-3. Boolean Value Tests for 0 and 1

```
>>> print(bool(0))
False
>>> print(bool(1))
True
```

In contrast SAS does not have a Boolean data type. As a result, SAS Data Step code is often constructed as a Series of cascading IF-THEN/DO blocks used to perform Boolean-style truth tests. SAS does have implied Boolean test operators, however. An example is the END= variable option on the SET statement. This feature is used as an end-of-file indicator when reading a SAS dataset. The value assigned to the END= variable option is initialized to 0 and set to 1 when the SET statement reads the last observation in a SAS dataset.

Other SAS functions also use implied Boolean logic. For example, the FINDC function used to search strings for characters returns a value of 0, or false, if the search excerpt is not found in the target string. Every Python object can be interpreted as a Boolean and is either True or False.

These Python objects are always False:

- None
- False
- 0 (for integer, float, and complex)
- Empty strings
- Empty collections such as " ", ( ), [ ], { }

Comparison Operators

Python has eight comparison operators shown in Table 2-2. They all have the same priority which is higher than that of the Boolean operators in Table 2-1.

Table 2-2. *Python Comparison Operations*

Operation	Meaning
<	Strictly less than
<=	Less than or equal
>	Strictly greater than
>=	Greater than or equal
==	Equal
!=	Not equal
is	Object identity
is not	Negated object identity

The last two Python comparison operators is and is not do not have direct analogs in SAS. You can think of Python's is and is not as testing object identity, that is, if two or more objects are the same. In other words, do both objects point to the same memory location? A Python object can be thought of as a memory location holding a data value and a set of associated operations. This concept is further illustrated in Listings 2-4 and 2-5.

Listing 2-4. Python Equivalence Test

```
>>> x = 32.0
>>> y = 32
>>> if (x == y):
...    print ("True. 'x' and 'y' are equal")
... else:
...    print("False. 'x' and 'y' are not equal")
...
True. 'x' and 'y' are equal
```

In this example, x is assigned the value 32.0 and y is assigned 32. Lines 3 through 6 illustrate the Python IF/ELSE construct. As one expects x and y evaluate to the same arithmetic value. Note Python uses == to test for equality in contrast to SAS which uses =.

Listing 2-5 illustrates Python's is identify test for x and y.

Listing 2-5. Python IS Comparison

```
>>> x = 32.0
>>> y = 32
>>> x is y
False
```

The is operator does not test if the values assigned to x and y are equivalent (we have already shown they are equivalent in Listing 2-4), rather we are testing to determine if the Python objects x and y are the same object. In other words, do x and y point to the same memory location? Listing 2-6 helps further illustrate this point.

Listing 2-6. Python IS Comparison 2

```
>>> x = 32.0
>>> y = x
>>> x is y
True
```

In the preceding example, x and y are the same object by virtue of the assignment statement

```
y = x
```

Let's further examine examples of Python's Boolean comparison operators along with contrasting SAS examples. As stated previously empty sets in Python return False. This is illustrated in Listing 2-7.

Listing 2-7. Boolean Tests for Empty and Non-empty Sets

```
>>> print(bool("))
False
>>> print(bool(' '))
True
>>> print(bool('Arbitrary String'))
True
```

The first Boolean test returns False given the string is empty or null. The results from the second Boolean test returns True. This is a departure for how SAS handles missing character variables. In SAS, zero or more whitespaces (ASCII 32) assigned to a character variable is considered a missing value.

Chapter 3, "pandas Library," goes into further detail on missing value detection and replacement.

Next let's examine simple Boolean comparison operations. In Python Boolean comparison operations can be chained together. This is illustrated in Listing 2-8.

Listing 2-8. Boolean Chained Comparisons

```
>>> x = 20
>>> 1 < x < 100
True
```

Boolean comparisons are performed between each pair of terms. In Listing 2-8, 1 < x evaluates True and x < 100 evaluates True making the expression True.

Listing 2-9. Boolean Chained Comparisons 2

```
>>> x = 20
>>> 10 < x < 20
False
```

In Listing 2-9, 10 < x evaluates True and x < 20 evaluates False making the expression False.

A fairly common type of Boolean expression is testing for equality and inequality among numbers and strings. For Python the inequality comparison uses != for evaluation and the SAS language uses ^=. Listing 2-10 illustrates a simple example.

Listing 2-10. Python Numeric Inequality

```
>>> x = 2
>>> y = 3
>>> x != y
True
```

Listing 2-11 illustrates this same program.

Listing 2-11. SAS Numeric Inequality

```
4    data _null_;
5    /* inequality comparison */
6    x = 2;
7    y = 3;
8
9    if x ^= y then
10        put 'True';
11    else put 'False';
12   run;
```

OUTPUT:

```
True
```

Using a NULL Data Step, variables x and y are assigned numeric values 2 and 3, respectively. The IF-THEN/ELSE statement is used along with a PUT statement to write to the SAS log. Since the value 2 does not equal 3, the inequality test with ^= evaluates true and 'True' is written. The ELSE condition is not executed.

Further in this chapter, we will discuss strings and string formatting in more detail. Python's Boolean tests for string equality and inequality follow the same pattern used for numerics. Listing 2-12 uses the Boolean comparison operator "==" in contrast to the SAS comparison operator "=".

Listing 2-12. Boolean String Equality

```
>>> s1 = 'String'
>>> s2 = 'string'
>>> s1 == s2
False
```

This Boolean comparison returns False since the first character in object s1 is "S" and the first character in object s2 is "s".

Listing 2-13 illustrates this same Python program written with SAS.

Listing 2-13. SAS String Equality

```
4   data _null_;
5
6   /* string equality comparison */
7   s1 = 'String';
8   s2 = 'string';
9
10  if s1 = s2 then
11     put 'True';
12  else put 'False';
13  run;
```

OUTPUT:
False

Using a NULL Data Step, the variables s1 and s2 are assigned the character values 'String' and 'string', respectively. The IF-THEN/ELSE statement is used along with a PUT statement to write to the SAS log. Since the character variable s1 value of 'String' does not match the character variable s2 value of 'string', the IF statement evaluates false. The ELSE statement is executed resulting in 'False' written to the SAS log.

IN/NOT IN

We can illustrate membership operators with in and not in with Listing 2-14.

Listing 2-14. IN and NOT IN Comparisons

```
>>> 'on' in 'Python is easy to learn'
True
>>> 'on' not in 'Python is easy to learn'
False
```

IN evaluates to True if a specified sequence is found in the target string. Otherwise it evaluates False. not in evaluates False if a specified sequence is found in the string. Otherwise it evaluates True.

AND/OR/NOT

The Python's Boolean operation order for and, or, and not is listed in Table 2-3. Python's evaluation rules for and and or operators behave as follows.

Table 2-3. *Python Boolean Operations Precedence*

Precedence	Operation	Results
1	not x	If x is false, then True; False otherwise.
2	x and y	If x is false, its value is returned; otherwise *y* is evaluated and the resulting value is returned False.
3	x or y	If x is true, its value is returned; otherwise, y is evaluated and the resulting value is returned.

The operator not yields True if its argument is false; otherwise, it yields False.

The expression x and y first evaluates x; if x is False, its value is returned; otherwise, y is evaluated and the resulting value is returned.

The expression x or y first evaluates x; if x is True, its value is returned; otherwise, y is evaluated and the resulting value is returned.

Let's examine how Boolean operation precedence work. This is illustrated in Listing 2-15.

Listing 2-15. Boolean AND/OR Precedence

```
>>> True and False or True
True
>>> (True or False) or True
True
```

The Boolean and operator precedence has a higher priority than that of or. In the first pair, True and False evaluate False. Therefore, the second evaluation becomes False or True which evaluates True. The second example in Listing 2-15 illustrates the use of parentheses to further clarify the Boolean operation. Parentheses have the highest precedence order.

The Python Boolean and operator returns True if both predicates evaluate True. Otherwise, it returns False. Listing 2-16 tests the condition for finding both the character 'r' and a blank in a Python sequence (string).

Listing 2-16. Python Boolean and

```
>>> s3 = 'Longer String'
>>> 'r' and " " in s3
True
```

The same logic is shown using SAS in Listing 2-17.

Listing 2-17. SAS Boolean AND Operator

```
4    data _null_;
5
6      /* SAS 'and' operator */
7      s3 = 'Longer String';
8
9      if findc(s3,'r') ^= 0 and findc(s3,' ') ^= 0 then
10             put 'True';
11        else put 'False';
12    run;
```

OUTPUT:
True

The FINDC function searches the character variable s3 left to right for the character 'r.' This function returns the location for the first occurrence where the character 'r' is found, in this case, position 6. This causes the first half of the IF predicate to evaluate true. Following AND is the second half of the IF predicate using the FINDC function to search for a blank character (ASCII 32) which is found at position 7. This predicate evaluates true. Since both IF predicates evaluate true, this results in the statement following THEN to execute and write 'True' to the SAS log.

The Python or Boolean operator returns True when one or the other predicate evaluates True. Listing 2-18 illustrates the Boolean or operation.

Listing 2-18. Python Boolean or

```
>>> s4 = 'Skinny'
>>> s5 = 'Hunger'
>>> 'y' in s4 or s5
True
```

This same logic is shown using SAS in Listing 2-19.

Listing 2-19. SAS Boolean OR

```
4    data _null_;
5
6    /* Equivalent in comparison with 'or operator */
7      s4 = 'Skinny';
8      s5 = 'hunger';
9
10   if findc(s4,'y') ^= 0 or findc(s5,'y') ^= 0 then
11       put 'True';
12   else put 'False';
13   run;
```

OUTPUT:

```
True
```

The FINDC function searches the character variable s4 left to right for the character 'y'. This function returns the location for the first occurrence of where the character 'y' is found, in this case, position 6. This results in the first half of the IF predicate to evaluate true. Since the first IF predicate evaluates true, this results in the statement following THEN statement to execute and write 'True' to the SAS log. The ELSE statement is not executed.

Numerical Precision

It is a mathematical truth that .1 multiplied by 10 produces 1 (for base-10, of course). Consider Listing 2-20.

Listing 2-20. Boolean Equivalence

```
>>> x = [.1] * 10
>>> x == 1
False
```

So how is this possible? Let's begin by closely examining the first line of the program. x defines a Python list. A list is a data structure containing an ordered collection of items. In this case, our list contains ten numeric floats with the value 0.1. When the Python interpreter executes the first line of the program, the list x is expanded to contain ten items (floats), each with the value of 0.1. This is illustrated in Listing 2-21 where we use the print() function to display the list.

Listing 2-21. Contents of List x

```
>>> x = [.1] * 10
>>> print(x)
[0.1, 0.1, 0.1, 0.1, 0.1, 0.1, 0.1, 0.1, 0.1, 0.1]
```

This intermediate summation step is illustrated in Listing 2-22.

Listing 2-22. Python Sum Operation

```
>>> .1 + .1 + .1 + .1 + .1 + .1 + .1 + .1 + .1 + .1
0.9999999999999999
```

As an aside, you can see another example illustrating the simplicity of Python. There are no variables to declare and in this case no expressions or assignments made.

The explanation for these results is how floating-point numbers are represented in computer hardware as base 2 fractions. And as it turns out 0.1 cannot be represented exactly as a base 2 fraction. It is an infinitely repeating fraction.[2]

Fortunately, there are straightforward remedies to this challenge. Similar to SAS, the Python Standard Library has a number of built-in numeric functions such as round().[3]

---

[2]Floating-Point Arithmetic: Issues and Limitations at https://docs.python.org/3.6/tutorial/floatingpoint.html

[3]Built-in Functions for Python. See https://docs.python.org/3.7/library/functions.html

A built-in function means it is available to the Python interpreter and does not require the importing of any additional packages.

Python's round() function returns a number rounded to a given precision after the decimal point. If *the number of digits after the decimal is omitted from the function call* or is None, the function returns the nearest integer to its input value.

Listing 2-23 is a re-write of the Python program from Listing 2-20.

Listing 2-23. Python round Function

```
>>> nl = '\n'
>>>
>>> total = 0
>>> list = [.1] * 10
>>>
>>> for i in list:
...     total += i
...
>>> print(nl,
...        "Boolean expression: 1 == total is:        ", 1 == total,
...        nl,
...        "Boolean expression: 1 == round(total) is:", 1 == round(total),
...        nl,
...        "total is:", total,
...        nl,
...    "total type is:", type(total))
 Boolean expression: 1 == total is:          False
 Boolean expression: 1 == round(total) is: True
 total is: 0.9999999999999999
 total type is: <class 'float'>
```

The object total is an accumulator used in the for loop. The construct += as part of the accumulation is equivalent to the SAS expression

```
total = total + i;
```

The print() function contains a Boolean comparison operation similar to the one found in Listing 2-20. Without the use of the built-in round() function, this Boolean equivalency test returns False.

The round() function rounds the total object to the nearest integer. In contrast to the line above it, here the Boolean equality operator == returns True since 0.999... has been rounded to the integer value of 1.

The numerical precision issue raised here is not unique to Python. The same challenge exists for SAS, or any other language utilizing floating-point arithmetic, which is to say nearly all computer languages. Listing 2-24 uses the same logic to illustrate numerical accuracy.

Listing 2-24. SAS Round Function

```
4    data _null_;
5    one = 1;
6    total = 0;
7    inc = .1;
8
9    do i = 1 to 10;
10       total + inc;
11       put inc ', ' @@;
12    end;
13
14    put;
15    if total = one then put 'True';
16      else put 'Comparison of "one = total" evaluates to False';
17
18    if round(total) = one then put 'Comparison of "one = round(total)"
     evaluates to True';
19      else put 'False';
20
21    put 'Total is: ' total 8.3;
22    run;
```

43

OUTPUT:

```
0.1 , 0.1 , 0.1 , 0.1 , 0.1 , 0.1 , 0.1 , 0.1 , 0.1 , 0.1 ,
Comparison of "one = total" evaluates to False
Comparison of "one = round(total)" evaluates to True
Total is:     1.000
```

This SAS program uses a DO/END loop to accumulate values into the total variable. The inc variable, set to a numeric value of 0.1, is a stand-in for the items in the Python list. The first IF statement on line 15 performs a comparison of the accumulated values into variable total with the numeric variable one having an integer value of 1. Similar to the Python example, the first half of this IF predicate (.999...= 1) evaluates false and the second half of the IF predicate executes indicating the comparison is false.

The IF statement on line 18 uses the ROUND function to round the variable total value (.999...) to the nearest integer value (1). This IF predicate now evaluates true and writes to the log. Line 19 does not execute.

The last line of the program writes the value of the variable total using the SAS-supplied 8.3 format which displays the value 1.000. The internal representation for the variable total remains .9999999999.

Strings

In Python strings are referred to as an ordered sequence of Unicode characters. Strings are immutable, meaning they cannot be updated in place. Any method applied to a string such as replace() or split() used to modify a string returns a copy of the modified string. Strings are enclosed in either single quotes (') or double quotes (").

If a string needs to include quotes as a part of the string literal, then backslash (\) is used as an escape character. Alternatively, like SAS, one can use a mixture of single quotes (') and double quotes (") assuming they are balanced.

Let's start with some simple examples for both Python and their SAS analogs. Listing 2-25 illustrates a "Hello World" example.

Listing 2-25. Python String Assignment and Concatenation

```
>>> s5 = 'Hello'
>>> s6 = "World"
>>>
```

```
>>> print(s5,s6)
Hello World
>>> print(s5 + s6)
HelloWorld
>>> print('Type() for s5 is:', type(s5))
Type() for s5 is: <class 'str'>
```

Python uses the plus symbol (+) for string concatenation operation. SAS provisions an extensive set of functions for string concatenation operations to provide finer controls for output appearances.

Listing 2-26 uses the CAT function to concatenate the character variables s5 and s6.

Listing 2-26. SAS Character Assignment and Concatenation

```
4   data _null_;
5       s5 = 'Hello';
6       s6 = 'World';
7
8   concat1 = cat(s5, s6);
9   concat2 = cat(s5, ' ', s6);
10
11  put s5= s6= /
12  concat1= /
13  concat2=;
14  run;
```

```
s5=Hello s6=World
concat1=HelloWorld
concat2=Hello World
```

Similar to SAS, Python has an extensive set of string manipulation methods. Listing 2-27 illustrates the Python upper() Method.

Listing 2-27. Python upper() Method

```
>>> print(s5 + " " + s6.upper())
Hello WORLD
```

The SAS program in Listing 2-28 illustrates the same program logic.

45

Listing 2-28. SAS UPCASE Function

```
4   data _null_;
5       s5 = 'Hello';
6       s6 = 'World';
7
8       upcase = cat(s5, ' ', upcase(s6));
9
10  put upcase;
11  run;
```

OUTPUT:

```
Hello WORLD
```

Listing 2-29 illustrates the ability to create strings that preserve spacing.

Listing 2-29. Python Multiline String

```
>>> s7 = "'Beautiful is better than ugly.
... Explicit is better than implicit.
... Simple is better than complex.
... Complex is better than complicated.
... Flat is better than nested.
... Sparse is better than dense.
... Readability counts, and so on..."'
>>> print(s7)
Beautiful is better than ugly.
Explicit is better than implicit.
Simple is better than complex.
Complex is better than complicated.
Flat is better than nested.
Sparse is better than dense.
Readability counts, and so on...
```

Observe how three consecutive single quotes (') are needed to define a multiline string. A Docstring preserves the spacing and line breaks in the string literal.

Continuing with the Python program from Listing 2-29, Listing 2-30 illustrates the use of the count() method for counting occurrences of an excerpt ('c' in this case) in a target string.

Listing 2-30. Python count Method

```
>>> print('Occurrences of the letter "c":', s7.count('c'))
Occurrences of the letter "c": 6
```

The count() method illustrated in the preceding example is one of a number of methods used by Python for sophisticated string manipulation tasks. You can think of these methods as being similar to SAS functions. In the case of Python, methods are associated with and act upon a particular object. In the preceding example, s7 is a string object used to hold the value of the Docstring. For the remainder of this book, we use the Python nomenclature object rather than variable when referring to code elements assigned values.

The methods available for the built-in string object are found in the Python Standard Library 3.7 documentation at https://docs.python.org/3/library/stdtypes.html#string-methods.

String Slicing

Python uses indexing methods on a number of different objects having similar behaviors depending on the object. With a sequence of characters (string), Python automatically creates an index with a start position of zero (0) for the first character in the sequence and increments to the end position of the string (length –1). The index can be thought of as one-dimensional array.

The general form for Python string slicing is

```
string[start : stop : step]
```

Python string slicing is a sophisticated form of parsing. By indexing a string using offsets separated by a colon, Python returns a new object identified by these offsets. start identifies the lower-bound position of the string which is inclusive; stop identifies the upper-bound position of the string which is non-inclusive; Python permits the use of a negative index values to count from right to left; step indicates every nth item, with a default value of one (1). Seeing a few examples will help to clarify.

At times you may find it easier to refer to characters toward the end of the string. Python provides an "end-to-beginning" indexer with a start position of –1 for the last character in the string and decrements to the beginning position.

Table 2-4 illustrates this concept.

Table 2-4. *Python Sequence Indexing*

Character	H	e	l	l	o		W	o	r	l	d
Index value	0	1	2	3	4	5	6	7	8	9	10
Index value R to L	–11	–10	–9	–8	–7	–6	–5	–4	–3	–2	–1

A number of SAS character handling functions have modifiers to enable scanning from right to left as opposed to the default behavior of scanning left to right.

Listing 2-31 illustrates finding the first character in a sequence (index 0 position).

Listing 2-31. Python String Slicing, Example 1

```
>>> s = 'Hello World'
>>> s[0]
'H'
```

In this example, the slicing operation contains no colon so the default is the "start" position being 0 as the index value which returns the first letter of the string.

Listing 2-32 is the analog example using the SUBSTR function to extract the first letter from the variable "s".

Listing 2-32. SAS SUBSTR Function

```
4   data _null_;
5       s = 'Hello World';
6       extract = substr(s, 1, 1);
7
8   put extract;
9   run;
```

OUTPUT:

H

In contrast to Python, with an index start position of 0, SAS uses an index start position of 1. The SAS SUBSTR function scans the character variable s (first argument), starts at position 1 (second argument), and extracts 1 character position (third argument).

Consider another example, Listing 2-33, having no start position which then defaults to 0. The stop position following the colon (:) goes up to but does include index position 5.

Listing 2-33. Python String Slicing, Example 2

```
>>> s = 'Hello World'
>>> s[:5]
'Hello'
```

In other words, in this example, index position 5 maps to the whitespace (blank) separating the two words and is not returned.

Listing 2-34 illustrates what happens when an index start value is greater than the length of sequence being sliced.

Listing 2-34. Python String Slicing, Example 3

```
>>> s = 'Hello World'
>>> print(len(s))
11
>>> empty = s[12:]
>>> print(empty)

>>>
>>> bool(empty)
False
```

When the index start value is greater than the length of the sliced sequence, Python does not raise an error, rather, it returns an empty (null) string. Recall from the preceding discussion on Boolean comparisons that empty objects evaluate False.

Now consider Listing 2-35 illustrating the case of when the stop value for string slicing is greater than the length of the actual string.

Listing 2-35. Python String Slicing, Example 4

```
>>> s = 'Hello World'
>>> s[:12]
'Hello World'
```

When the index stop value is greater than the length of the sliced sequence, then the entire sequence is returned.

Listing 2-36 identifies the start index position 3 which is included and the stop index position of –1 (indicating the last character in the sequences) which is not included.

Listing 2-36. Python String Slicing, Example 5

```
>>> s = 'Hello World'
>>> s[3:-1]
'lo Worl'
```

Since the stop index position is not inclusive, the last character in the sequence is not included.

If we want to include the last letter in this sequence, then we would leave the stop index value blank. Listing 2-37 illustrates how to return a sequence beginning at start position 3 to the end of the sliced sequence.

Listing 2-37. Python String Slicing, Example 6

```
>>> s = 'Hello World'
>>> s[3:]
'lo World'
```

Listing 2-38 illustrates scanning a sequence from right to left.

Listing 2-38. Python String Slicing, Example 7

```
>>> s = 'Hello World'
>>> s[-11]
'H'
>>> s[-12]
IndexError: string index out of range
```

With the first slice operation, because there is a single index value, it defaults to the `start` value. With a negative value, the slice operation begins at the end of the sequence and proceeds right to left decrementing the index value by 1 (assuming the `step` value remains the default value of 1).

In the second slice operation, a negative `start` value larger than the sequence length to be sliced is out of range and therefore raises an IndexError.

Listing 2-39 illustrates use of the backslash (\) to escape the single quote (') to be a part of the returned sequence.

Listing 2-39. Python String Quoting

```
>>> q = 'Python\'s capabilities'
>>> print(q)
Python's capabilities
>>> q1 = "Python's features"
>>> print(q1)
Python's features
```

Formatting

In the day-to-day work of data analysis, a good deal of energy is devoted to formatting of numerics and strings in our reports and analysis. We often need values used in our program output formatted for a more pleasing presentation. This often includes aligning text and numbers, adding symbols for monetary denominations, and mapping numerics into character strings. In this section we introduce the basics of Python string formatting. Throughout the rest of the book, we will encounter additional examples.

In the preceding examples, we saw illustrations of basic string manipulation methods. Python also provisions string formatting method calls and methods.

Formatting Strings

Formatting Python strings involve defining a string constant containing one or more format codes. The format codes are fields to be replaced enclosed by curly braces ({ }). Anything not contained in the replacement field is considered literal text, which is unchanged on output. The format arguments to be substituted into the replacement field can use either keyword ({gender}, e.g.) or positional ({0}, {1} e.g.) arguments.

A simple example for calling the format() method with a positional argument is illustrated in Listing 2-40.

Listing 2-40. Format Method with a Positional Argument

```
>>> 'The subject\'s gender is {0}'.format("Female")
"The subject's gender is Female"
```

The argument "Female" from the format() method is substituted into the replacement field designated by {0} contained inside the string constant literal text. Also notice the use of the backslash (\) to escape the single quote to indicate a possessive apostrophe for the string literal 'subject'.

Format specifications separated by a colon (:) are used to further enhance and control output appearances. This is illustrated in Listing 2-41.

Listing 2-41. Format Method Specification

```
>>> 'The subject\'s gender is {0:>10}'.format("Female")
"The subject's gender is     Female"
```

In Listing 2-41, the format specification in the replacement field uses the alignment option {0:>10} to force the replacement field to be right aligned with a width of ten characters. By default the field width is the same size as the string used to fill it. In subsequent examples we use this same pattern for format specifications to control the field width and appearances of numerics.

Listing 2-42 illustrates multiple positional arguments. Further, these positional arguments can be called in any order.

Listing 2-42. Format Method with Positional Arguments

```
>>> scale = 'Ratings are: {0} {1} or {2}'
>>> scale.format('1. Agree', '2. Neutral', '3. Disagree')
'Ratings are: 1. Agree 2. Neutral or 3. Disagree'
>>>
>>> scale = 'Ratings are: {2} {0} {1}'
>>> scale.format('1. Agree', '2. Neutral', '3. Disagree')
'Ratings are: 3. Disagree 1. Agree 2. Neutral'
```

The following syntax calls the string format() method to create three positional arguments

```
scale.format('1. Agree', '2. Neutral', '3. Disagree')
```

The format() method also accepts keyword= arguments as illustrated in Listing 2-43.

Listing 2-43. Format Method with Keyword Arguments

```
>>> location = 'Subject is in {city}, {state} {zip}'
>>> location.format(city='Denver', state='CO', zip='80218')
'Subject is in Denver, CO 80218'
```

Combining positional and keyword arguments together is illustrated in Listing 2-44.

Listing 2-44. Combining Format Method Keyword and Positional Arguments

```
>>> location = 'Subject is in {city}, {state}, {0}'
>>> location.format(80218, city='Denver', state='CO')
'Subject is in Denver, CO, 80218'
```

Notice when combining positional and keyword arguments together, keyword arguments are listed first followed by positional arguments.

Beginning with Python 3.6, formatted string literals or f-strings were introduced as an improved method for formatting. f-strings are designated with a preceding f and curly braces containing the replacement expression. f-strings are evaluated at runtime allowing the use of any valid expression inside the string. Consider Listing 2-45.

Listing 2-45. f-string Formatting

```
>>> radius = 4
>>> pi     = 3.14159
>>>
>>> print("Area of a circle with radius:", radius,
...       '\n',
...    f"is: {pi * radius **2}")
Area of a circle with radius: 4
 is: 50.26544
```

In this example, the formula for calculating the area of a circle is enclosed within a set of curly braces ({ }). At execution time, the results are calculated and printed as a result of calling the print() function.

Formatting Integers

The pattern for applying formats to integers is similar to that of strings. The main difference being the replacement field deals with formatting numeric values. And as indicated previously, some format specifications have values independent of the data types to be formatted. For example, field padding is common to all data types, whereas a comma separator (to indicate thousands) is only applied to integers and floats.

Consider Listing 2-46.

Listing 2-46. Decimal Right Aligned

```
>>> int = 123456789
>>> nl   = '\n'
>>> print(nl,
...         'int unformatted:', int,
...         nl,
...         'int formatted:' , "{:,d}".format(int))

 int unformatted: 123456789
 int formatted: 123,456,789
```

In this example, we use a positional argument for the format() method along with the format specification {:>20} to indicate we want the decimal value right aligned with a field width of 20.

Listing 2-47 illustrates combining multiple format specifications to achieve the desired appearance.

Listing 2-47. Combining Format Specifications

```
>>> print("{:>10,d}\n".format(123456789),
... "{:>10,d}".format(1089))
123,456,789
     1,089
```

In this example, the format specification {:>10,d} indicates the field is right justified with a width of 10. The ,d part of the specification indicates the digits use a comma as the thousands separator. This example uses a single print() function requiring a new line \n indicator after the first number in order to see the effect of the alignment.

Integers can be displayed with their corresponding octal, hexadecimal, and binary representation. This feature is illustrated in Listing 2-48.

Listing 2-48. Python Displaying Different Base Values

```
>>> int = 99
>>> nl = '\n'
>>>
>>> print (nl,
...          'decimal:     ', int,
...          nl,
...          'hexidecimal:', "{0:x}".format(int),
...          nl,
...          'octal:       ', "{0:o}".format(int),
...          nl,
...          'binary:      ', "{0:b}".format(int))

 decimal:      99
 hexidecimal: 63
 octal:       143
 binary:      1100011
```

The analog SAS program is shown in Listing 2-49.

Listing 2-49. SAS Displaying Different Base Values

```
4    data _null_;
5      input int 8.;
6      int_left = left(put(int, 8.));
7      put 'int:      ' int_left /
8          'hex:      ' int hex2. /
9          'octal:    ' int  octal. /
10         'binary:   ' int binary8. /
11         'Original: ' _infile_;
```

```
12  list;
13  datalines;
```

OUTPUT:

```
int:      99
hex:      63
octal:    143
binary:   01100011
Original: 99
RULE:        ----+----1----+----2----+----3----+----4----+----5
14           99

244  ;;;;
245  run;
```

This example reads on input the numeric value 99 and uses a PUT statement to write this value to the log using 8., hex2., octal., and binary8. formats.

For both Python and SAS, the default is to display integer values without leading zeros or a plus (+) sign to indicate positive integer values. Listing 2-50 illustrates how to alter these default behaviors.

Listing 2-50. Python Format for Leading 0's

```
>>> 'Integer 99 displayed as {:04d}'.format(99)
'Integer 99 displayed as 0099'
```

The format specifier :04d indicates leading zeros (0) are to be added in the field width of 4. The analog SAS program is shown in Listing 2-51.

Listing 2-51. SAS Format for Leading 0's

```
4   data _null_;
5     input int 8.;
6     /* display_int is a character variable */
7     display_int = put(int, z4.);
8     put 'int:      ' display_int/
9         'Original: ' _infile_;
10  list;
11  datalines;
```

```
int:       0099
Original: 99
RULE:        ----+----1----+----2----+----3----+----4----+----5
12           99
13   ;;;;
14   run;
```

This example uses the SAS-supplied z4. format shown on line 7.

In order to display the plus (+) sign for integers in Python, consider Listing 2-52.

Listing 2-52. Python Leading Plus Sign

```
>>> '{:+3d}'.format(99)
'+99'
```

The format specification {:+3d} indicates a preceding plus sign (+) using a field width of 3.

The corresponding SAS program in Listing 2-53 illustrates creating and calling a user-defined plussign. format.

Listing 2-53. SAS Leading Plus Sign

```
4  proc format;
5     picture plussign
6            0 - 99 = '  00' (prefix='+');
NOTE: Format PLUSSIGN has been output.
7
8  data _null_;
9     input int 8.;
10
11 put 'int:      ' int plussign. /
12       'Original: ' _infile_;
13 list;
14 datalines;

int:       +99
Original: 99
RULE:        ----+----1----+----2----+----3----+----4----+----5
```

```
15           99
16  ;;;;
17  run;
```

PROC FORMAT is used to create a PICTURE format and is called on line 11.

Formatting Floats

Consider Listing 2-54. This example illustrates a format specification for floats to display one digit after the decimal using {0:.1f} or four places after the decimal {0:.4f}. Regardless of how the value is displayed using one or four places to the right of the decimal, the internal representation of the value remains the same.

Listing 2-54. Python Decimal Places

```
>>> "precision: {0:.1f} or {0:.4f}".format(3.14159265)
'precision: 3.1 or 3.1416'
```

Listing 2-55 illustrates a format specification for percentages. In the case of both Python and SAS, the percent format multiplies the resulting number by 100 and places a trailing percent (%) sign.

Listing 2-55. Python Percent Format

```
>>> "6.33 as a Percentage of 150: {0:.2%}".format(6.33/150)
'6.33 as a Percentage of 150: 4.22%'
```

The analog SAS program, in Listing 2-56, uses the SAS-supplied percent 8.2 format to indicate two places after the decimal are displayed followed by a percent sign (%).

Listing 2-56. SAS Percent Format

```
4  data _null_;
5     pct = 6.33 / 150;
6
7  put '6.33 as a percentage of 150: ' pct percent8.2;
8  run;
```

OUTPUT:
```
6.33 as a percentage of 150:    4.22%
```

58

Datetime Formatting

Strictly speaking, datetime is not a Python built-in type but instead refers to the datetime module and their corresponding objects which supply classes for manipulating date and datetime values. These next examples illustrate using the strftime(format) for date, datetime, and time handling. Python date, datetime, and time objects support the strftime(format) method which is used to derive a string representing either dates or times from date and time objects. This string is then manipulated with directives to produce the desired appearances when displaying output. In other words, the strftime(format) method constructs strings from the date, datetime, and time objects rather than manipulating these objects directly.

We will see a good deal in more detail for date and time arithmetic in Chapter 7, "Date and Time." For now, consider Listing 2-57.

Listing 2-57. Python Import Datetime

```
>>> from datetime import datetime, date, time
>>> now = datetime.now()
>>> print(now)
2018-08-01 12:19:47.326261
>>> print(type(now))
<class 'datetime.datetime'>
```

Up to this point all of the Python examples we have seen are executed using a built-in interpreter. We have not needed to rely on additional Python modules or programs. In order to load other Python programs or modules, we use the import statement. Here, the first line in our example imports the objects datetime, date, and time from the Python module datetime.

In our example we also create the now object on line 2. In our program, the value associated with the now object is like a snapshot of time (assuming we did not execute line 2 again).

Calling the print() method for the now object displays the current data and time this program executed.

Consider Listing 2-58. Here we introduce formatting directives for date and time formatting.

Listing 2-58. STRFTIME(format)

```
>>> from datetime import datetime, date, time
>>>
>>> nl = '\n'
>>> now = datetime.now()
>>>
>>> print('now: ' , now,
...       nl      ,
...       'Year:' , now.strftime("%Y"),
...       nl      ,
...       'Month:' , now.strftime("%B"),
...       nl      ,
...       'Day:  ' , now.strftime("%d"),
...       nl, nl  ,
...       'concat1:'    , now.strftime("%A, %B %d, %Y A.D."),
...       nl,
...       'datetime:'    , now.strftime("%c"))
now:    2019-02-19 17:14:17.752075
Year:   2019
Month:  February
Day:    19

concat1: Tuesday, February 19, 2019 A.D.
datetime: Tue Feb 19 17:14:17 2019
```

The strftime(format) directives are used to control the appearances of the value associated with the now object created in Listing 2-57. The now object holds the datetime returned from the datetime.now() function. These formatting directives are able to parse as well as format and control the appearances of the output.

Also notice the nl object assigned the value '\n' used in this example. This is a new line indicator for the print() function to go to a new line enabling a single call of the print() function to print multiple, physical lines of output.

For example, the format directive %Y returns the century and year, for example, 2018. Table 2-5 calls out the formatting directive and the corresponding line number location for the preceding example.[4]

Table 2-5. *Formatting Directives Used in Listing 2-58*

Directive	Meaning
%A	Weekday
%B	Month
%d	Day of month
%Y	Century and year
%c	Date and time

Listing 2-59 is the analog program to the Python example.

Listing 2-59. SAS Datetime Example

```
4          data _null_;
5
6          * Get Year;
7          date = today();
8          year_pt = year(date);
9
10         * Get Month;
11         month_nm = put(date, monname.);
12         month_pt2 = put(date, monname3.);
13
14         * Get Day;
15         day_pt = put(day(date), z2.);
16         date2 = day(date);
17         dow1 = put(date, downame.);
18         dow2 = put(date, downame3.);
```

---

[4]The table of all formatting directives for strftime and strptime() is located at https://docs.python.org/3/library/datetime.html#strftime-and-strptime-behavior

```
19
20          * Get time;
21          now = time();
22          tm = put(now, time8.);
23
24          * whitespace, comma, suffix;
25          ws = ' ';
26          comma = ',';
27          ad = 'A.D.';
28
29          put 'Default output: ' date ' for time ' now;
30          put 'Year: ' year_pt;
31          put 'Month: ' month_nm;
32          put 'Day: ' day_pt ;
33
34          concat1 = cat(dow1, comma, month_nm, ws, day_pt, comma, ws,
            year_pt, ws, ad);
35          concat2 = cat(dow2, ws, month_pt2, ws, date2, ws, tm, ws, year_pt);
36
37          put 'concat1: ' concat1;
38          put 'current datetime: ' concat2;
39          run;
```

OUTPUT:
```
Default output: 20736  for time 71660.228
Year: 2016
Month: October     Day: 09

concat1: Sunday,   October 09, 2016 A.D.
current datetime: Sun Oct 9 19:54:20 2016
```

The output for the SAS variable date of 20736 is obviously not the actual date, rather, it represents the number of days since January 1, 1960, which is the epoch start used by SAS. Likewise, the output for the SAS variable now 71660.228 is the number of seconds from the epoch start.

Summary

In this chapter we covered Python types and basic formatting. We understand how Python and SAS variable assignments can be made without declarations and that types need not be declared as they are inferred. We also introduced Python string slicing and formatting. Throughout the remainder of the book, we will build on these concepts.

Up to this point, we have discussed various features from the Python Standard Library related to data analysis. Chapter 3, "pandas Library," describes the pandas data structure. The pandas library is a "higher-level" capability which makes Python an outstanding language for conducting real-world data analysis tasks.

CHAPTER 3

pandas Library

In this chapter we introduce a new library called pandas which in turn offers the DataFrame data structure. The pandas library evolved from the use of arrays in Python's NumPy package used in mathematical and scientific computing applications. The pandas library opens a new world of possibilities for data analysis. The main structure from the pandas library is the Series and DataFrame offering a structure to organize dissimilar types of data (strings, integers, and floats) into a single data structure and has the ability to easily apply methods or functions to all or portions of the data.

Some of the key features for pandas library include

- Provisions two array-like data structures, Series and DataFrame

- Easy detection and handling of missing data

- Easy slicing and subsetting operations

- Merging and joining of multiple DataFrames

- Automatic index objects for both rows and columns with multi-level/ hierarchical indexing

- Date range capabilities for custom date frequencies used in time Series analysis

- Loaders for input/output accepting a wide range of tabular data sources

- Wide range of built-in analysis methods

- Moving window statistics for rolling averages, rolling standard deviations, and so on

In many ways pandas DataFrames are very similar to and behave much like SAS datasets. See Table 3-1.

© Randy Betancourt, Sarah Chen 2019
R. Betancourt and S. Chen, *Python for SAS Users*, https://doi.org/10.1007/978-1-4842-5001-3_3

Table 3-1. *pandas and SAS Nomenclature*

pandas	SAS
DataFrame	Dataset
Row	Observation
Column	Variable
Groupby	By-Group
NaN	. (period)
Slice	Subset

For the remainder of the book, pandas are central to understanding Python in a data analysis context. pandas are not built-in to Python Standard Library and must be imported as shown in Listing 3-1. For our introduction to pandas, we import the numpy and pandas library. We also import the numpy.random.randn random number generator to draw a sample from the "standard normal" distribution.[1]

Listing 3-1. Importing Libraries

```
>>> import numpy as np
>>> import pandas as pd
>>> from numpy.random import randn
```

The first two import statements are followed by the keyword as followed by an identifier functioning as a short-hand for calling methods and functions associated with the library. The third import statement loads the randn random number generator from the numpy.random library. The numpy.random library provides an extensive set of generators for creating distributions and permutations. On line 3 the from statement imports just the randn generator feature. Later if we need to draw a sample using a binomial distribution, then the import statement to use is

```
from numpy.random import binomial
```

---

[1]See https://docs.scipy.org/doc/numpy-1.14.0/reference/routines.random.html

We begin by examining the Series data structure followed by the detailed examination of the DataFrame. The Series is a one-dimensional array container for a collection of either numerics or strings (but not both together). In a Series the numerics must be the same data type. A DataFrame is a container for a Series. DataFrames may contain strings and numerics with different data types.

Column Types

Before examining the details for Series and DataFrames, an overview of column types is useful. Previously in Chapter 2, "Python Types and Formatting," we discussed Python types. The pandas library is built on top of Python's NumPy library and inherits many of the NumPy types. Table 3-2 lists the column types encountered in this book.

Table 3-2. *Common pandas Types*

pandas Data Type	Python Data Type	Usage
Object	Str	Sequence of text
int64	Int	Integer value
float64	Float	Floating-point value
bool	Boolean	True/False
datetime64	N/A	Date and time values
timedelta	N/A	Difference between two datetimes
category	N/A	Corresponds to statistical categorical variables, e.g, gender

In general, we do not need to concern ourselves with types. Occasionally a program raises an error, perhaps as a result of an illegal operation using mismatched types. An example is summing numerical values from two different columns where unbeknownst to you, both columns have a type of "object". Rather than resulting in the summing of values, the results are concatenated values since the plus (+) symbol is used for string concatenation. Clearly not the results you are excepting. Later in the book, we encounter the DataFrame astype() method for converting types.

In the following examples, we encounter the types object, int64, and float64. In Chapter 7, "Date and Time," we discuss the datetime64 and timedelta types. The pandas type object is similar to a SAS character variable used to manipulate string values. The int64 and float64 are pandas types for integers and floating-point numbers respectfully. Both of these types are similar to a SAS numeric.

Series

From a SAS context, a Series can be thought of as a one-dimensional array with labels. A Series includes a default index used as a key to locate element values. Let's begin by constructing a Series with ten randomly generated numeric elements. Listing 3-2 illustrates the construction of a Series by calling the numpy.random function randn(). The randn() function draws a sample from the "standard normal" distribution. In order to make the Series reproducible, the random number generator is seeded with an initial value of 54321.

In this example, s1 is the Series name containing ten numeric elements with a type of float64. Notice the assignment statement on the second line. pd.Series is being called using pd as the identifier assigned following the keyword as from the import statement in Listing 3-1.

The print() method is combined with the head() function with the argument 5 to display the first five elements in the Series. Series are automatically indexed beginning at position 0. This index position is displayed to the left of the element values.

Listing 3-2. Create Series of Random Values

```
>>> np.random.seed(54321)
>>> s1 = pd.Series(randn(10))
>>> print(s1.head(5))
0    0.223979
1    0.744591
2   -0.334269
3    1.389172
4   -2.296095
dtype: float64
```

Contrast the Series created in Listing 3-2 with Listing 3-3.

Listing 3-3. SAS Array of Random Values

```
4 data _null_;
5    call streaminit(54321);
6
7  array s2 {10};
8     do i = 1 to 10;
9        s2{i} = rand("Normal");
10       if i <= 5 then put s2{i};
11    end;
12 run;
```

OUTPUT:

```
-1.364866914
1.9696792198
0.5123294653
-0.597981097
-0.895650739
```

Unlike most other programming languages, an array in the SAS language is not a data structure. Rather, an array in SAS is used as a convenience to iterate over groups of similar variables or values assigned to the array elements. While our analogy is imperfect, it remains useful for contrasting the two languages.

In Listing 3-3 we use a _NULL_ Data Step with a DO/END loop to generate ten random values from the normal random number generator. Similar to the preceding Python example, the call STREAMINIT function is used to supply a seed value to enable a reproducible stream of random numbers.

Line 7

```
array s2 {10};
```

defines a one-dimensional array called s2 containing ten elements.

Line 9

```
s2{i} = rand("Normal");
```

iterates over the array where i is the loop index variable calling the SAS rand("Normal") function and loads the generated values into the ten array elements.

Listing 3-4 illustrates the creation of a Series and with a user-defined index. Elements from a Series can be returned by the index value as illustrated here.

Index values are assigned to the Series using the Python list ([ ]) structure as a container. A Python list is a mutable structure for holding a collection of items. In this example, the syntax

```
index=['a', 'b', 'c', 'd', 'e', 'f', 'g', 'h', 'i', 'j']
```

creates a Python list called index to hold these values.

Listing 3-4. Series Index Labels

```
>>> np.random.seed(54321)
>>> s2 = pd.Series(randn(10), index=['a', 'b', 'c', 'd', 'e', 'f', 'g',
'h', 'i', 'j'])
>>> print(s2.head(5))
a    0.223979
b    0.744591
c   -0.334269
d    1.389172
e   -2.296095
dtype: float64
```

Series elements are returned either by their default index position or by a user-defined index value shown in Listing 3-5. In this example, the first element of the Series is returned.

Listing 3-5. Returning Series Elements

```
>>> print(s2[0])
0.22397889127879958
>>> print(s2['a'])
0.22397889127879958
```

In contrast, arrays in SAS must use a non-zero index start position for element retrieval. The same logic is shown using SAS in Listing 3-6.

Listing 3-6. SAS Array Indexed Retrieval

```
4 data _null_;
5   call streaminit(54321);
6
7 array s2 {10} ;
8    do i = 1 to 10;
9      s2{i} = rand("Normal");
10     if i = 1 then put s2{i};
11   end;
12 run;
```

OUTPUT:

-1.364866914

The DO/END block executes once based on the IF statement and writes the array element value to the SAS log.

Retrieval of values from a Series follows the string-slicing pattern presented in Chapter 2, "Python Types and Formatting." Listing 3-7 illustrates this syntax.

Listing 3-7. Series Returning First Three Elements

```
>>> print(s2[:3])
a    0.223979
b    0.744591
c   -0.334269
dtype: float64
>>> print(s2[:'c'])
a    0.223979
b    0.744591
c   -0.334269
dtype: float64
```

The value to the left of the colon (:) separator is the start position for the Series' index location, and values to the right identify the stop position for the element location. An empty value at the start position defaults to the first element (position 0), and an empty value for the stop value defaults to the last element (Series length –1).

71

Listing 3-8 is the SAS program with similar logic. It uses an IF statement within the DO/END block to return the first three array elements and print their values to the SAS log.

Listing 3-8. Array Returning First Three Elements

```
4 data _null_;
5    call streaminit(54321);
6
7 array s2 {10} ;
8    do i = 1 to 10;
9       s2{i} = rand("Uniform");
10      if i <= 3 then put s2{i};
11   end;
12 run;
```

OUTPUT:
```
0.4322317771
0.5977982974
0.7785986471
```

pandas allows mathematical operations to be combined with Boolean comparisons as a condition for returning elements from a Series. This is illustrated in Listing 3-9.

Listing 3-9. Series Mathematical Operation

```
>>> s2[s2 < s2.mean()]
2    -0.334269
4    -2.296095
7    -0.082760
8    -0.651688
9    -0.016022
dtype: float64
```

In the preceding example, the Boolean < operator is used to return any element in the Series whose value is less than the arithmetic mean value for all the Series elements.

DataFrames

You can think of a pandas DataFrame as a collection of Series into a relational-like structure with labels. There are a number of different constructor methods for creating DataFrames. DataFrames have a number of different readers to load values from a wide range of input sources including .csv files, DBMS tables, web scrapping, REST APIs, and SAS datasets (.sas7bdat files), to name a few. These DataFrame readers are similar to the SAS/Access product line.

The following is a basic introduction to the DataFrame reader `read_csv()` method. Chapter 6, "pandas Readers and Writers," covers this topic in more detail. This example uses the publicly available UK Accidents Report Data from January 1, 2015, to December 31, 2015, available from

```
https://data.gov.uk/dataset/cb7ae6f0-4be6-4935-9277-47e5ce24a11f/road-safety-data
```

Listing 3-10 illustrates the syntax.

Note   Since the time of this writing, the data available at this web site has changed, and the remaining examples utilize a copy of this data at

```
https://raw.githubusercontent.com/RandyBetancourt/
PythonForSASUsers/master/data/uk_accidents.csv
```

Listing 3-10. DataFrame read_csv Method, Example 1

```
>>> import pandas as pd
>>> file_loc = "C:\\Data\\uk_accidents.csv"
>>> df = pd.read_csv(file_loc)
```

Line 2 from this example defines the `file_loc` object to identify the path location to read the .csv file from the local filesystem. Note the double backslashes (\\) in the pathname for normalizing the Windows pathname. Without the double backslashes, a syntax error is raised. Line 3 constructs the DataFrame `df` by calling the `read_csv()` method. Unlike SAS, the read operation is silent with no status information returned after the read is completed unless an error is raised.

Listing 3-11 illustrates reading the same .csv file directly without needing to download the file manually.

Listing 3-11. DataFrame read_csv Method, Example 2

```
>>> df = pd.read_csv("https://raw.githubusercontent.com/RandyBetancourt/
PythonForSASUsers/master/data/uk_accidents.csv")
>>> print(df.shape)
(266776, 27)
```

The remainder of the examples in this chapter are dependent on executing Listing 3-11.

The print() function displays the value from the DataFrame shape attribute to indicate the number of rows and columns in the DataFrame.

Listing 3-12 illustrates the syntax for PROC IMPORT from Base SAS software to read the UK accident .csv file stored on GitHub.

Listing 3-12. SAS PROC IMPORT

```
4   filename git_csv temp;
5   proc http
6       url="https://raw.githubusercontent.com/RandyBetancourt/
        PythonForSASUsers/master/data/uk_accidents.csv"
7       method="GET"
8       out=git_csv;
9
10  proc import datafile = git_csv
11      dbms=csv
12      out=uk_accidents;
13  run;

NOTE: 266776 records were read from the infile GIT_CSV.
      The minimum record length was 65.
      The maximum record length was 77.
NOTE: The dataset WORK.UK_ACCIDENTS has 266776 observations and 27
variables.

266776 rows created in WORK.UK_ACCIDENTS from GIT_CSV.

NOTE: WORK.UK_ACCIDENTS dataset was successfully created.
```

74

The `filename` statement on line 4 defines the fileref `git_csv` as a temporary location on the local filesystem to output the .csv file. The syntax

```
proc import datafile = git_csv
```

reads the .csv file downloaded by PROC HTTP.

DataFrame Validation

pandas provide a number of methods to begin the process of validation. As an example, the shape attribute returns a DataFrame's row and column count. This is illustrated in Listing 3-13.

Listing 3-13. DataFrame Characteristics

```
>>> print(df.shape)
(266776, 27)
```

In this example, the DataFrame `df` has 266,777 rows and 27 columns.

In order to understand how the data is physically organized, use the info() method to display information such as column names, column count, index structure, and so on.

Listing 3-14 illustrates the use of the info() method to return detailed information on the contents of a DataFrame. The DataFrame info() method returns output similar to that from PROC CONTENTS for understanding physical characteristics of a SAS dataset.

Listing 3-14. Examining the DataFrame's Organization

```
>>> print(df.info())
<class 'pandas.core.frame.DataFrame'>
RangeIndex: 266776 entries, 0 to 266775
Data columns (total 27 columns):
Accident_Severity          266776 non-null int64
Number_of_Vehicles         266776 non-null int64
Number_of_Casualties       266776 non-null int64
Day_of_Week                266776 non-null int64
Time                       266752 non-null object
Road_Type                  266776 non-null int64
Speed_limit                266776 non-null int64
```

```
Junction_Detail                  266776 non-null int64
Light_Conditions                 266776 non-null int64
Weather_Conditions               266776 non-null int64
Road_Surface_Conditions          266776 non-null int64
Urban_or_Rural_Area              266776 non-null int64
Vehicle_Reference                266776 non-null int64
Vehicle_Type                     266776 non-null int64
Skidding_and_Overturning         266776 non-null int64
Was_Vehicle_Left_Hand_Drive_     266776 non-null int64
Sex_of_Driver                    266776 non-null int64
Age_of_Driver                    266776 non-null int64
Engine_Capacity__CC_             266776 non-null int64
Propulsion_Code                  266776 non-null int64
Age_of_Vehicle                   266776 non-null int64
Casualty_Class                   266776 non-null int64
Sex_of_Casualty                  266776 non-null int64
Age_of_Casualty                  266776 non-null int64
Casualty_Severity                266776 non-null int64
Car_Passenger                    266776 non-null int64
Date                             266776 non-null object
dtypes: int64(25), object(2)
memory usage: 55.0+ MB
None
```

The first line of output identifies the DataFrame as belonging to the object class `pandas.core.frame.DataFrame`.

Next, information about the RangeIndex object is presented. The RangeIndex object is used as a row label. Like a SAS dataset, DataFrames can be subset by rows, by columns, or some combination of both. DataFrame row labels are identifiers for performing certain row-based subsetting operations similar to the behavior of the SAS automatic variable _N_. Chapter 5, "Data Management," covers this topic in more detail.

When a DataFrame is constructed and no column, or collection of columns is defined as the index, then by default, the RangeIndex object is created using a start position of 0 and an end position of DataFrame length –1. Alternatively, a DataFrame can be constructed designating a column or collection of columns as the index using the syntax

```
df = pd.read_csv('d:\\data\\Customers.csv', index_col = ['Last_Name,
First_Name'])
```

Further, the DataFrame index can be altered dynamically. The DataFrame method set_index() is used to designate any column or collection of columns as the index after the DataFrame is created.

The bulk of the output from the info() method displays the column attribute information. The last column from the info() method output displays the DataFrame column types. In this example, there are 25 numeric columns with type int64 and 2 columns with type object, similar to a character variable in a SAS dataset.

The dtype attribute is used to return the type for any DataFrame column as shown in Listing 3-15.

Listing 3-15. DataFrame dtype Attribute

```
>>> df['Date'].dtype
dtype('O')
```

This rather sparse output indicates the Date column in the df DataFrame is type object; in other words the column values are strings. Of course, in order to do any meaningful time-based analysis with the Date column, it must have datetime64 as its type.

In Listing 3-10 and Listing 3-11 examples, the read_csv() method uses a default type mappings when constructing the DataFrame from the .csv file. In Chapter 6, "pandas Readers and Writers," we will illustrate in detail how to take advantage of date parsers in order to load datetime values stored as strings directly into DataFrame columns with a datetime64 type.

For example, the syntax

```
file_loc = "C:\\Data\\uk_accidents.csv"
df = pd.read_csv(file_loc, parse_dates=['Date'])
```

uses the parse_dates= list data structure to designate the .csv column named Date is read using the default date parser and results in a datetime64 DataFrame column type without the need for an intermediate conversion step.

DataFrame Inspection

Inspection refers to the task of displaying portions of the values contained by the DataFrame to increase the understanding of the data contents. With SAS this is accomplished with features like PROC PRINT and PROC SQL. The head() and tail() functions display by default the first ten rows and the last ten rows, respectively, of a DataFrame. If you are familiar with Unix, then you will recognize that these DataFrame function names derive from the head command to display the first five rows of a file and the tail function to display the last five rows of a file. You can pass an integer argument to the tail() function, for example:

```
df.tail(24)
```

displays the last 24 rows of the df DataFrame.

Listing 3-16 illustrates use of an integer argument of 10 to return the last ten rows.

Listing 3-16. DataFrame tail() method

```
>>> df.tail(10)
        Accident_Severity      ...           Date
266766                   2     ...       8/30/2015
266767                   3     ...      11/29/2015
266768                   3     ...      11/29/2015
266769                   3     ...      11/29/2015
266770                   3     ...       7/26/2015
266771                   3     ...       7/26/2015
266772                   3     ...      12/31/2015
266773                   3     ...       7/28/2015
266774                   3     ...       7/28/2015
266775                   3     ...       7/15/2015

[10 rows x 27 columns]
```

Notice the first column of output from the tail(10) function displays the RangeIndex values. As an analogy, SAS uses the FIRSTOBS and OBS dataset option followed by a value for _N_ with most procedures as a means to determine which observations to include for processing.

For example, consider Listing 3-17.

Listing 3-17. PROC PRINT Firstobs =

```
4 proc print data = uk_accidents (firstobs = 266767);
5   var Accident_Severity Date;
6 run;
```

```
NOTE: There were 10 observations read from the dataset WORK.UK_ACCIDENTS.
```

The FIRSTOBS= dataset option is set to 266767 in order to display the last ten observations in the SAS dataset WORK.uk_accidents created in Listing 3-12. The SAS Note indicates ten rows were read from the dataset. Figure 3-1 displays the output.

Obs	Accident_Severity	Date
266767	2	08/30/2015
266768	3	11/29/2015
266769	3	11/29/2015
266770	3	11/29/2015
266771	3	07/26/2015
266772	3	07/26/2015
266773	3	12/31/2015
266774	3	07/28/2015
266775	3	07/28/2015
266776	3	07/15/2015

Figure 3-1. *Print Last Ten OBS*

Notice that the last row label for the DataFrame in Listing 3-16, DataFrame tail function is 266775, while the last observation number in the SAS output is 266776. Recall the default row index value for a DataFrame starts at 0, and the SAS automatic variable _N_ starts at 1.

As one would expect, the head(5) function returns the first five rows from a DataFrame as illustrated in Listing 3-18.

Listing 3-18. DataFrame head() Function

```
>>> df.head(5)
   Accident_Severity      ...          Date
0                  3      ...      1/9/2015
1                  3      ...      1/9/2015
2                  3      ...     2/23/2015
3                  3      ...     2/23/2015
4                  3      ...     2/23/2015

[5 rows x 27 columns]
```

The syntax for displaying the first five observations in a SAS dataset is

```
proc print data=uk_accidents (obs = 5);
```

Listing 3-19 illustrates the DataFrame describe() function to report measures of central tendencies, dispersion, and shape for all numeric types. Due to space limitations, only the first two columns of output are displayed. The describe() function display is similar to output produced with PROC MEANS in SAS.

Listing 3-19. DataFrame describe() Function

```
>>> df.describe()
       Accident_Severity  Number_of_Vehicles       ...
count      266776.000000       266776.000000       ...
mean            2.871529            4.103994       ...
std             0.361889            4.388495       ...
min             1.000000            1.000000       ...
25%             3.000000            2.000000       ...
50%             3.000000            2.000000       ...
75%             3.000000            3.000000       ...
max             3.000000           37.000000       ...

[8 rows x 25 columns]
```

Listing 3-20 returns output similar to that of the describe() function.

Listing 3-20. PROC MEANS

```
4 proc means data = uk_accidents;
5    var Accident_Severity Number_of_Vehicles;
6 run;
```

The output from Listing 3-20 is shown in Figure 3-2.

The MEANS Procedure

Variable	N	Mean	Std Dev	Minimum	Maximum
Accident_Severity	266776	2.8715289	0.3618894	1.0000000	3.0000000
Number_of_Vehicles	266776	4.1039936	4.3884950	1.0000000	37.0000000

Figure 3-2. PROC MEANS Output

DataFrames have a variety of methods to slice and dice (subset) data. We will review these features in detail in Chapter 4, "Indexing and GroupBy." For now we introduce the slicing operator [[ ]] to select a set of rows and/or columns from a DataFrame.

Listing 3-21 illustrates the [[ ]] slicing operator returning columns by labels chained with the head() function to display the first ten rows.

Listing 3-21. DataFrame Column Slicing

```
>>> df[['Sex_of_Driver', 'Time']].head(10)
   Sex_of_Driver    Time
0              1   19:00
1              1   19:00
2              1   18:30
3              2   18:30
4              1   18:30
5              1   17:50
6              1   17:50
7              1    7:05
8              1    7:05
9              1   12:30
```

In SAS, the syntax for displaying the first ten observations for the Sex_of_Driver and Time variables is

```
proc print data=uk_accidents (obs = 10);
    var Sex_of_Driver Time;
```

As one would expect, there are a large number of statistical and visualization techniques that can be applied to all or portions of a DataFrame to derive meaningful information and insights. One such example is the hist() method to render a histogram.

Listing 3-22 displays the Python code used to create the histogram in Figure 3-3.

Listing 3-22. Histogram of Accident Rates by Gender

```
>>> import matplotlib.pyplot as plt
>>> df.hist(column='Sex_of_Driver', grid=False)
>>> plt.show()
```

From the supplied metadata, we know the variable Sex_of_Driver value of 1 maps to males, 2 to females, 3 to not known and –1 to data missing or out of range.

Figure 3-3. *Histogram of Accident Rates by Gender*

From this simple histogram, we see males have an accident rate over twice that of females.

Missing Data

One of the more challenging aspects for data analysis is the treatment of missing data. Data may be missing for a wide range of reasons. It may be the data is not available or the data was not collected. Sometime values are recorded inaccurately. Whatever the reasons for encountering missing data, we need a good strategy for dealing with this challenge.

pandas use two built-in values or sentinel values for handling missing data, the Python None object and NaN (not a number) object. The None object is often used to indicate missing values in Python code. The None object is used as a missing value indicator for DataFrame columns with a type of object (character strings). In contrast NaN is a special floating-point value used to indicate missing values for the float64 type. This means NaN is specifically for floating-point values with no equivalent for strings, integers, or other pandas types.

However, this is generally not an issue. To use missing data with an integer column, the column will be upcasted to a type float. pandas does this conversion transparently for you if you assign the None object into a column of data type int.

As an example consider Listing 3-23 and Listing 3-24 together.

Listing 3-23. Construct df1 DataFrame

```
>>> import pandas as pd
>>> df1 = pd.DataFrame([['cold', 9],
...                     ['warm', 4],
...                     [None , 4]],
...                     columns=['Strings', 'Integers'])
>>> print(df1)
  Strings  Integers
0    cold         9
1    warm         4
2    None         4
>>> print(df1.dtypes)
Strings     object
Integers     int64
```

Listing 3-23 creates the df1 DataFrame with two columns labeled Strings and Integers. The type for the Strings column is object and the type for the column Integers is int64.

The first print() function displays the df1 DataFrame. The second print() function returns the column types. Since all values for the Integers column are integer values, the type for the column is naturally int64. On row 2 the value for the Strings column is missing as indicated by the None object for its value.

Now consider Listing 3-24. This example illustrates how pandas automatically upcasted the DataFrame's column Integers from int64 to float64 in order to accommodate the update of the value 9 to None indicating a missing value.

Listing 3-24. Update df1 DataFrame

```
>>> df1.loc[df1.Integers == 9, 'Integers'] = None
>>> print(df1)
   Strings  Integers
0    cold       NaN
1    warm       4.0
2    None       4.0
>>> print(df1.dtypes)
Strings      object
Integers    float64
```

The first line of this example uses the DataFrame loc() indexer and Boolean logic to locate and update the Integers column on the row where its value is 9 and updates this value to missing using the None object. The corresponding SAS syntax in a Data Step is used to update a numerical value to missing is

```
if integers = 9 then integers = .;
```

In Listing 3-23 the type for the Integers column is int64. As a result of the in-place update of the value 9 to the Python object None, the type for this column is now float64. Also notice how the output from the print() function in Listing 3-24 displays the updated value as a NaN, the missing value indicator for float64 even though the None object is assigned. This is a result of automatically upcasting the column type to accommodate missing values and how NaNs are used as a missing data indicator for columns with type float64.

To further the understanding of missing value treatment by pandas, consider
Listing 3-25 to create the df2 DataFrame.

Listing 3-25. pandas Missing Values

```
>>> import pandas as pd
>>> df2 = pd.DataFrame([['cold','slow', None, 2.7, 6.6, 3.1],
...                     ['warm', 'medium', 4.2, 5.1, 7.9, 9.1],
...                     ['hot', 'fast', 9.4, 11.0, None, 6.8],
...                     ['cool', None, None, None, 9.1, 8.9],
...                     ['cool', 'medium', 6.1, 4.3, 12.2, 3.7],
...                     [None, 'slow', None, 2.9, 3.3, 1.7],
...                     [None, 'slow', None, 2.9, 3.3, 1.7]],
...                     columns=['Temp', 'Speed', 'Measure1', 'Measure2',
...                              'Measure3', 'Measure4'])
>>> print(df2)
    Temp   Speed  Measure1  Measure2  Measure3  Measure4
0   cold    slow       NaN       2.7       6.6       3.1
1   warm  medium       4.2       5.1       7.9       9.1
2    hot    fast       9.4      11.0       NaN       6.8
3   cool    None       NaN       NaN       9.1       8.9
4   cool  medium       6.1       4.3      12.2       3.7
5   None    slow       NaN       2.9       3.3       1.7
6   None    slow       NaN       2.9       3.3       1.7
>>> print(df2.dtypes)
Temp         object
Speed        object
Measure1    float64
Measure2    float64
Measure3    float64
Measure4    float64
```

In this example, the Python None object is used to indicate NA's or missing values for
columns with type object (character data) and columns with the type float64 (numeric
data). Even though we use the Python None object to indicate a missing value for
columns Measure1–Measure4, the sentinel value NaN is used to represent these missing
values. That is because columns Measure1–Measure4 have a type of float64.

Missing Value Detection

With this basic knowledge of missing values for pandas, the next step is understanding missing value detection along with missing value replacement. Table 3-3 lists the functions applied to a pandas DataFrame or Series to detect and replace missing values.

Table 3-3. *pandas Missing Replacement Functions*

Function	Action Taken
isnull()	Generates a Boolean mask indicating missing values
notnull()	Opposite of isnull()
dropna()	Returns a filtered copy of the original DataFrame
fillna()	Returns a copy of the original DataFrame with missing values filled or imputed

Each of these functions is examined in detail in the following text.

In SAS there are a number of different approaches to use for missing value detection and replacement. One approach with SAS is to write a Data Step to traverse along variables and use IF/THEN logic to test for and replace missing values reading the entire dataset observation by observation.

Python permits a similar approach using the isnull() function illustrated in Listing 3-26.

Listing 3-26. Count Missing Values Iteratively

```
>>> for col_name in df2.columns:
...       print (col_name, end="---->")
...       print (sum(df2[col_name].isnull()))
...
Temp---->2
Speed---->1
Measure1---->4
Measure2---->1
Measure3---->1
Measure4---->0
```

In this example, a Python `for` loop iterates over the columns in the `df2` DataFrame (created in Listing 3-25) and uses the `sum()` method combined with the `isnull()` method to return a count of missing values for each column. While this example returns the correct results, there is a more Pythonic approach for achieving the same results.

As an aside, if you find yourself devising programming algorithms in Python using iterative methods, stop and take time to do research. Chances are a method or function for the object, in this case, a DataFrame, already exists.

Listing 3-27 is a case in point. Rather than iterating over the columns in `df2` DataFrame shown in Listing 3-26, a more direct and efficient approach is to use the DataFrame `isnull()` method combined with the sum() method for the entire `df2` DataFrame.

Listing 3-27. isnull Returning Missing Count

```
>>> df2.isnull().sum()
Temp        2
Speed       1
Measure1    4
Measure2    1
Measure3    1
Measure4    0
```

Only three lines of Python code in Listing 3-26 are used to iterate over the `df2` columns and call the `isnull()` method combined with the `sum()` method. In contrast, Listing 3-27 requires only one line of code.

An approach to identifying missing values with SAS is illustrated in Listing 3-28. In this example, `PROC FORMAT` bins all values into missing and non-missing "buckets." By default SAS uses a period (.) for missing numeric values and a blank (ASCII 32) to indicate missing for character variables. Therefore, a user-defined format is needed for both numeric and character variables.

Listing 3-28. PROC FORMAT to Identify Missing Values

```
4   data df;
5      infile cards;
6      input temp $4.
7             speed $7.
8          @14 measure1
```

```
9        @18 measure2
10       @23 measure3
11       @28 measure4 ;
12   list;
13   datalines;
```

RULE:	----+----1----+----2----+----3----+----4----+----5

```
14       cold slow    .    2.7  6.6   3.1
15       warm medium  4.2  5.1  7.9   9.1
16       hot  fast    9.4  11.0 .     6.8
17       cool         .    .    9.1   8.9
18       cool medium  6.1  4.3  12.2  3.7
19            slow    .    2.9  3.3   1.7
20            slow    .    2.9  3.3   1.7
```

NOTE: The dataset WORK.DF has 7 observations and 6 variables.

```
21   ;;;;
22   proc print;
```

NOTE: There were 7 observations read from the dataset WORK.DF.

```
23   proc format;
24     value $missfmt ' '='Missing' other='Not Missing';
```
NOTE: Format $MISSFMT has been output.
```
25     value  missfmt  . ='Missing' other='Not Missing';
```
NOTE: Format MISSFMT has been output.
```
26 proc freq data=df;
27     format _CHARACTER_ $missfmt.;
28     tables _CHARACTER_ / missing missprint nocum nopercent;
29
30     format _NUMERIC_ missfmt.;
31     tables _NUMERIC_ / missing missprint nocum nopercent;
32 run;
```

The user-defined $missfmt.$ format bins character variable values into two buckets: those with a blank value (ASCII 32) to indicate a missing value labeled "Missing" and all other values labeled "Not Missing". Similarly, the user-defined missfmt. format bins numeric variables into two buckets: those with a period (.) labeled "Missing" and all other values labeled "Not Missing".

Figure 3-4 displays the output from PROC PRINT. The character variables temp and speed use blanks (ASCII 32) to indicate missing values. The numeric variables measure1–measure4 use a period (.) to indicate missing values.

Obs	temp	speed	measure1	measure2	measure3	measure4
1	cold	slow	.	2.7	6.6	3.1
2	warm	medium	4.2	5.1	7.9	9.1
3	hot	fast	9.4	11.0	.	6.8
4	cool		.	.	9.1	8.9
5	cool	medium	6.1	4.3	12.2	3.7
6		slow	.	2.9	3.3	1.7
7		slow	.	2.9	3.3	1.7

Figure 3-4. *SAS Dataset df*

Figure 3-5 displays output from PROC FREQ calling the user-defined $missfmt. format for binning missing/non-missing character variables and the missfmt. for binning missing/non-missing numeric variables. The missing option for table statement is required in order for PROC FREQ to include missing values in the output.

The FREQ Procedure

temp	Frequency
Missing	2
Not Missing	5

speed	Frequency
Missing	1
Not Missing	6

measure1	Frequency
Missing	4
Not Missing	3

measure2	Frequency
Missing	1
Not Missing	6

measure3	Frequency
Missing	1
Not Missing	6

measure4	Frequency
Not Missing	7

Figure 3-5. *SAS Missing Value Detection with PROC FREQ*

isnull() Method

Calling the isnull() method returns a DataFrame of Boolean values. This is illustrated in Listing 3-29.

Listing 3-29. isnull() Boolean Mask

```
>>> print(df2)
    Temp   Speed  Measure1  Measure2  Measure3  Measure4
0   cold    slow       NaN       2.7       6.6       3.1
1   warm  medium       4.2       5.1       7.9       9.1
2    hot    fast       9.4      11.0       NaN       6.8
3   cool    None       NaN       NaN       9.1       8.9
4   cool  medium       6.1       4.3      12.2       3.7
5   None    slow       NaN       2.9       3.3       1.7
6   None    slow       NaN       2.9       3.3       1.7
>>> df2.isnull()
    Temp   Speed  Measure1  Measure2  Measure3  Measure4
0  False   False      True     False     False     False
1  False   False     False     False     False     False
2  False   False     False     False      True     False
3  False    True      True      True     False     False
4  False   False     False     False     False     False
5   True   False      True     False     False     False
6   True   False      True     False     False     False
```

The isnull() method returns a DataFrame of Boolean values with None objects and NaN's returned as True while non-missing values are returned as False. Unlike SAS, empty or blank values for DataFrame columns with an object type are not considered missing.

The notnull() method is the inverse of the isnull() method. It produces a Boolean mask where null or missing values are returned as False and non-missing values are returned as True.

The behavior of missing values for DataFrames used in mathematical operations and functions is similar to SAS' behavior. In the case of DataFrames

- Row-wise operations on missing data propagate missing values.

- For methods and function, missing values are treated as zero.

- If all data values are missing, the results from methods and functions will be 0.

To illustrate, consider the following examples. Listing 3-30 illustrates the syntax for creating a new column labeled Sum_M3_M4 with a row-wise summing of columns Col4 and Col5 together.

Listing 3-30. Addition Data with NaN's

```
>>> df2['Sum_M3_M4'] = df2['Measure3'] + df2['Measure4']
>>> print(df2[['Measure3', 'Measure4', 'Sum_M3_M4']])
   Measure3  Measure4  Sum_M3_M4
0       6.6       3.1        9.7
1       7.9       9.1       17.0
2       NaN       6.8        NaN
3       9.1       8.9       18.0
4      12.2       3.7       15.9
5       3.3       1.7        5.0
6       3.3       1.7        5.0
```

In a row-wise arithmetic operation, missing values (NaNs) are propagated. Also observe the print() function used to display a subset of columns from DataFrame df2. Chapter 5, "Data Management," details indexing and slicing operations for DataFrames. The syntax

```
print(df2[['Measure3', 'Measure4', 'Sum_M3_M4']])
```

is a form of DataFrame slicing [[ ]], in this case, columns Measure3, Measure4, and Sum_M3_M4 are returned as a DataFrame, then passed to the print() method.

This is analogous to the var statement in PROC PRINT for SAS:

```
proc print data=df2;
   var measure3 measure4 sum_m3_m4;
```

Also recall how variable names in Python are case-sensitive and case-insensitive in SAS.

Listing 3-31 returns the arithmetic sum for the column labeled Sum_M3_M4. The sum() method is applied to the column Sum_M3_M4, and in this operation, a NaN is mapped to zero. In general Python methods will ignore missing data; however, that is not always the case.

Listing 3-31. Sum Function with NaN's, Example 1

```
>>> print(df2[['Sum_M3_M4']])
   Sum_M3_M4
0        9.7
1       17.0
2        NaN
3       18.0
4       15.9
5        5.0
6        5.0
>>> df2['Sum_M3_M4'].sum()
70.6
```

In this example, the sum() method is combined with the column df2[Sum_M3_M4] returning the value 70.6. Strictly speaking, df2[Sum_M3_M4] is a Series.

Listing 3-32 illustrates this same behavior with respect to missing values.

Listing 3-32. SAS Sum Function with Missing

```
4  proc sql;
5    create table df_sum as
6      select *
7              , (measure3 + measure4) as Sum_M3_M4
8      from df;
NOTE: Table WORK.DF_SUM created, with 7 rows and 7 columns.
9
10     select Sum_M3_M4
11       from df_sum;
NOTE: Writing HTML Body file: sashtml.htm
12
13     select 'Sum Function Applied to Measure 5'
14             ,sum(Sum_M3_M4)
15       from df_sum;
16 quit;
```

The `PROC SQL SELECT` statement creates the variable `Sum_M3_M4` on the SAS dataset `df_sum`. Observe how this sum operation is analogous to Listing 3-31. Like the Python example, the addition of SAS performs on observation 3 with

```
(measure3 + measure4) as Sum_M3_M4
```

as the second variable in the `SELECT` statement propagates a missing value. For observation 3, `measure3` is missing and `measure4` has a value of 6.8 resulting in a missing value for the variable `Sum_M3_M4` displayed as the first piece of output in Figure 3-6.

The second `SELECT` statement displays the values for the variable `Sum_M3_M4`. The third `SELECT` statement uses the `SUM` function to add the values in the column `Sum_M3_M4`. The output is displayed as the second piece of output in Figure 3-6.

Sum_M3_M4
9.7
17
.
18
15.9
5
5

Sum Function Applied to Sum_M3_M4	70.6

Figure 3-6. *SAS SUM Function with Missing Values*

Consider Listing 3-33. As discussed previously the default behavior for the `sum()` method is to map the NaN value on row 2 to the value 0. Listing 3-33, illustrates how to override this default behavior.

Listing 3-33. Sum Method with NaN's, Example 2

```
>>> print(df2[['Sum_M3_M4']])
    Sum_M3_M4
0         9.7
1        17.0
2         NaN
3        18.0
4        15.9
5         5.0
6         5.0
>>> df2['Sum_M3_M4'].sum(skipna=False)
nan
```

The parameter skipna=False forces the sum() method to return a NaN if a value of NaN is encountered in the operation.

Listing 3-34 illustrates adding the column labeled Measure5 to DataFrame df2 with all values set to missing using the None object. Applying the sum() method to Measure5 returns a value of zero (0) since all values in this column are missing.

Listing 3-34. Sum Method with All Missing Values

```
>>> df2['Measure5'] = None
>>> print(df2['Measure5'])
0    None
1    None
2    None
3    None
4    None
5    None
6    None
Name: Measure5, dtype: object
>>> df2['Measure5'].sum()
0
```

Likewise, the behavior for the SAS SUM function returns zero in the case where all input values are missing. Consider Listing 3-35.

Listing 3-35. SAS Sum Function with All Missing Values

```
4    data _null_;
5      do i= 1 to 7;
6         measure5 = .;
7         put measure5;
8         sum_m5 = sum(measure5);
9         sum_0_m5 = sum(0, measure5);
10     end;
11     put 'SUM(measure5) Returns:' sum_m5;
12     put 'SUM(0, measure5) Returns:' sum_0_m5;
```

OUTPUT:

```
.

.

.

.

.

.

.

SUM(measure5) Returns:.
SUM(0, measure5) Returns:0
```

A _NULL_ Data Step iterates seven times by setting all instances for variable measure5 to missing value and prints the default SAS sentinel missing value for numerics, a period (.) to the log. The statement on line 8

```
sum_m5 = sum(measure5);
```

illustrates the default behavior of the SAS SUM function returning missing (.) since all values for the variable measure5 are set to missing. The syntax

```
sum_0_m5 = sum(0, measure5);
```

illustrates overriding this default behavior and having the SUM function return zero (0) when all input values to the function are missing.

Dropping Missing Values

One method for dealing with missing values is to drop the row or column in which the missing value is found. This approach is illustrated in Listing 3-36.

Listing 3-36. dropna() Method

```
>>>df2['Measure5'] = 0
>>>df3 = df2.dropna()
>>> print(df3)
   Temp   Speed  Measure1  Measure2  Measure3  Measure4
1  warm  medium       4.2       5.1       7.9       9.1
4  cool  medium       6.1       4.3      12.2       3.7
```

Calling the dropna() method without any parameters drops those rows where one or more values are missing regardless of the column's type. The default behavior for dropna() is to operate along rows or axis 0 and return a new DataFrame with the original DataFrame unmodified. In this example, DataFrame df3 is derived from DataFrame df2 and excludes dropped values from DataFrame df2. Alternatively, the default inplace=False parameter can be set to True in order to perform an in-place update to the original DataFrame.

Listing 3-37 illustrates an in-place update for the dropna() method dropping rows with missing values.

Listing 3-37. dropna() Update in Place

```
>>> import pandas as pd
>>> df4 = pd.DataFrame([['cold','slow', None, 2.7, 6.6, 3.1],
...                 ['warm', 'medium', 4.2, 5.1, 7.9, 9.1],
...                 ['hot', 'fast', 9.4, 11.0, None, 6.8],
...                 ['cool', None, None, None, 9.1, 8.9],
...                 ['cool', 'medium', 6.1, 4.3, 12.2, 3.7],
...                 [None, 'slow', None, 2.9, 3.3, 1.7],
...                 [None, 'slow', None, 2.9, 3.3, 1.7]],
...                 columns=['Temp', 'Speed', 'Measure1',
...                 'Measure2', 'Measure3', 'Measure4'])
```

```
>>> print(df4)
   Temp   Speed  Measure1  Measure2  Measure3  Measure4
0  cold    slow       NaN       2.7       6.6       3.1
1  warm  medium       4.2       5.1       7.9       9.1
2   hot    fast       9.4      11.0       NaN       6.8
3  cool    None       NaN       NaN       9.1       8.9
4  cool  medium       6.1       4.3      12.2       3.7
5  None    slow       NaN       2.9       3.3       1.7
6  None    slow       NaN       2.9       3.3       1.7
>>> df4.dropna(inplace=True)
>>> print(df4)
   Temp   Speed  Measure1  Measure2  Measure3  Measure4
1  warm  medium       4.2       5.1       7.9       9.1
4  cool  medium       6.1       4.3      12.2       3.7
```

Unlike Listing 3-34, this example does not make an assignment to create a new DataFrame. Instead, the original DataFrame df4 is updated in place with the inplace=True parameter.

The SAS CMISS function can be used to detect and then delete observations containing one or more missing values as illustrated in Listing 3-38.

Listing 3-38. CMISS Delete Observation with Any Missing Values

```
4    data df4;
5        set df;
6        if cmiss(of _all_) then delete;
7
NOTE: There were 7 observations read from the dataset WORK.DF.
NOTE: The dataset WORK.DF4 has 2 observations and 6 variables.

8    proc print data = df4;
9    run;
```

The argument to the CMISS function uses the automatic SAS variable _ALL_ to designate all variables in the dataset. In this case, the of parameter to the CMISS function is required; otherwise, the code produces the error

```
Cannot use _all_ as a variable name.
```

Figure 3-7 displays the resulting SAS dataset df4.

Obs	temp	speed	measure1	measure2	measure3	measure4
1	warm	medium	4.2	5.1	7.9	9.1
2	cool	medium	6.1	4.3	12.2	3.7

Figure 3-7. *Results from CMISS Function*

The dropna() method also works along a column axis. DataFrames refer to rows as axis 0 and columns as axis 1. The default behavior for the dropna() method is to operate along axis 0 or rows.

Listing 3-39 illustrates dropping any column containing missing values.

Listing 3-39. dropna() Along Axis 1

```
>>> print(df2)
    Temp   Speed  Measure1  Measure2  Measure3  Measure4
0   cold   slow       NaN       2.7       6.6       3.1
1   warm   medium     4.2       5.1       7.9       9.1
2   hot    fast       9.4      11.0       NaN       6.8
3   cool   None       NaN       NaN       9.1       8.9
4   cool   medium     6.1       4.3      12.2       3.7
5   None   slow       NaN       2.9       3.3       1.7
6   None   slow       NaN       2.9       3.3       1.7
>>> df2.dropna(axis=1)
    Measure4
0        3.1
1        9.1
2        6.8
3        8.9
4        3.7
5        1.7
6        1.7
```

This example returns a DataFrame by dropping any column containing one or more missing values. The same results can be accomplished with the following syntax.

```
df2.dropna(axis = 'columns')
```

The parameter `axis = 'columns'` is an alternative to `axis = 1`.

Listing 3-40 illustrates dropping any variable containing one or more missing values. One approach is to

- Create an ODS output table using PROC FREQ NLEVELS option to identify those variables in the SAS dataset containing one or more missing values. Figure 3-8 displays the results of this step.

- Execute the PROC SQL SELECT INTO : to create the Macro variable &drop containing the variable names with missing values separated by a blank (ASCII 32). The FROM clause identifies the output dataset created by the ODS Table Output created with PROC FREQ.

- A SAS Data Step creates the output dataset df2, in this case, by reading the input dataset df using the SAS dataset option DROP followed by the Macro variable &drop containing the DROP list created in the PROC SQL step. Figure 3-9 displays the resulting SAS dataset.

Listing 3-40. Dropping SAS Variables with Missing Values

```
4 ods output nlevels=nlvs;
5   proc freq data=df nlevels;
6       tables _all_;
7 ods select nlevels;

NOTE: The dataset WORK.NLVS has 6 observations and 4 variables.
NOTE: There were 7 observations read from the dataset WORK.DF.

8 proc print data=nlvs;run;

NOTE: There were 6 observations read from the dataset WORK.NLVS.

9   proc sql noprint ;
10     select tablevar into :drop separated by ' '
11         from nlvs
12       where NMissLevels ne 0;
13 quit;
14
```

```
15 data df2;
16    set df(drop=&drop);
```

NOTE: There were 7 observations read from the dataset WORK.DF.
NOTE: The dataset WORK.DF2 has 7 observations and 1 variables.

```
17  proc print data=df2;run;
```

NOTE: There were 7 observations read from the dataset WORK.DF2.

The SAS statements

```
ods output nlevels=nlvs;
   proc freq data=df nlevels;
      tables _all_;
ods select nlevels;
```

opens a SAS dataset called nlvs. PROC FREQ with the NLEVELS option executes to produce the desired output. By default, PROC FREQ produces a number of different pieces of tabular output. The statement ODS SELECT NLEVELS selects the NLEVELS object from PROC FREQ and outputs its values as a Series of observations and variables into the SAS dataset nlvs.

Figure 3-8 illustrates the results of executing the syntax

```
proc print data=nlvs;
run;
```

Obs	TableVar	NLevels	NMissLevels	NNonMissLevels
1	temp	5	1	4
2	speed	4	1	3
3	measure1	4	1	3
4	measure2	6	1	5
5	measure3	6	1	5
6	measure4	6	0	6

Figure 3-8. ODS Table Output from PROC FREQ

The PROC SQL step uses the

```
select tablevar into :drop separated by ' '
```

to build the Macro variable &drop containing names of the variables to be dropped separated by a blank (ASCII 32). The WHERE clause

```
NMissLevels ne 0
```

selects those variable names containing one or more missing values. The variable tablevar holds the names of the variables in the SAS dataset df.

Figure 3-9 displays the PROC PRINT output for the SAS dataset df2 created by dropping the variables with missing values held in the Macro variable &drop.

Obs	measure4
1	3.1
2	9.1
3	6.8
4	8.9
5	3.7
6	1.7
7	1.7

Figure 3-9. *Results from Dropping Variables with Missing Values*

Listing 3-41 illustrates the removal of duplicate rows in a DataFrame.

Listing 3-41. drop_duplicates()

```
>>> df6 = df2.drop_duplicates()
>>> print(df6)
   Temp   Speed  Measure1  Measure2  Measure3  Measure4
0  cold   slow        NaN       2.7       6.6       3.1
1  warm   medium      4.2       5.1       7.9       9.1
2  hot    fast        9.4      11.0       NaN       6.8
```

```
3   cool    None      NaN      NaN      9.1      8.9
4   cool  medium      6.1      4.3     12.2      3.7
5   None    slow      NaN      2.9      3.3      1.7
```

This example creates the DataFrame df6 by applying the drop_duplicates() method to the df2 DataFrame. In DataFrame df2 rows 5 and 6 have identical values.

PROC SORT in SAS has a number of different options for handling duplicate observations in a SAS dataset. Listing 3-42 illustrates the NODUPRECS option for PROC SORT.

Listing 3-42. Drop Duplicate Records with SAS

```
4         proc sort data = df
5             out = df6
6             noduprecs;
7         by measure1;
NOTE: 7 observations were read from "WORK.df"
NOTE: 1 duplicate observation were found
NOTE: Dataset "WORK.df6" has 6 observation(s) and 6 variable(s)
8         proc print data=df6;run;
NOTE: 6 observations were read from "WORK.df6"
```

The NODUPRECS option identifies observations with identical values for all variables and removes from the output dataset.

As you can see from the preceding examples, the dropna() method drops a fair amount of "good" data. Rather than dropping the entire row or column if a missing value is encountered, the dropna() method uses the thresh= parameter to specify the minimum number of non-missing values for a row or column to be kept when dropping missing values. Listing 3-43 illustrates this feature.

Listing 3-43. dropna(thresh=4)

```
>>> print(df2)
    Temp   Speed  Measure1  Measure2  Measure3  Measure4
0   cold    slow       NaN       2.7       6.6       3.1
1   warm  medium       4.2       5.1       7.9       9.1
2    hot    fast       9.4      11.0       NaN       6.8
3   cool    None       NaN       NaN       9.1       8.9
```

```
4  cool   medium        6.1          4.3          12.2         3.7
5  None   slow          NaN          2.9          3.3          1.7
6  None   slow          NaN          2.9          3.3          1.7
>>> df7 = df2.dropna(thresh=4)
>>> print(df7)
    Temp   Speed  Measure1  Measure2  Measure3  Measure4
0   cold   slow       NaN       2.7       6.6       3.1
1   warm   medium     4.2       5.1       7.9       9.1
2   hot    fast       9.4      11.0       NaN       6.8
4   cool   medium     6.1       4.3      12.2       3.7
5   None   slow       NaN       2.9       3.3       1.7
6   None   slow       NaN       2.9       3.3       1.7
```

The example creates the DataFrame df7 by setting the thresh= parameter to 4. The thresh=4 parameter iterates through all rows and keeps each row that has at least four non-missing values. Row 3 is dropped since it contains only three non-missing values.

Imputation

Of course, rather than dropping an entire row or column, missing values can be replaced or imputed using mathematical and statistical functions. The fillna() method returns a Series or DataFrame by replacing missing values with derived values. One approach is to replace all missing numerical values (NaN) with zeros. Listing 3-44 illustrates the fillna() method.

Listing 3-44. Replacing NaN's with Zeros

```
>>> print(df2)
    Temp   Speed  Measure1  Measure2  Measure3  Measure4
0   cold   slow       NaN       2.7       6.6       3.1
1   warm   medium     4.2       5.1       7.9       9.1
2   hot    fast       9.4      11.0       NaN       6.8
3   cool   None       NaN       NaN       9.1       8.9
4   cool   medium     6.1       4.3      12.2       3.7
5   None   slow       NaN       2.9       3.3       1.7
6   None   slow       NaN       2.9       3.3       1.7
```

```
>>> df8 = df2.fillna(0)
>>> print(df8)
```

	Temp	Speed	Measure1	Measure2	Measure3	Measure4
0	cold	slow	0.0	2.7	6.6	3.1
1	warm	medium	4.2	5.1	7.9	9.1
2	hot	fast	9.4	11.0	0.0	6.8
3	cool	0	0.0	0.0	9.1	8.9
4	cool	medium	6.1	4.3	12.2	3.7
5	0	slow	0.0	2.9	3.3	1.7
6	0	slow	0.0	2.9	3.3	1.7

In this example, the fillna() method is applied to the entire DataFrame. The None objects in columns Temp and Speed are replaced with the string zero ('0'). The NaN's in columns Measure1–Measure4 are replaced with the numeric value zero (0).

Listing 3-45 illustrates mapping NaN's for the numeric columns only.

Listing 3-45. fillna() Method Over Column Subset

```
>>> print(df2)
```

	Temp	Speed	Measure1	Measure2	Measure3	Measure4
0	cold	slow	NaN	2.7	6.6	3.1
1	warm	medium	4.2	5.1	7.9	9.1
2	hot	fast	9.4	11.0	NaN	6.8
3	cool	None	NaN	NaN	9.1	8.9
4	cool	medium	6.1	4.3	12.2	3.7
5	None	slow	NaN	2.9	3.3	1.7
6	None	slow	NaN	2.9	3.3	1.7

```
>>> df9 = df2[['Measure1', 'Measure2', 'Measure3', 'Measure4']].fillna(0)
>>> print(df9)
```

	Measure1	Measure2	Measure3	Measure4
0	0.0	2.7	6.6	3.1
1	4.2	5.1	7.9	9.1
2	9.4	11.0	0.0	6.8
3	0.0	0.0	9.1	8.9
4	6.1	4.3	12.2	3.7
5	0.0	2.9	3.3	1.7
6	0.0	2.9	3.3	1.7

The `fillna(0)` method with a parameter value of zero (0) replaces NaN's in columns Measure1–Measure4 with a numeric zero (0).

Listing 3-46 passes a Series of different replacement values into a single DataFrame to handle missing values. The `fillna()` method accepts a Dictionary of values as a parameter.

A Python Dictionary is a collection of `key:value` pairs where keys have unique values within the Dictionary. A pair of braces creates an empty Dictionary: { }. Placing a comma-separated list of `key:value` pairs within the braces adds `key:value` pairs to the Dictionary.

Listing 3-46. fillna() Method Using a Dictionary

```
>>> df10 = df2.fillna({
...        'Temp'  : 'cold',
...        'Speed' : 'slow',
...        'Measure1' : 0,
...        'Measure2' : 0,
...        'Measure3' : 0,
...        'Measure4' : 0,
... })
>>> print(df10)
   Temp   Speed  Measure1  Measure2  Measure3  Measure4
0  cold    slow       0.0       2.7       6.6       3.1
1  warm  medium       4.2       5.1       7.9       9.1
2   hot    fast       9.4      11.0       0.0       6.8
3  cool    slow       0.0       0.0       9.1       8.9
4  cool  medium       6.1       4.3      12.2       3.7
5  cold    slow       0.0       2.9       3.3       1.7
6  cold    slow       0.0       2.9       3.3       1.7
```

In the Temp column, the string `'cold'` replaces the None object, and in the Speed column, the string `'slow'` replaces the None object. Columns Measure1–Measure4 map the NaN's to zero (0).

Another imputation method is to replace NaN's with the arithmetic mean from a column having few or no missing values. This assumes the columns have nearly equal measures of dispersion. Listing 3-47 illustrates this approach.

Listing 3-47. fillna() with Arithmetic Mean

```
>>> print(df2)
    Temp   Speed  Measure1  Measure2  Measure3  Measure4
0   cold    slow       NaN       2.7       6.6       3.1
1   warm  medium       4.2       5.1       7.9       9.1
2    hot    fast       9.4      11.0       NaN       6.8
3   cool    None       NaN       NaN       9.1       8.9
4   cool  medium       6.1       4.3      12.2       3.7
5   None    slow       NaN       2.9       3.3       1.7
6   None    slow       NaN       2.9       3.3       1.7
>>> df11 = df2[["Measure1", "Measure2", "Measure3"]].fillna(df2.Measure4.mean())
>>> print(df11)
   Measure1  Measure2  Measure3
0       5.0       2.7       6.6
1       4.2       5.1       7.9
2       9.4      11.0       5.0
3       5.0       5.0       9.1
4       6.1       4.3      12.2
5       5.0       2.9       3.3
6       5.0       2.9       3.3
```

In this example, NaN's in columns Measure1–Measure3 are replaced with the arithmetic mean value derived from the column Measure4 which is 5.0.

Listing 3-48 illustrates the same logic in SAS.

Listing 3-48. Replace Missing Values with Arithmetic Mean

```
4 data df2;
5   infile cards dlm=',';
6   input Temp $
7         Speed $
8           Measure1
9           Measure2
10          Measure3
11          Measure4 ;
12 list;
13 datalines;
```

```
RULE:        ----+----1----+----2----+----3----+----4----+----5-
14           cold, slow, ., 2.7, 6.6, 3.1
15           warm, medium, 4.2, 5.1, 7.9, 9.1
16           hot, fast, 9.4, 11.0, ., 6.8
17           cool, , ., ., 9.1, 8.9
18           cool, medium, 6.1, 4.3, 12.2, 3.7
19           , slow, ., 2.9, 3.3, 1.7
20           , slow, ., 2.9, 3.3, 1.7
NOTE: The dataset WORK.DF2 has 7 observations and 6 variables.

21 ;;;;
22 proc sql noprint;
23    select mean(Measure4) into :M4_mean
24    from df2;
25  quit;

26 data df11(drop=i);
27    set df2;
28 array x {3} Measure1-Measure3;
29   do i = 1 to 3;
30      if x(i) = . then x(i) = &M4_mean;
31   end;
32 format Measure1-Measure4 8.1;

NOTE: There were 7 observations read from the dataset WORK.DF2.

38 proc print data = df11; run;
NOTE: There were 7 observations read from the dataset WORK.DF11.
```

This example uses the PROC SQL SELECT INTO : syntax to create the Macro variable &M4_mean. The SAS Data Step in lines 26 to 31 create an ARRAY with variables Measure1–Measure3 as elements. The DO/END block iterates over the ARRAY executing the statement

```
if x(i) = . then x(i) = &M4_mean;
```

If any observation value in the variables Measure1–Measure3 equals missing, the observation value of the variable is assigned the value from the Macro variable &M4_mean which is 5.0.

The results from this program are displayed in Figure 3-10.

Obs	Temp	Speed	Measure1	Measure2	Measure3	Measure4
1	cold	slow	5.0	2.7	6.6	3.1
2	warm	medium	4.2	5.1	7.9	9.1
3	hot	fast	9.4	11.0	5.0	6.8
4	cool		5.0	5.0	9.1	8.9
5	cool	medium	6.1	4.3	12.2	3.7
6		slow	5.0	2.9	3.3	1.7
7		slow	5.0	2.9	3.3	1.7

Figure 3-10.   *Replace Missing Using PROC SQL*

Summary

In this chapter we introduced the pandas library and the roles for DataFrame which is essential to using Python for data analysis tasks. We covered critical topics such as column types and how pandas handle missing values along with discussing methods for detecting and replacing missing values. With this foundation set, we can begin the exploration of new methods to expand the repertoire of data exploration and analysis.

CHAPTER 4

Indexing and GroupBy

SAS users tend to think of indexing SAS datasets to either improve query performance or as a method to avoid dataset sorting. Another use case for using SAS indexes is to provide direct access to a specific observation in a dataset. For example, in order to retrieve an observation whose value for the variable name is 'Lassiter', absent an index, SAS performs a sequential read starting with the first observation in the dataset. SAS normally begins reading at observation 1 reading the dataset in sequence for name = 'Lassiter' until all observations are read.

Alternatively, if an index on the variable name is present, SAS may use the index to directly access those observations containing these values without performing a sequential read of the dataset. A SAS index stores values in ascending order for a specific variable or variables and manages information on how to locate a given observation(s) in the dataset.

In contrast, pandas automatically create an index structure at DataFrame creation time for both rows and columns. In Chapter 3, "pandas Library," we encountered the RangeIndex object used as the default row index. These index objects are responsible for holding the axis labels and other metadata like integer-based location identifiers, axis name, and so on.

One or more columns in DataFrame can be used to define an index. Assigning more than one column as an index creates a MultiIndex object discussed later in this chapter. New users to pandas often get confused about the role of an index, since most of their prior associations consider an index to be an auxiliary structure for columns.

The way we like to think about a pandas index is to consider it as a means for labeling DataFrame rows. Recall from Chapter 3, "pandas Library," that at DataFrame creation time, the RangeIndex object is created as the default index similar to the automatic _N_ variable SAS establishes at SAS dataset creation time. In a DataFrame, the values from a column or columns may be used as an index to supply values as row labels augmenting the default integer values assigned by the RangeIndex object. Just as you are able to return SAS dataset observations using the automatic variable _N_, a DataFrame's default RangeIndex is used to return rows using a zero-based offset. By explicitly setting

111

© Randy Betancourt, Sarah Chen 2019
R. Betancourt and S. Chen, *Python for SAS Users*, https://doi.org/10.1007/978-1-4842-5001-3_4

a DataFrame index from column or multiple column values, you can return rows using these column values in addition to returning rows using the RangeIndex object.

Create Index

When a DataFrame is assigned an index, the rows remain accessible by supplying a collection of integer values as well as accessible by the row labels defined by the index. Listing 4-1 illustrates the set_index() method using the ID column. In this example, the values from the ID column supply labels for the DataFrame rows.

Listing 4-1. Create DataFrame Index

```
>>> import pandas as pd
>>> df = pd.DataFrame([['0071', 'Patton'  , 17,  27],
...                     ['1001', 'Joyner'  , 13,  22],
...                     ['0091', 'Williams', 111, 121],
...                     ['0110', 'Jurat'   , 51,  55]],
...          columns = ['ID',   'Name', 'Before', 'After'])
>>> print(df)
     ID      Name  Before  After
0  0071    Patton      17     27
1  1001    Joyner      13     22
2  0091  Williams     111    121
3  0110     Jurat      51     55
>>> df.set_index('ID', inplace=True)
>>> print(df)
          Name  Before  After
ID
0071    Patton      17     27
1001    Joyner      13     22
0091  Williams     111    121
0110     Jurat      51     55
```

The DataFrame df is constructed using the DataFrame() constructor method. The first print() function returns all of the rows labeled with the default RangeIndex object labeling rows starting with the integer 0 to axis (length –1). The syntax

```
df.set_index('ID', inplace = True)
```

selects the ID column as the index and performs an `inplace` operation indicated by the argument: `inplace = True` updates the index in place rather than creating a new DataFrame. The default value for the `set_index()` method is `inplace = False`. In the case where the `inplace=` argument is `False`, you must assign the results to a new DataFrame. For example,

```
df_idx = df.set_index('ID', inplace=False)
```

creates the `df_idx` DataFrame with the ID column as its index. The original `df` DataFrame remains unaltered.

The second `print()` function illustrates how the DataFrame rows are labeled with values from the ID column. The overhead for creating and dropping indexes is minimal, and it is not unusual to do so repetitively in a single Python program.

Next, we consider subsetting DataFrames. Subsetting data by rows and/or columns is an essential task for any form of data analysis. pandas DataFrames offer three choices for subsetting operations. They are

1. [ ] operator enables selection by columns or by rows.

2. `loc()` indexer uses row and column labels for subsetting. A column label is the column name and row labels are assigned with an index (either with the `index=` parameter at DataFrame creation time or with the `set_index()` method. If no index is explicitly assigned, then the integer-based RangeIndex object is the default. If no names are assigned to columns, then the RangeIndex object labels the columns with the first column as 0, the second column as 1, and so on.

3. `iloc()` indexer uses integer positions (from 0 to axis (length - 1)) for subsetting rows and columns. This method remains available even if a user-defined index or MultiIndex is defined. MultiIndexes or hierarchical indexes are discussed later in this chapter.

Both the `loc()` and `iloc()` indexers accept Boolean logic to perform complex subsetting. The [ ] operator and the `iloc()` indexers can access rows using the default RangeIndex object, that is, integer values indicating a position along the index. The `loc()` indexer requires a user-defined index for creating row labels in order to operate.

All three indexers return a DataFrame.

Return Columns by Position

Consider Listing 4-2. This example constructs the i DataFrame using a single print()
function to display the DataFrame values, default row index, and the default column
index. The '\n' syntax inserts a new line to display the desired results.

Listing 4-2. DataFrame Default Indexes

```
>>> i = pd.DataFrame([['Patton'    , 17,  27],
...                   ['Joyner'    , 13,  22],
...                   ['Williams'  , 111, 121],
...                   ['Jurat'     , 51,  55],
...                   ['Aden'      , 71,  70]])
>>> print(i)
          0    1    2
0    Patton   17   27
1    Joyner   13   22
2  Williams  111  121
3     Jurat   51   55
4      Aden   71   70
>>>
>>> print(' Row Index:    ',    i.index, '\n', 'Column Index:', i.columns)
 Row Index:    RangeIndex(start=0, stop=5, step=1)
 Column Index: RangeIndex(start=0, stop=3, step=1)
```

We begin with subsetting using the [ ] operator. Observe that both columns and
rows in DataFrame i use the default RangeIndex as their labels.

The default RangeIndex is used to select rows or columns using integers to locate
their positions along the index. Consider Listing 4-3.

Listing 4-3. Returning Column 0 from the DataFrame

```
>>> i[0]
0      Patton
1      Joyner
2    Williams
3       Jurat
4        Aden
```

The call to [ ] operator returns the first column (0) from the DataFrame i. In most cases, DataFrame columns will have labels to return the columns of interest.

The [ ] operator also accepts a Python list of columns to return. Recall that a Python list is a mutable data structure for holding a collection of items. List literals are written within square brackets [ ] with commas (,) to indicate multiple items in the list.

Consider Listing 4-4. Each of the values supplied to the DataFrame() constructor method is a Python list and the columns= argument passes a list.

Listing 4-4. Create df DataFrame

```
>>> df = pd.DataFrame([['I','North', 'Patton', 17, 27],
...                     ['I', 'South','Joyner', 13, 22],
...                     ['I', 'East', 'Williams', 111, 121],
...                     ['I', 'West', 'Jurat', 51, 55],
...                     ['II','North', 'Aden', 71, 70],
...                     ['II', 'South', 'Tanner', 113, 122],
...                     ['II', 'East', 'Jenkins', 99, 99],
...                     ['II', 'West', 'Milner', 15, 65],
...                     ['III','North', 'Chang', 69, 101],
...                     ['III', 'South','Gupta', 11, 22],
...                     ['III', 'East', 'Haskins', 45, 41],
...                     ['III', 'West', 'LeMay', 35, 69],
...                     ['III', 'West', 'LeMay', 35, 69]],
...                     columns=['District', 'Sector', 'Name', 'Before',
                        'After'])
>>>
>>> df[['Name', 'After']].head(4)
       Name  After
0    Patton     27
1    Joyner     22
2  Williams    121
3     Jurat     55
```

In this example, the syntax

```
df[['Name', 'After']].head(4)
```

is a column subsetting operation returning the columns Name and After. Notice how the Python list with ['Name', 'After'] inside the DataFrame slice operator results in a pair of square brackets [[ ]]. The outer pair is the syntax for the DataFrame [ ] operator, while the inner pair holds the literal values to form the Python list of column names.

Clearly, using a list of column names rather than a list of column integer index positions is a more convenient method for subsetting.

The equivalent SAS program is displayed in Listing 4-5. It is used in subsequent examples in this chapter.

Listing 4-5. Create df SAS Dataset

```
4 data df;
5 length region $ 6
6        name $ 8
7        district $ 3;
8 infile cards dlm=',';
8 input district $
10        region $
11        name $
12        before
13        after;
14 list;
15 datalines;

RULE:       ----+----1----+----2----+----3----+----4----+----5
16       I,   North, Patton,    17,  27
17       I,   South, Joyner,    13,  22
18       I,   East,  Williams, 111, 121
19       I,   West,  Jurat,     51,  55
20       II,  North, Aden,      71,  70
21       II,  South, Tanner,   113, 122
22       II,  East,  Jenkins,   99,  99
23       II,  West,  Milner,    15,  65
24       III, North, Chang,     69, 101
```

```
25          III, South, Gupta,     11,  22
26          III, East,  Haskins,   45,  41
27          III, West,  LeMay,     35,  69
28          III, West,  LeMay,     35,  69
NOTE: The dataset WORK.DF has 13 observations and 5 variables.

29 ;;;;
30 proc print data = df(obs=4);
31    var name after;
32 run;

NOTE: There were 4 observations read from the dataset WORK.DF
```

The output from PROC PRINT with data=df(obs=4) is displayed in Figure 4-1.

Obs	name	after
1	Patton	27
2	Joyner	22
3	Williams	121
4	Jurat	55

Figure 4-1. *PROC PRINT displays the output of the df SAS Dataset*

Return Rows by Position

The general syntax for DataFrame row slicing (subsetting rows) using the [ ] operator is

```
df:[start : stop : step]
```

The start position is included in the output, and the stop position is not included in the output.

For example, consider Listing 4-6.

Listing 4-6. DataFrame Row Slicing, Example 1

```
>>> df[:3]
  District Sector      Name  Before  After
0        I  North    Patton      17     27
1        I  South    Joyner      13     22
2        I   East  Williams     111    121
```

This example returns the first three rows from the df DataFrame. A null value for the start position defaults to start position zero (0). The value following the colon (:) indicates the stop position and goes up to but does not include the row in the slicing operation.

Listing 4-7 illustrates returning every other row from the df DataFrame.

Listing 4-7. DataFrame Row Slicing, Example 2

```
>>> df[::2]
   District Sector      Name  Before  After
0         I  North    Patton      17     27
2         I   East  Williams     111    121
4        II  North      Aden      71     70
6        II   East   Jenkins      99     99
8       III  North     Chang      69    101
10      III   East   Haskins      45     41
12      III   West     LeMay      35     69
```

The start and stop positions are null causing the slice df[::2] to default to the first and last row, respectively, in the DataFrame. The value of two (2) for the step position returns every other row.

This same logic is displayed in Listing 4-8.

Listing 4-8. SELECT Every Other Row

```
4 data df1;
5    set df;
6    if mod(_n_, 2) ^= 0 then output;
7 run;
```

NOTE: There were 13 observations read from the dataset WORK.DF.
NOTE: The dataset WORK.DF1 has 7 observations and 5 variables.

The example creates the df1 dataset with a subsetting IF statement to perform modulo division by 2 on the automatic SAS _N_ variable assigned to each observation. Modulo division by 2 on even integers returns 0 (zero). By using the IF statement's inequality evaluation of ^= 0 every odd _N_ value (1, 3, 5, etc.) evaluates true and is written to the output df1 dataset.

Calling PROC PRINT displays the output shown in Figure 4-2.

Obs	sector	name	district	before	after
1	North	Patton	I	17	27
2	East	Williams	I	111	121
3	North	Aden	II	71	70
4	East	Jenkins	II	99	99
5	North	Chang	III	69	101
6	East	Haskins	III	45	41
7	West	LeMay	III	35	69

Figure 4-2. Output from SELECT Every Other Row

Return Rows and Columns by Label

The loc() indexer is a method primarily used for returning rows and columns using labels. Allowed inputs to loc() are

- A single label such as 12 or 'Name'. Note that 12 is interpreted as the row label and not as the integer location along the index.

- A Python list of labels ['A', 'B', 'C'].

- A slice object with labels 'a' : 'z'. Both start, in this case, 'a', and stop, 'z', are included when present in the index.

- Conditional evaluations.

Each of these methods is illustrated.

Up to this point, the index for the df DataFrame relies on the default RangeIndex object for returning rows by an integer position along the index. In order to retrieve rows from the df DataFrame by labels, the Name column is set as the DataFrame index. This action assigns the values from the Name column as labels for the DataFrame rows. Said another way, a DataFrame index maps column values onto rows as labels.

The syntax and default values for the set_index() method is

df.set_index(*keys, drop=True, append=False, inplace=False, verify_integrity=False*)

Listing 4-9 illustrates defining an index for an existing DataFrame.

Listing 4-9. Add Index to DataFrame

```
>>> print(df)
    District Sector      Name  Before  After
0          I  North    Patton      17     27
1          I  South    Joyner      13     22
2          I   East  Williams     111    121
3          I   West     Jurat      51     55
4         II  North      Aden      71     70
5         II  South    Tanner     113    122
6         II   East   Jenkins      99     99
7         II   West    Milner      15     65
8        III  North     Chang      69    101
9        III  South     Gupta      11     22
10       III   East   Haskins      45     41
11       III   West     LeMay      35     69
12       III   West     LeMay      35     69
>>> print(df.index)
RangeIndex(start=0, stop=13, step=1)
>>>
>>> df.set_index('Name', inplace = True, drop = True)
>>> print(df.head(4))
```

```
         District Sector  Before  After
Name
Patton            I  North      17      27
Joyner            I  South      13      22
Williams          I   East     111     121
Jurat             I   West      51      55
>>> print(df.index)
Index(['Patton', 'Joyner', 'Williams', 'Jurat', 'Aden', 'Tanner',
'Jenkins','Milner', 'Chang', 'Gupta', 'Haskins', 'LeMay', 'LeMay'],
dtype='object', name='Name')
```

In this example, the first `print()` function displays all rows from the df DataFrame. The syntax

```
print(df.index)
```

returns the default RangeIndex in use for the rows with integer values between 0 and 13. The syntax

```
df.set_index('Name', inplace=True, drop=True)
```

selects the values from the Name column label as row labels. The argument `inplace=True` updates the df DataFrame in place, and the `drop=True` argument drops the Name column from the DataFrame.

With this defined index, the `loc()` indexer uses the Name column values to return rows rather than using row position.

Notice how the third `print()` function displays the values for the Name column as row labels in the leftmost column of the output. The syntax

```
print(df.index)
```

returns the index values as a Python list. An index may have non-unique values which we illustrate with this example. Some DataFrame operations require the index keys be in sorted order, while others may require unique values. We cover the details for sorting in Chapter 5, "Data Management." Chapter 7, "Date and Time," covers details for unique index values.

With an index in place as row labels, we can slice rows using the `loc()` indexer. As well, columns can be sliced with the `loc()` indexer since they have labels (i.e., names).

The syntax for the loc() indexer is

```
df.loc[row selection, column selection]
```

The row selection is listed first, separated by a comma (,) followed by the column selection. For both the row and column selections, a colon (:) is used to request a range of items. Consider Listing 4-10.

Listing 4-10. Return Row Slices

```
>>> df.loc['Patton': 'Aden', ]
          District Sector  Before  After
Name
Patton          I  North      17     27
Joyner          I  South      13     22
Williams        I   East     111    121
Jurat           I   West      51     55
Aden           II  North      71     70
```

This example slices rows beginning with the row labeled 'Patton' and ending with the row labeled 'Aden' inclusive. The empty value for the column selector, following the comma (,), implies all columns. The same DataFrame can be returned by stating the column selector explicitly with the syntax

```
df.loc['Patton' : 'Aden', 'District' : 'After']
```

Listing 4-11 illustrates supplying a single label to the row selector followed by a Python list of labels as the column selector.

Listing 4-11. Return Row and Column Slices

```
>>> df.loc['LeMay', ['Before','After']]
        Before  After
Name
LeMay       35     69
LeMay       35     69
```

Notice how the row labels are not unique.

Conditionals

Listing 4-12 illustrates returning rows and columns based on a Boolean comparison.

Listing 4-12. Return Rows Conditionally

```
>>> df.loc[(df['Sector'] == 'West') & (df['Before'] > 20)]
      District Sector  Before  After
Name
Jurat        I   West      51     55
LeMay      III   West      35     69
LeMay      III   West      35     69
```

The Boolean comparisons are enclosed with parentheses ( ) and utilize any of the comparison operators listed in Table 2-2 from Chapter 2, "Python Types and Formatting." In this example, the Boolean comparisons contain two predicates; the first is (df['Sector'] == 'West') and the second is (df['Before'] > 20). The Boolean operator & (and) joins the predicates, and therefore both must return True in order to meet the row selection criteria.

Note the syntax differences between Listing 4-11 and Listing 4-12. In the former rows are sliced based on labels. The latter uses the df['Sector'] and df['Before'] to designate column names for the conditional expression.

Suppose we wish to subset rows based on the last letter of the value for the Name column ending with the letter 'r.' Listing 4-13 combines the loc() indexer with the .str.endswith attribute to satisfy the request.

Listing 4-13. Conditionally Return Rows with String Manipulation

```
df.loc[df['Name'].str.endswith("r"), ['District', 'Sector']]
KeyError: 'the label [Name] is not in the [index]'
```

Unfortunately, this example raises a KeyError since the column Name was dropped when the df.index was initially created in Listing 4-9. Note this error message is truncated here. One remedy for the KeyError is to "return" the Name column using the reset_index() function illustrated in Listing 4-14.

Listing 4-14. Drop DataFrame Index

```
>>> df.reset_index(inplace = True)
>>> df.loc[df['Name'].str.endswith("r"), ['Name', 'Before', 'After']]
     Name  Before  After
1  Joyner      13     22
5  Tanner     113    122
7  Milner      15     65
```

In this example, the syntax

```
df.reset_index(inplace = True)
```

calls the reset_index() method to "drop" the index and return the Name column as one of the columns on the df DataFrame. The inplace = True argument performs the operation in place. The second line in the program chains the .str.endswith("r") attribute to the Name column and returns True for any value whose last letter in the sequence is 'r'.

The purpose of this example is to simply illustrate resetting an index with the reset_index() method. The more Pythonic remedy for the KeyError illustrated in Listing 4-13 is

```
df.loc[df.index.str.endswith('r'), ['District', 'Sector']]
```

The analog SAS program is shown in Listing 4-15.

Listing 4-15. Conditionally Return Observations with String Manipulation

```
4  proc sql;
5    select name
6            ,before
7            ,after
8    from df
9    where substr(reverse(trim(name)),1,1) = 'r';
10 quit;
```

The nested functions in the WHERE clause work from the inside out by

1. Calling the TRIM function to remove trailing blanks

2. Calling the REVERSE function to reverse the letters in the variable name

3. Calling the SUBSTR (left of =) function to test if the first letter is 'r'

Figure 4-3 displays the output from PROC SQL.

name	before	after
Joyner	13	22
Tanner	113	122
Milner	15	65

Figure 4-3. *Last Name Ends with 'r'*

Another method for conditional testing is to combine the loc() indexer with the isin attribute. The isin attribute returns a Boolean indicating if elements in the DataFrame column are contained in a Python list of values. As an example, consider Listing 4-16.

Listing 4-16. Select Rows with isin List of Values

```
>>> df.set_index('Name', inplace=True)
>>> df.loc[df['Sector'].isin(['North', 'South'])]
        District Sector  Before  After
Name
Patton         I  North      17     27
Joyner         I  South      13     22
Aden          II  North      71     70
Tanner        II  South     113    122
Chang        III  North      69    101
Gupta        III  South      11     22
```

Because the index was "dropped" in Listing 4-14, the index is set again, this time with the syntax

```
df.set_index('Name', inplace=True)
```

to enable slicing with labels using the loc() indexer.

Listing 4-17 illustrates the same capability using the IN operator. The IN operator performs an implied truth test by including values from a list that match values from the sector variable. The IN operator is also valid with an IF statement in a Data Step. Figure 4-4 displays the subset row.

Listing 4-17. SAS IN Operator

```
4 proc sql;
5   select *
6   from df
7 where sector in ('North', 'South');
8 quit;
```

sector	name	district	before	after
North	Patton	I	17	27
South	Joyner	I	13	22
North	Aden	II	71	70
South	Tanner	II	113	122
North	Chang	III	69	101
South	Gupta	III	11	22

Figure 4-4. *IN Operator Results*

Updating

The loc() indexer can update or set values (the term used with pandas documentation). Consider Listing 4-18.

Listing 4-18. Set Values Matching a List of Labels

```
>>> df.loc[['Patton', 'Jurat', 'Gupta'], 'After']
Name
Patton    27
Jurat     55
Gupta     22
Name: After, dtype: int64
>>> df.loc[['Patton', 'Jurat', 'Gupta'], ['After']] = 100
>>> df.loc[['Patton', 'Jurat', 'Gupta'], 'After']
```

```
Name
Patton    100
Jurat     100
Gupta     100
Name: After dtype: int64
```

The first call to the loc() indexer supplies a Python list of Name labels for three individuals along with their corresponding After values and returns a Series. Recall that a Series is analogous to a single DataFrame column. The second call to the loc() indexer sets (updates) the After column for each of the labels in the Python list

```
['Patton', 'Jurat', 'Gupta']
```

The SAS analog is illustrated in Listing 4-19.

Listing 4-19. IN Operator Conditionally Select Rows.

```
4   data df;
5       set df;
6   if _n_ = 1 then put
7       'Name      After';
8   if name in ('Patton', 'Jurat', 'Gupta') then do;
9       after = 100;
10      put @1 name @10 after;
11      end;
12  run;
```

OUTPUT:

```
Name      After
Patton    100
Jurat     100
Gupta     100
NOTE: There were 13 observations read from the dataset WORK.DF.
NOTE: The dataset WORK.DF has 13 observations and 5 variables.
```

This example uses the IN operator with an IF/THEN DO/END block updating the After variable conditionally.

Setting values for an entire DataFrame column is illustrated in Listing 4-20.

127

Listing 4-20. Set Values for a Column

```
>>> df.loc[: , 'After'] = 100
>>> print(df.head(5))
         District Sector  Before  After
Name
Patton          I  North      17    100
Joyner          I  South      13    100
Williams        I   East     111    100
Jurat           I   West      51    100
Aden           II  North      71    100
```

The call to the loc() indexer slices all rows from the df DataFrame since no start and stop values are supplied indicated by a colon (:). The column slice After is set to 100.

Return Rows and Columns by Position

The iloc() indexer uses integer positions (from 0 to axis (length –1)) for slicing rows and columns. Allowed inputs to iloc() are

- An integer, for example, 12.

- A Python list of integers [4, 2, 22].

- A slice object with integers 2 : 22. The start, in this case, 2, is inclusive and the stop position 22 is exclusive.

The stop position for the iloc() indexer is exclusive, meaning not included. This is in contrast to the loc() indexer which is inclusive.

The syntax for the iloc() indexer is

```
df.iloc[row selection, column selection]
```

A comma (,) is used to separate the request of row slices from column slices. A colon (:) is used to request a range of items. The absence of either a column or row selector is an implicit request for all columns or rows, respectively.

These features are illustrated in Listing 4-21 introducing the iloc() indexer.

Listing 4-21. Return df First and Last Row

```
>>> df.iloc[[0, -1]]
      District Sector    Name  Before  After
Name
Patton        I  North  Patton      17    100
LeMay       III   West   LeMay      35     69
```

In this example, a Python list of row values based on their position is passed to the iloc() indexer. Row 0 is the first row and row –1 is the last row in the df DataFrame.

The same logic for SAS is illustrated in Listing 4-22.

Listing 4-22. Return First and Last Observation

```
4  data df1;
5    set df end = last;
6
7  if name in ('Patton', 'Jurat', 'Gupta') then after = 100;
8  if _n_ = 1 then output;
9  if last = 1 then output;
10 run;

NOTE: There were 12 observations read from the dataset WORK.DF.
NOTE: The dataset WORK.DF1 has 2 observations and 5 variables.

11 proc print data = df1 noobs;
12 run;
```

The input dataset df uses the END= dataset option to detect the last observation reading the df dataset. The END= dataset option initializes a variable's value to 0 and is set to 1 when the last observation is read. Subsetting IF statements are used to output the first and last observation to the output dataset df1. The output dataset is displayed in Figure 4-5. The NOOBS option for PROC PRINT suppresses the display of the SAS observation number contained in the automatic SAS variable _N_.

sector	name	district	before	after
North	Patton	I	17	100
West	LeMay	III	35	69

Figure 4-5. *First and Last Observation*

The `iloc()` indexer accommodates a Python list of integers as well as a slice object to define row and column selections. Listing 4-23 illustrates combining these selectors.

Listing 4-23. iloc() Using List and Slice Object

```
>>> df.reset_index(inplace = True)
>>> df.iloc[[2, 10, 12], :2]
         Name District
2    Williams        I
10    Haskins      III
12      LeMay      III
```

While it is possible to call the `iloc()` indexer with an index preset, in order to understand the effect, the `Name` index is dropped with

```
df.reset_index(inplace = True)
```

The row selector uses a Python list of integers selecting rows 2, 10, and 12 followed by a comma (,) to define the column slicer. The column slicer `0:2` selects two columns (column 0 and column 1). Remember, for the `iloc()` indexer, the `stop` values used as slicers for row and column values go up to but do not include the `stop` value.

The syntax for selecting the first three columns and all rows in the DataFrame is

```
df.iloc[ : , :3]
```

If the column slicer stop position exceeds the number of columns in the DataFrame, then all columns are returned.

The iloc() indexer accepts the value –1 to indicate the last object in a sequence, –2 as second to last, and so on. Listing 4-24 illustrates this feature.

Listing 4-24. Return Last Row from Last Column

```
>>> df.iloc[-1, -1]
100
```

This example returns the last row from the last column in DataFrame df.

MultiIndexing

Thus far, the use of indexes involves a single column labeling DataFrame rows. See Listing 4-9 as an illustration. This section introduces MultiIndexing, also known as hierarchical indexing. Often the data for analysis is captured at the detail level. As part of performing an exploratory analysis, a MultiIndex DataFrame provides a useful multi-dimensional "view" of data.

These actions are accomplished using the pandas' MultiIndex object. Simply put, a MultiIndex allows multiple index levels within a single index. Higher-dimensional data can be represented by a one-dimensional Series or a two-dimensional DataFrame.

In a DataFrame, rows and columns may have multiple levels of indexes defined with a MultiIndex object.

Later in this chapter, we will see the benefits from MultiIndexing for "pivoting" DataFrames much the same way an Excel spreadsheet can be pivoted. We will also discuss "stacking" data as a means for "flattening" DataFrames and "unstacking" to perform the reverse operation.

To begin, consider Listing 4-25. The example creates a hierarchical index for the columns in the df DataFrame.

Listing 4-25. MultiIndex Details, Part 1

```
>>> import pandas as pd
>>> import numpy as np
>>> pd.options.display.float_format = '{:,.2f}'.format
>>> cols = pd.MultiIndex.from_tuples([ (x,y) for x in
['Test1','Test2','Test3'] for y in ['Pre','Post']])
>>>
>>> nl = '\n'
>>> np.random.seed(98765)
```

```
>>> df = pd.DataFrame(np.random.randn(2,6),index = ['Row 1','Row 2'],
columns = cols)
>>>
>>> print(nl,
...       df)
```

```
       Test1        Test2        Test3
       Pre  Post   Pre   Post   Pre   Post
Row 1  -0.65 0.85  1.08 -1.79  0.94 -0.76
Row 2   0.72 1.02  0.97 -0.04 -0.07  0.81
```

To control the output, `options.display.float_format=` displays floats two places to the right of the decimal. There are several different constructors for defining a MultiIndex. This example uses `MultiIndex.from_tuples()` to define a hierarchical index for the DataFrame columns.

A Python tuple is a data structure similar to a list used to hold unlike items such as strings, ints, floats, and so on. Unlike a list, tuples are immutable and are defined using a pair of parentheses ( ). In this example, the `for` loops are shortcuts creating the strings to populate the tuples. Without the `for` loops, the syntax is

```
pd.MultiIndex.from_tuples([('Test1', 'Pre'), ('Test1', 'Post'), ('Test2',
'Pre'), ('Test2', 'Post'), ('Test3', 'Pre'), ('Test3', 'Post')])
```

The df DataFrame in this example uses the `DataFrame()` constructor assigning row labels with `index=['Row 1','Row 2']` and `columns = col` creating the MultiIndexed or hierarchical columns.

With the df DataFrame constructed along with its hierarchical columns and row labels, let's examine the constituent components closely by considering Listing 4-26.

Listing 4-26. MultiIndex Details, Part 2

```
>>> print(nl,
...          'Index:        '  , df.index,
...    nl                ,
...          'Columns:      '  , df.columns,
...    nl                ,
...          'Col Level 1:' , df.columns.levels[0],
```

```
...    n1              ,
...          'Col Level 2:'  , df.columns.levels[1])

Index:        Index(['Row 1', 'Row 2'], dtype='object')
Columns:      MultiIndex(levels=[['Test1', 'Test2', 'Test3'], ['Post', 'Pre']],
              codes=[[0, 0, 1, 1, 2, 2], [1, 0, 1, 0, 1, 0]])
Col Level 1: Index(['Test1', 'Test2', 'Test3'], dtype='object')
Col Level 2: Index(['Post', 'Pre'], dtype='object')
```

Begin with the index. Recall a pandas index is simply a method to assign labels to rows. In this example, df.index returns the row labels, 'Row1' and 'Row2'.

The statement df.columns returns the DataFrame's column labels. In this case, a Python list of lists which are the unique levels from the MultiIndex assigned as columns. The labels return a Python list of lists referencing these levels on the index.

This df DataFrame MultiIndex has two levels. The statement

```
df.columns.levels[0]
```

returns a Python list of column labels used in the outermost level of the hierarchical index. The statement df.columns.levels[1] returns the innermost level of the hierarchical index. Whether assigned to the DataFrame rows or columns, a hierarchical index can have an arbitrary number of levels.

To further understand MultiIndexes, we construct a more elaborate DataFrame. Listing 4-27 illustrates a hierarchical index for both the DataFrame's rows and columns. The MultiIndex for the columns has a depth of two with values for Area and When as levels. The second hierarchical index on the rows has a depth of two with Year and Month values as levels. The tickets DataFrame holds values for traffic violation tickets.

Since our objective is to understand hierarchical indexes, the explanation for the Python code creating the tickets DataFrame is found in Appendix A at the end of this book. Note that the script in Appendix A must be executed as a part of the examples in this section.

Listing 4-27. Create tickets DataFrame

```
>>> import pandas as pd
>>> import numpy as np
>>> np.random.seed(654321)
```

```
>>> idx = pd.MultiIndex.from_product([[2015, 2016, 2017, 2018],
...                          [1, 2, 3]],
...               names = ['Year', 'Month'])
>>> columns=pd.MultiIndex.from_product([['City' , 'Suburbs', 'Rural'],
...                          ['Day' , 'Night']],
...               names = ['Area', 'When'])
>>>
>>> data = np.round(np.random.randn(12, 6),2)
>>> data = abs(np.floor_divide(data[:] * 100, 5))
>>>
>>> tickets = pd.DataFrame(data, index=idx, columns = columns).sort_
index().sort_index(axis=1)
>>> print(tickets)
Area           City        Rural         Suburbs
When           Day Night   Day Night     Day Night
Year Month
2015 1         15.0  18.0   9.0   3.0      3.0   3.0
     2         11.0  18.0   3.0  30.0     42.0  15.0
     3          5.0  54.0   7.0   6.0     14.0  18.0
2016 1         11.0  17.0   1.0   0.0     11.0  26.0
     2          7.0  23.0   3.0   5.0     19.0   2.0
     3          9.0  17.0  31.0  48.0      2.0  17.0
2017 1         21.0   5.0  22.0  10.0     12.0   2.0
     2          5.0  33.0  19.0   2.0      7.0  10.0
     3         31.0  12.0  19.0  17.0     14.0   2.0
2018 1         25.0  10.0   8.0   4.0     20.0  15.0
     2         35.0  14.0   9.0  14.0     10.0   1.0
     3          3.0  32.0  33.0  21.0     24.0   6.0
```

Notice the output from the print function in Listing 4-27. The results display the hierarchical columns Area as the outer level and When as the inner level. Likewise, with the hierarchical row index, where Year is the outer level and Month is the inner level.

The print(tickets.index) statement returns the MultiIndex levels and labels assigned to the rows. To subset DataFrame rows, we refer to

```
[2015, 2016, 2017, 2018]
```

as the outer level of the MultiIndex to indicate Year and

```
[1, 2, 3]
```

as the inner level of the MultiIndex to indicate Month to compose the row slices.

Similarly, to subset columns, we refer to

```
['City', 'Rural', 'Suburbs']
```

as the outer levels of the of the MultiIndex to indicate Area and

```
['Day', 'Night']
```

as the inner portion of the MultiIndex to indicate When for the column slices.

Together, row and column slices determine the DataFrame subset.

Listing 4-28 produces the analog tickets SAS dataset using PROC TABULATE to render output shaped like the tickets DataFrame. Since the Python code and SAS code call different random number generators, the values created, while similar, differ between the DataFrame and the SAS dataset.

Listing 4-28. Tickets Dataset from PROC TABULATE

```
4  data tickets;
5  length Area $ 7
6          When $  9;
7  call streaminit(123456);
8  do year = 2015, 2016, 2017, 2018;
9    do month = 1, 2, 3;
10        do area = 'City', 'Rural', 'Suburbs';
11            do when = 'Day', 'Night';
12                tickets = abs(int((rand('Normal')*100)/5));
13                output;
14            end;
15          end;
16      end;
17  end;
```

```
NOTE: The dataset WORK.TICKETS has 72 observations and 5 variables.
18 proc tabulate;
19    var tickets;;
20    class area when year month;
21          table year * month ,
22                  area=' ' * when=' ' * sum=' ' * tickets=' ';
23  run;
```

The Data Step uses nested DO/END blocks generating the class variables area, when, year, and month. The tickets variable is created with nested functions working from the inside out:

1. The RAND function draws values from the normal distribution random number generator. These values are then multiplied by 100 and the product is divided by 5.

2. The INT function returns the integer portion of the value.

3. The ABS function returns the absolute value.

Figure 4-6 illustrates the TABLE statement syntax

```
table year * month ,
      area=' ' * when=' ' * sum=' ' * tickets=' ';
```

that constructs this particular output.

The row dimension crosses (*) the month variable with the year variable. The column dimension crosses (*) values for tickets with the area variable which in turn is crossed (*) with the when variable and together they are crossed with the summed value for the tickets variable.

		City		Rural		Suburbs	
		Day	Night	Day	Night	Day	Night
year	month						
2015	1	14.00	5.00	18.00	21.00	15.00	21.00
	2	13.00	37.00	8.00	7.00	1.00	31.00
	3	5.00	26.00	2.00	17.00	1.00	23.00
2016	1	15.00	14.00	1.00	6.00	7.00	17.00
	2	19.00	2.00	46.00	1.00	21.00	1.00
	3	26.00	4.00	16.00	2.00	3.00	16.00
2017	1	25.00	5.00	4.00	15.00	7.00	15.00
	2	17.00	0.00	2.00	12.00	5.00	1.00
	3	5.00	2.00	21.00	17.00	3.00	35.00
2018	1	16.00	12.00	0.00	2.00	11.00	15.00
	2	27.00	18.00	14.00	5.00	17.00	5.00
	3	21.00	6.00	6.00	3.00	23.00	9.00

Figure 4-6. *PROC TABULATE OUTPUT*

Basic Subsets with MultiIndexes

With the tickets DataFrame created having hierarchical indexes for rows and columns, we can apply a range of methods for subsetting as well as applying condition-based logic as filtering criteria.

An important feature of hierarchical indexing is the ability to select data by a "partial" label identifying a subgroup in the data. Partial selection "drops" levels of the hierarchical index from the results using methods analogous to row and column slicing for regular DataFrames.

Consider Listing 4-29.

Listing 4-29. Identify Subgroups with MultiIndexing, Example 1

```
>>> tickets['Rural']
When          Day  Night
Year Month
2015 1        9.0    3.0
     2        3.0   30.0
     3        7.0    6.0
2016 1        1.0    0.0
     2        3.0    5.0
     3       31.0   48.0
2017 1       22.0   10.0
     2       19.0    2.0
     3       19.0   17.0
2018 1        8.0    4.0
     2        9.0   14.0
     3       33.0   21.0
```

In this example, the [ ] operator returns a subset of the tickets DataFrame from the level Rural. In this case, Rural designates one of three values from the outer level of the column hierarchical index. Because there is no explicit row selection, all rows are returned.

Listing 4-30 answers the question: for each month how many tickets were issued in the city at night?

Listing 4-30. Identify Subgroups with MultiIndexing, Example 2

```
>>> tickets['City', 'Night']
Year  Month
2015  1         18.0
      2         18.0
      3         54.0
2016  1         17.0
      2         23.0
      3         17.0
2017  1          5.0
      2         33.0
      3         12.0
```

```
2018   1          10.0
       2          14.0
       3          32.0
```

This example illustrates selecting with both levels of the column MultiIndex. City is from the outermost level of the hierarchical index and Night is from the innermost level.

Recall that most subsetting and slicing operations return a DataFrame. Listing 4-31 illustrates creating a new DataFrame. In this example, the sum() function is applied to the tickets DataFrame elements returning the sum of all tickets by year. These summed values create the new DataFrame sum_tickets.

Listing 4-31. Sum Tickets to New DataFrame

```
>>> sum_tickets = tickets.sum(level = 'Year')
>>> print(sum_tickets)
Area   City         Rural       Suburbs
When   Day  Night  Day  Night Day  Night
Year
2015   31.0 90.0   19.0  39.0 59.0  36.0
2016   27.0 57.0   35.0  53.0 32.0  45.0
2017   57.0 50.0   60.0  29.0 33.0  14.0
2018   63.0 56.0   50.0  39.0 54.0  22.0
```

Use the axis = 1 argument to apply the sum() function along a column with the syntax

```
sum_tickets2 = tickets.sum(level = 'Area', axis=1)
```

Listing 4-32 illustrates PROC TABULATE to render the same report as Listing 4-29 as well as create the sum_tickets datasets using ODS OUTPUT TABLE=.

Listing 4-32. PROC TABULATE Report and New Dataset

```
4 ods output
5     table = sum_tickets (keep = area
6                                 when
7                                 year
8                                 tickets_sum);
9 proc tabulate data=tickets;
10    var tickets;
```

```
11    class area when year;
12         table year,
13             area=' ' * when=' ' * sum=' ' * tickets=' ';run;
```

NOTE: The dataset WORK.SUM_TICKETS has 24 observations and 4 variables.
NOTE: There were 72 observations read from the dataset WORK.TICKETS.

```
14 ods output close;
15 proc print data = sum_tickets;
16 run;
```

NOTE: There were 24 observations read from the dataset WORK.SUM_TICKETS.

The default statistic for PROC TABULATE is sum and is applied to the variable tickets using the VAR statement. The TABLE statement arranges the output similar to the output in Listing 4-30. The PROC TABULATE output is presented in Figure 4-7.

	City		Rural		Suburbs	
	Day	Night	Day	Night	Day	Night
year						
2015	32.00	68.00	28.00	45.00	17.00	75.00
2016	60.00	20.00	63.00	9.00	31.00	34.00
2017	47.00	7.00	27.00	44.00	15.00	51.00
2018	64.00	36.00	20.00	10.00	51.00	29.00

Figure 4-7. *Tickets Summed with PROC TABULATE*

In order to create the output dataset sum_tickets, the syntax

```
ods output
   table = sum_tickets (keep = area
                               when
                               year
                               tickets_sum);
```

opens the ODS destination sum_tickets, as an output SAS dataset with a KEEP list of variables. This method for summarization is an alternative to calling PROC SUMMARY/ MEANS or PROC SQL.

Listing 4-33 illustrates the more conventional method for producing the same "rolled up" or summarized dataset.

Listing 4-33. Summarizing tickets Dataset with PROC SUMMARY

```
4   proc summary data = tickets
5                 nway
6                 noprint;
7      class area
8           when
9           year;
10     output out=sum_tickets(keep=area when year tickets_sum)
11            sum(tickets)=tickets_sum;
```

```
NOTE: There were 72 observations read from the dataset WORK.TICKETS.
NOTE: The dataset WORK.SUM_TICKETS has 24 observations and 4 variables.
```

The NWAY option requests a combination for all levels of variable values listed on the CLASS statement. The SUM(tickets)=tickets_sum option then sums the number of tickets for each NWAY crossing.

Advanced Indexing with MultiIndexes

Earlier in the chapter, we detailed the loc() indexer for slicing rows and columns with indexed DataFrames. See the section "Return Rows and Columns by Label" in this chapter. Slicing rows and columns with the loc() indexer can be used with a MultiIndexed DataFrame using similar syntax. The loc() indexer supports Boolean logic for filtering criteria.

The loc() indexer enables partial slicing using hierarchically indexed rows and/ or columns. Begin by returning the DataFrame along with its index and column information illustrated in Listing 4-34.

Listing 4-34. Return Ticket Index and Column Levels

```
>>> print(tickets.index)
MultiIndex(levels=[[2015, 2016, 2017, 2018], [1, 2, 3]],
           codes=[[0, 0, 0, 1, 1, 1, 2, 2, 2, 3, 3, 3], [0, 1, 2, 0, 1, 2,
           0, 1, 2, 0, 1, 2]],
```

```
                 names=['Year', 'Month'])
>>> print(tickets.columns)
MultiIndex(levels=[['City', 'Rural', 'Suburbs'], ['Day', 'Night']],
           codes=[[0, 0, 1, 1, 2, 2], [0, 1, 0, 1, 0, 1]],
           names=['Area', 'When'])
```

The loc() indexer takes as arguments, slicers to determine the DataFrame subset of interest. Consider Listing 4-35 illustrates returning all rows for year 2018.

Listing 4-35. Year Slice 2018

```
>>> tickets.loc[2018]
Area    City          Rural        Suburbs
When    Day Night    Day Night    Day Night
Month
1       25.0  10.0     8.0   4.0    20.0  15.0
2       35.0  14.0     9.0  14.0    10.0   1.0
3        3.0  32.0    33.0  21.0    24.0   6.0
```

In this case, the rows are sliced returning those with the MultiIndex level for Year equal to 2018. And because no column slicer is provided, all columns are returned.

We can slice Year level for 2018 and Month level for 3 illustrated in Listing 4-36.

Listing 4-36. Slice Year 2018 and Month 3

```
>>> tickets.loc[2018, 3, :]
Area         City          Rural        Suburbs
When         Day Night    Day Night    Day Night
Year Month
2018 3        3.0  32.0    33.0  21.0    24.0   6.0
```

In this example, level 2018 denotes the outer row slice and 3 denotes the inner row slice. This subset sets the DataFrame by returning month 3 for every year. The column slice follows the second comma. Again, with no column slice provided, denoted by the colon (:), all columns are returned.

Slicing Rows and Columns

Consider Listing 4-37. In this example, we wish to return the third month for each year. Based on what we have learned about row and column slicing up to this point, it is reasonable to conclude the statement

```
tickets.loc[(:,3),:]
```

is the appropriate syntax. However, this syntax raises an error since it is illegal to use a colon inside a tuple constructor. Recall a tuple is an immutable sequence of items enclosed by parenthesis. As a convenience the Python's built-in slice(None) function selects all the content for a level. In this case, we want month level 3 for all years.

Listing 4-37. Slice Month 3 for All Years

```
>>> tickets.loc[(slice(None), 3), :]
Area          City        Rural       Suburbs
When        Day Night   Day Night   Day Night
Year Month
2015 3        5.0  54.0   7.0   6.0   14.0  18.0
2016 3        9.0  17.0  31.0  48.0    2.0  17.0
2017 3       31.0  12.0  19.0  17.0   14.0   2.0
2018 3        3.0  32.0  33.0  21.0   24.0   6.0
```

The syntax slice(None) is the slicer for the Year column which includes all values for a given level, in this case, 2015 to 2018 followed by 3 to designate the level for month. All columns are returned since no column slicer was given.

Another way to request this same subset is

```
tickets.loc[(slice(None), slice(3,3)), :]
```

Consider the request for all years and months 2 and 3 as the row slicer in Listing 4-38.

Listing 4-38. Slice Months 2 and 3 for All Years

```
>>> tickets.loc[(slice(None), slice(2,3)), :]
```

Area		City		Rural		Suburbs	
When		Day	Night	Day	Night	Day	Night
Year	Month						
2015	2	11.0	18.0	3.0	30.0	42.0	15.0
	3	5.0	54.0	7.0	6.0	14.0	18.0
2016	2	7.0	23.0	3.0	5.0	19.0	2.0
	3	9.0	17.0	31.0	48.0	2.0	17.0
2017	2	5.0	33.0	19.0	2.0	7.0	10.0
	3	31.0	12.0	19.0	17.0	14.0	2.0
2018	2	35.0	14.0	9.0	14.0	10.0	1.0
	3	3.0	32.0	33.0	21.0	24.0	6.0

Alternatively, the same results are accomplished with the syntax

```
idx_obj = ((slice(None), slice(2,3)), slice(None))
tickets.loc[idx_obj]
```

This syntax helps in further understanding exactly how the slicing operation is performed. The first slice(None) requests all of the rows for the outer row label, years 2015 to 2018. slice(2,3) returns months 2 and 3 for inner row label. The last slice(None) requests all columns, that is, both the outer column Area and the inner column When.

Fairly quickly, however, we begin to have difficulty supplying a collection of tuples for the slicers used by the loc() indexer. Fortunately, pandas provides the IndexSlice object to deal with this situation.

Consider Listing 4-39 as an alternative to Listing 4-38.

Listing 4-39. IndexSlice Object

```
>>> idx = pd.IndexSlice
>>> tickets.loc[idx[2015:2018, 2:3], :]
>>>
```

Area		City		Rural		Suburbs	
When		Day	Night	Day	Night	Day	Night
Year	Month						
2015	2	11.0	18.0	3.0	30.0	42.0	15.0
	3	5.0	54.0	7.0	6.0	14.0	18.0

2016 2	7.0	23.0	3.0	5.0	19.0	2.0
3	9.0	17.0	31.0	48.0	2.0	17.0
2017 2	5.0	33.0	19.0	2.0	7.0	10.0
3	31.0	12.0	19.0	17.0	14.0	2.0
2018 2	35.0	14.0	9.0	14.0	10.0	1.0
3	3.0	32.0	33.0	21.0	24.0	6.0

The IndexSlice object provides a more natural syntax for slicing operations on MultiIndexed rows and columns. In this case, the slice

```
tickets.loc[idx[2015:2018, 2:3], :]
```

returns years 2015:2018 inclusive on the outer level of the MultiIndex for the rows and months 2 and 3 inclusive on the inner level. The colon (:) designates the start and stop positions for these row labels. Following the row slicer is a comma (,) to designate the column slicer. With no explicit column slices defined all columns are returned.

Consider Listing 4-40.

Listing 4-40. Slicing Rows and Columns, Example 1

```
>>> idx = pd.IndexSlice
>>> tickets.loc[idx[2018:, 2:3 ], 'City' : 'Rural']
Area          City        Rural
When          Day Night   Day Night
Year Month
2018 2        35.0  14.0   9.0  14.0
     3         3.0  32.0  33.0  21.0
```

The row slicer returns levels 2018 for Year on the outer level of the MultiIndex and 2 and 3 from Month on the inner level. The column slicer returns the levels City and Rural from Area on the outer level of the MultiIndex. In this example, the column slicer did not slice along the inner level of the MultiIndex on When.

Listing 4-41 illustrates details for slicing columns.

Listing 4-41. Slicing Rows and Slicing Columns, Example 2

```
>>> idx = pd.IndexSlice
>>> tickets.loc[idx[2018:, 2:3 ], idx['City', 'Day' : 'Night']]
Area         City
When         Day Night
Year Month
2018 2       35.0  14.0
     3        3.0  32.0
```

The row slicer returns levels 2018 for Year on the outer level of the MultiIndex and 2 and 3 from Month on the inner level. The column slicer returns the level City for Area on the outer level of the MultiIndex and the levels Day and Night on the inner level from When.

Conditional Slicing

Oftentimes we need to subset based on conditional criteria. pandas allows the loc() indexer to permit a Boolean mask for slicing based on criteria applied to values in the DataFrame. We introduced the concept of a Boolean mask in Chapter 3, "pandas Library," in the section on isnull().

We can identify instances where the number of tickets relates to a given threshold by creating a Boolean mask and applying it to the DataFrame using the loc() indexer. Specifically, we want to know when the number of tickets issued in the city during the day is greater than 25.

Listing 4-42 illustrates this feature.

Listing 4-42. Conditional Slicing

```
>>> mask = tickets[('City' ,'Day' )] > 25
>>> tickets.loc[idx[mask], idx['City', 'Day']]
Year   Month
2017   3         31.0
2018   2         35.0
Name: (City, Day), dtype: float64
```

In this example, we define the mask object using the column slicing syntax followed by the Boolean operator greater than (>) and 25 as the threshold value. Rows are sliced using the conditional with the mask object. The columns are sliced using the City level from Area and the Day level from When. Area is the outer level of the column MultiIndex and When is the inner level.

Another form of conditional slicing uses the pandas where attribute. The where attribute returns a DataFrame the same size as the original whose corresponding values are returned when the condition is True. When the condition is False, the default behavior is to return NaN's. This feature is illustrated in Listing 4-43.

Listing 4-43. DataFrame where Attribute

```
>>> missing = "XXX"
>>> tickets.where(tickets> 30, other = missing)
```

Area		City		Rural		Suburbs	
When		Day	Night	Day	Night	Day	Night
Year	Month						
2015	1	XXX	XXX	XXX	XXX	XXX	XXX
	2	XXX	XXX	XXX	XXX	42	XXX
	3	XXX	54	XXX	XXX	XXX	XXX
2016	1	XXX	XXX	XXX	XXX	XXX	XXX
	2	XXX	XXX	XXX	XXX	XXX	XXX
	3	XXX	XXX	31	48	XXX	XXX
2017	1	XXX	XXX	XXX	XXX	XXX	XXX
	2	XXX	33	XXX	XXX	XXX	XXX
	3	31	XXX	XXX	XXX	XXX	XXX
2018	1	XXX	XXX	XXX	XXX	XXX	XXX
	2	35	XXX	XXX	XXX	XXX	XXX
	3	XXX	32	33	XXX	XXX	XXX

The other = argument assigns an arbitrary value for the False condition, in this case, 'missing'. Also notice how the returned DataFrame is the same shape as the original.

Cross Sections

pandas DataFrames provision a cross section method called xs as another means for returning rows and columns from an indexed DataFrame or partial data in the case of a MultiIndexed DataFrame. The compact syntax offered by the xs() method makes it fairly easy to subset MultiIndexed DataFrames. The xs() method is read only.

Consider Listing 4-44.

Listing 4-44. xs Cross Section, Example 1

```
>>> tickets.xs((1), level='Month')
Area  City        Rural        Suburbs
When   Day Night   Day Night    Day Night
Year
2015  15.0  18.0   9.0   3.0    3.0    3.0
2016  11.0  17.0   1.0   0.0   11.0   26.0
2017  21.0   5.0  22.0  10.0   12.0    2.0
2018  25.0  10.0   8.0   4.0   20.0   15.0
```

The xs() cross section method has two arguments. The first argument in this example is level 1 and the second argument level = 'Month' returning the rows for month 1 for all years with all columns. Recall the Month column is a component of the MultiIndex to form the row labels.

The xs() cross section method works along a column axis illustrated in Listing 4-45.

Listing 4-45. xs() Cross Section, Example 2

```
>> tickets.xs(('City'), level='Area', axis = 1)
When         Day  Night
Year Month
2015 1      15.0   18.0
     2      11.0   18.0
     3       5.0   54.0
2016 1      11.0   17.0
     2       7.0   23.0
     3       9.0   17.0
```

```
2017 1      21.0     5.0
     2       5.0    33.0
     3      31.0    12.0
2018 1      25.0    10.0
     2      35.0    14.0
     3       3.0    32.0
```

In this example, we return all rows for the level City. The axis = 1 argument returns just the columns for the level City.

Because the xs() cross section method returns a DataFrame, we can apply mathematical and statistical functions as attributes. Listing 4-46 returns the sum of all tickets issued during daylight hours in each of the three areas.

Listing 4-46. xs() Cross Section, Example 3

```
>>> tickets.xs(('Day'), level='When', axis = 1).sum()
Area
City       178.0
Rural      164.0
Suburbs    178.0
```

Listing 4-47 is the analog program for Listing 4-46.

Listing 4-47. Summed Tickets Where Day over Area

```
4 proc sql;
5 select unique area
6       , sum(tickets) as Sum_by_Area
7 from tickets
8     where when = 'Day'
9 group by area;
10 quit;
```

The WHERE clause selects those rows for when = 'Day'. The results from the query are displayed in Figure 4-8.

Area	Sum_by_Area
City	203
Rural	138
Suburbs	114

Figure 4-8. *Tickets Issued During Daylight for Each Area*

The GROUP BY clause sums the variable ticket into the unique levels for the area variable. As we will see in the next section, grouping operations are essential for data analysis.

GroupBy

A common pattern for data analysis familiar to SAS users is BY-group processing. SAS defines BY-group processing as

> *a method of processing observations from one or more SAS datasets that are grouped or ordered by values of one or more common variables. The most common use of BY-group processing in the DATA step is to combine two or more SAS datasets by using the BY statement with a SET, MERGE, MODIFY, or UPDATE statement.*[1]

pandas uses the term "Group By" to describe the task in terms of three steps:

- Splitting values into groups based on some criteria

- Applying a function to each of these groups

- Combining the results into a data structure

Within the Apply step, we often wish to do one or more of the following actions:

- Aggregate to compute summary statistics, such as

  - Compute group sums or means.

  - Compute group counts.

---

[1]SAS 9.2 Language Reference: Concepts, 2nd Edition.

- Transform to perform group-specific calculations, such as

  - Normalize data within the group.

  - Replace missing values with a value derived from each group.

- Filter to discard some groups based on group-wise calculation, such as

  - Drop data whose values are sparse.

  - Filter out data based on the group statistic.

To accomplish these types of operation, the pandas library includes a GroupBy object.

When a GroupBy object is created, it contains instructions to map rows and columns to named groups. A crucial benefit for GroupBy is eliminating the need to handle each of the resulting splits, or sub-groups explicitly. Instead GroupBy applies operations to the entire DataFrame often with a single pass of the data. The benefit being the user does not focus on group processing details, but instead benefits from a more-abstracted processing method.

The syntax for defining a GroupBy object is

```
DataFrame.groupby(by=None, axis=0, level=None, as_index=True,
sort=True, group_keys=True, squeeze=False, observed=False,
**kwargs)
```

As an example, consider Listing 4-48.

Listing 4-48. Create GroupBy gb

```
>>> import numpy as np
>>> import pandas as pd
>>> df = pd.DataFrame(
...      [['I',   'North', 'Patton',    17,  27,  22],
...      ['I',    'South', 'Joyner',    13,  22,  19],
...      ['I',    'East',  'Williams', 111, 121,  29],
...      ['I',    'West',  'Jurat',     51,  55,  22],
...      ['II',   'North', 'Aden',      71,  70,  17],
...      ['II',   'South', 'Tanner',   113, 122,  32],
...      ['II',   'East',  'Jenkins',   99,  99,  24],
...      ['II',   'West',  'Milner',    15,  65,  22],
...      ['III',  'North', 'Chang',     69, 101,  21],
```

```
...       ['III', 'South', 'Gupta',    11,  22,  21],
...       ['III', 'East',  'Haskins',  45,  41,  19],
...       ['III', 'West',  'LeMay',    35,  69,  20],
...       ['III', 'West',  'LeMay',    35,  69,  20]],
...        columns=['District', 'Sector', 'Name', 'Before', 'After', 'Age'])
>>> gb = df.groupby(['District'])
>>> print(gb)
<pandas.core.groupby.generic.DataFrameGroupBy object at 0x000002592A6A3B38>
```

The gb object is defined as a GroupBy object using the District column as the by =
parameter. In this case, the three unique values from the District column define the
groups. Notice a DataFrameGroupBy object is returned rather than a DataFrame. The gb
object is analogous to an SQL view containing instructions for executing SQL statement
to materialize rows and columns when the view is applied.

The SQL analogy is

```
CREATE VIEW GB as
   SELECT distinct District
                 , mean(Before)
                 , sum(After)
   FROM DF
   GROUP BY District
```

Only when the GroupBy object is applied are results produced. Consider Listing 4-49.

Listing 4-49. Applying sum( ) over GroupBy

```
>>> d_grby_sum = df.groupby(['District']).sum()
>>> print(d_grby_sum)
         Before  After  Age
District
I           192    225   92
II          298    356   95
III         195    302  101
>>> print(d_grby_sum.index)
Index(['I', 'II', 'III'], dtype='object', name='District')
```

All numeric columns in the underlying df Dataframe are grouped by the unique levels from the District column and then summed within each group. Of course, the sum() method is just one possibility here. Later in this chapter, we will illustrate examples for selecting individual columns and applying different aggregation methods as well as applying nearly any valid DataFrame operation.

Also observe how output from the District column appears like what one sees with an indexed DataFrame to define row labels.

A GroupBy object returns a DataFrame. Observe what happens when the d_grby_sum DataFrame is created from the GroupBy object in Listing 4-50.

Listing 4-50. Create DataFrame from GroupBy Object

```
>>> d_grby_sum = df.groupby(['District']).sum()
>>> print(d_grby_sum)
         Before  After  Age
District
I            192    225   92
II           298    356   95
III          195    302  101
>>> print(d_grby_sum.index)
Index(['I', 'II', 'III'], dtype='object', name='District')
```

The d_grby_sum DataFrame is indexed with values from the District column. GroupBy objects also have attributes allowing examination of their keys and groups. These object attributes are illustrated in Listing 4-51.

Listing 4-51. Keys and Groups for GroupBy Object

```
>>> gb = df.groupby(['District'])
>>> gb.groups.keys()
dict_keys(['I', 'II', 'III'])
>>>
>>> gb.groups
{'I': Int64Index([0, 1, 2, 3], dtype='int64'),
 'II': Int64Index([4, 5, 6, 7], dtype='int64'),
 'III': Int64Index([8, 9, 10, 11, 12], dtype='int64')}
```

The syntax `groups.keys()` returns a Python list for the keys' values. The syntax `gb.`
`groups` returns a Python Dictionary of key:value pairs for each key, mapped to a group,
along with a corresponding list of values indicating which rows compose a given group.
In this example, rows 0, 1, 2, and 3 define the groupby level for `District = 'I'`.

Listing 4-52 illustrates similar logic calling `PROC SUMMARY` to create a "grouped"
dataset summing the numeric variables by `district`.

Listing 4-52. Summary by District

```
4 data df;
5  infile cards dlm = ',';
6  length district $ 3
7         sector   $ 5
8         name     $ 8;
9  input  district $
10        sector   $
11        name     $
12        before
13        after
14        age;
15 list;
316 datalines;

RULE:          ----+----1----+----2----+----3----+----4----+----
17         I,   North, Patton,    17,  27,  22
18         I,   South, Joyner,    13,  22,  19
19         I,   East,  Williams, 111, 121,  29
20         I,   West,  Jurat,     51,  55,  22
21         II,  North, Aden,      71,  70,  17
22         II,  South, Tanner,   113, 122,  32
23         II,  East,  Jenkins,   99,  99,  24
24         II,  West,  Milner,    15,  65,  22
25         III, North, Chang,     69, 101,  21
26         III, South, Gupta,     11,  22,  21
27         III, East,  Haskins,   45,  41,  19
28         III, West,  LeMay,     35,  69,  20
29         III, West,  LeMay,     35,  69,  20
```

NOTE: The dataset WORK.DF has 13 observations and 6 variables.

```
30 ;;;;
31
32 proc summary data=df nway;
33     class district;
34     var before after age;
35     output out=gb_sum (drop = _TYPE_ _FREQ_)
36        sum=;
37  run;
```

NOTE: There were 13 observations read from the dataset WORK.DF.
NOTE: The dataset WORK.GB_SUM has 3 observations and 4 variables.

Figure 4-9 displays the resulting "groups" created using PROC SUMMARY. The CLASS statement defines the unique levels for the district variable.

district	before	after	age
I	192	225	92
II	298	356	95
III	195	302	101

Figure 4-9. *Grouped Summary by District*

Iteration Over Groups

The GroupBy object supports iterating over the defined groups. As an example, consider Listing 4-53.

Listing 4-53. Iterate Over Groups

```
>>> gb = df.groupby(['District'])
>>> for name, group in gb:
...     print('Group Name===> ',name)
...     print(group)
...     print('='*47)
...
```

Group Name===> I

	District	Sector	Name	Before	After	Age
0	I	North	Patton	17	27	22
1	I	South	Joyner	13	22	19
2	I	East	Williams	111	121	29
3	I	West	Jurat	51	55	22

===

Group Name===> II

	District	Sector	Name	Before	After	Age
4	II	North	Aden	71	70	17
5	II	South	Tanner	113	122	32
6	II	East	Jenkins	99	99	24
7	II	West	Milner	15	65	22

===

Group Name===> III

	District	Sector	Name	Before	After	Age
8	III	North	Chang	69	101	21
9	III	South	Gupta	11	22	21
10	III	East	Haskins	45	41	19
11	III	West	LeMay	35	69	20
12	III	West	LeMay	35	69	20

===

In this example, a for loop iterates over the GroupBy object to produce a custom report. As we have seen previously, iterating manually over objects can be useful; however, the apply() method discussed later in this chapter may be a more productive alternative for applying methods and functions to grouped values in a DataFrame.

With SAS, the same report is easily produced using the Data Step by group processing as shown in Listing 4-54. While we could have called PROC PRINT for this example, the goal of the example is to illustrate how FIRST.district and LAST.district behave for By Group processing.

Listing 4-54. Iterative By Group Processing

```
4  proc sort data = df presorted;
5     by district;
6
```

```
NOTE: Sort order of input dataset has been verified.
NOTE: There were 13 observations read from the dataset WORK.DF.

7 data _null_;
8 file print;
9    set df;
10   by district;
11
12 if first.district then
13    put 'Group Name====> ' district /
14         'District Sector    Name      Pre  Post  Age';
15 put @1 district @10 sector @20 name
16     @29 pre @34 post @40 age;
17
18 if last.district then
19    put '==========================================';
20 run;
NOTE: 22 lines were written to file PRINT.
```

In general, SAS By Group processing is established with either PROC SORT or an ORDER BY statement in PROC SQL. For Data Step processing when a BY statement is encountered, SAS creates the automatic variables FIRST.<by_variable> and LAST.<by_variable> to permit truth testing to control logic by identifying observations as first or last in the by group. The statement fragment

```
if first.district then
```

is a truth test with an implied Boolean evaluation of 0 for false and 1 for true. In our example, the preceding statement can also be written as

```
if first.distrct = 1 then
```

Figure 4-10 displays the report output.

```
Group Name====> I
District Sector     Name       Before   After   Age
I          North    Patton     17          27    22
I          South    Joyner     13          22    19
I          East     Williams  111         121    29
I          West     Jurat      51          55    22
========================================================
Group Name====> II
District Sector     Name       Before   After   Age
II         North    Aden       71          70    17
II         South    Tanner    113         122    32
II         East     Jenkins    99          99    24
II         West     Milner     15          65    22
========================================================
Group Name====> III
District Sector     Name       Before   After   Age
III        North    Chang      69         101    21
III        South    Gupta      11          22    21
III        East     Haskins    45          41    19
III        West     LeMay      35          69    20
III        West     LeMay      35          69    20
========================================================
```

Figure 4-10. *SAS By Group Processing*

Similarly, pandas provisions the first() and last() methods for the GroupBy object as illustrated in Listing 4-55 returning the first and last row, respectively, for each group.

Listing 4-55. Return First and Last Rows from GroupBy

```
>>> df.groupby('District').first()
         Sector    Name   Before   After   Age
District
I          North   Patton     17      27    22
II         North   Aden       71      70    17
III        North   Chang      69     101    21
```

```
>>> df.groupby('District').last()
        Sector   Name  Before  After  Age
District
I         West  Jurat      51     55   22
II        West  Milner     15     65   22
III       West  LeMay      35     69   20
```

GroupBy Summary Statistics

As mentioned earlier a GroupBy feature is the ability to accept most methods applicable to a DataFrame by applying the methods to individual groups. Consider Listing 4-56.

Listing 4-56. Summary Statistics by Group

```
>>> pd.options.display.float_format = '{:,.2f}'.format
>>> gb.describe()
          Age                                          ...
          count  mean  std   min   25%   50%   75%   max  ...

District                                               ...
I          4.00 23.00 4.24 19.00 21.25 22.00 23.75 29.00 ...
II         4.00 23.75 6.24 17.00 20.75 23.00 26.00 32.00 ...
III        5.00 20.20 0.84 19.00 20.00 20.00 21.00 21.00 ...

[3 rows x 24 columns]
```

This example illustrates how methods not specifically implemented for the GroupBy object are passed through allowing groups to call the method. Here the DataFrame's describe() method performs the aggregation describing values for each group. Due to page width limitations, only a portion of the actual output is presented here.

We can apply different aggregation methods to different columns defined by the GroupBy object. In Listing 4-49, the sum() method is applied to all numeric columns. In contrast, Listing 4-57 illustrates different statistics applied to columns.

Listing 4-57. Different Statistics Over Group Columns

```
>>> gb = df.groupby(['District'])
>>> gb.agg({'Age' : 'mean',
...         'Before' : 'median',
...         'After' : ['sum', 'median', 'std']
...             })
          Age Before After
          mean median  sum median    std
District
I         23.00     34  225  41.00 45.54
II        23.75     85  356  84.50 26.62
III       20.20     35  302  69.00 30.20
```

In this example, the agg() function is applied to the gb GroupBy object using a Python Dictionary to identify aggregation methods applied to designated columns. Recall a Python Dictionary is a data structure for holding key:value pairs. To accommodate multiple statistics for a given column, we pass a Python list of methods as the value for the Dictionary. For example, the After column has as its value a Python list of aggregation methods, sum(), median(), and std().

Listing 4-58 illustrates the same approach using SAS.

Listing 4-58. By Group Statistics over Different Variable

```
4 proc summary data=df nway;
5     class district;
6     output out=gb_sum (drop = _TYPE_ _FREQ_)
7         mean(age)        = age_mean
8         median(before)  = bfr_median
9         sum(after)      = aft_sum
10        median(after)   = aft_median
11        std(after)      = aft_std;
12 run;

NOTE: There were 13 observations read from the dataset WORK.DF.
NOTE: The dataset WORK.GB_SUM has 3 observations and 6 variables.

13 proc print data = gb_sum noobs;
14 run;
```

Figure 4-11 displays the output created by PROC SUMMARY.

district	age_mean	bfr_median	aft_sum	aft_median	aft_std
I	23.00	34	225	41.0	45.5439
II	23.75	85	356	84.5	26.6208
III	20.20	35	302	69.0	30.1960

Figure 4-11. *By Group Statistics for Different Variables Output*

The OUTPUT OUT= syntax applies summary statistics to the input variables and permits the naming of the resulting output variables.

Filtering by Group

A common coding pattern for data analysis is applying actions to a set of data based on a group's statistic. As an example, consider Listing 4-59.

Listing 4-59. Group By Filtering on a Statistic

```
>>> print(df)
   District Sector     Name  Before  After  Age
0        I  North    Patton      17     27   22
1        I  South    Joyner      13     22   19
2        I   East  Williams     111    121   29
3        I   West     Jurat      51     55   22
4       II  North      Aden      71     70   17
5       II  South    Tanner     113    122   32
6       II   East   Jenkins      99     99   24
7       II   West    Milner      15     65   22
8      III  North     Chang      69    101   21
9      III  South     Gupta      11     22   21
10     III   East   Haskins      45     41   19
11     III   West     LeMay      35     69   20
12     III   West     LeMay      35     69   20
```

```
>>> def std_1(x):
...     return x['Age'].std() < 5
...
>>> df.groupby(['District']).filter(std_1)
   District Sector      Name  Before  After  Age
0        I  North    Patton      17     27   22
1        I  South    Joyner      13     22   19
2        I   East  Williams     111    121   29
3        I   West     Jurat      51     55   22
8      III  North     Chang      69    101   21
9      III  South     Gupta      11     22   21
10     III   East   Haskins      45     41   19
11     III   West     LeMay      35     69   20
12     III   West     LeMay      35     69   20
```

This example removes groups with a group standard deviation for Age less than five (5). To do this, we define the std_1 function containing the filter criteria as

```
def std_1(x):
    return x['Age'].std() < 5
```

def is used to define a Python function followed by the function's name, in this case, std_1(). Inside this function definition, x is a local variable holding the group passed in when called.

A new DataFrame is created by passing the std_1() function to filter method of the GroupBy object.

Notice how no rows are returned from the District column with a value of 'II'.

Group by Column with Continuous Values

Sometimes the desire is to use columns with continuous values as a GroupBy object. Consider the case of age where these values are continuous. To create a meaningful GroupBy object, the first step is mapping continuous values into "buckets" and applying these binned values to a GroupBy operation. The binned values are mapped using the apply() method to create the GroupBy object. This action allows aggregations to be performed based on group values determined by bin ranges formed with the Age column.

Here we illustrate this pattern using the pandas cut() method for segmenting and sorting data values into bins. Consider Listing 4-60.

Listing 4-60. GroupBY Column with Continuous Values

```
>>> def stats(group):
...       return {'count' : group.count(),
...               'min'   : group.min(),
...               'max'   : group.max(),
...               'mean'  : group.mean()}
...
>>> bins = [0, 25, 50, 75, 200]
>>> gp_labels = ['0 to 25', '26 to 50', '51 to 75', 'Over 75']
>>>
>>> df['Age_Fmt'] = pd.cut(df['Age'], bins, labels=gp_labels)
>>> df['Age'].groupby(df['Age_Fmt']).apply(stats).unstack()
>>>
           count    max   mean    min
Age_Fmt
0 to 25    11.00  24.00  20.64  17.00
26 to 50    2.00  32.00  30.50  29.00
51 to 75    0.00    nan    nan    nan
Over 75     0.00    nan    nan    nan
```

In the example we begin by defining the stats() function using the def statement and naming this function stats. It simply returns a Python Dictionary of aggregation methods as a convenience for passing this Dictionary to the apply() method when creating the GroupBy object.

The syntax

```
bins = [0, 25, 50, 75, 200]
gp_labels = ['0 to 25', '26 to 50', '51 to 75', 'Over 75']
```

assigns the "cut-points" to the bins object as a Python list of values representing the upper and lower bounds for the bins created with the cut() method. The gp_labels object is another Python list of values holding the labels assigned to these bins. These objects are passed to the cut() method with the syntax

```
df['Age_Fmt'] = pd.cut(df['Age'], bins, labels=gp_labels)
```

defining the Age_Fmt column in the df DataFrame. This assignment creates column values by calling the cut() method for the df['Age'] column (with bins and labels defined). Note that pd.cut() uses the syntax pd to refer to the name for the pandas library that is loaded into the namespace with

```
import pandas as pd
```

The syntax

```
df['Age'].groupby(df['Age_Fmt']).apply(stats).unstack()
```

creates the GroupBy object using unique values from the Age_Fmt column as the group's levels and is attached to the df['Age'] column. The apply() method calls the defined function stats() applying the statistics column values within each group. The unstack() method reshapes the returned object from a stacked form (in this case, a Series object) to an unstacked form (a "wide" DataFrame).

The same logic in SAS is shown in Listing 4-61. In this example, the aggregation functions for the age variable statistics are produced with PROC SQL.

Listing 4-61. By Group with Continuous Variable

```
4 proc format cntlout = groups;
5     value age_fmt
6         0  - 25   = '0-25'
7        26 - 50   = '26-50'
8        51 - 75   = '51-75'
9        76 - high = 'Over 75';
NOTE: Format AGE_FMT has been output.

NOTE: The dataset WORK.GROUPS has 4 observations and 21 variables.

10 proc sql;
11     select fmt.label      label = 'Group'
12            , count(dat.age) label = 'Count'
13            , min(dat.age)   label = 'Min'
14            , max(dat.age)   label = 'Max'
15            , mean(dat.age)  label = 'Mean'
16 from
17     groups as fmt
```

```
18        left join df as dat
19        on fmt.label = put(dat.age, age_fmt.)
20 group by fmt.label;
21 quit;
```

PROC FORMAT provides similar binning logic as the cut() method in the Python example in Listing 4-59. The CNTLOUT = groups option outputs a dataset containing several variables including the label variable holding the value labels for the user-defined agefmt. format. The aggregation functions are applied to the age variable using PROC SQL. PROC SQL uses a left join to combine rows on the label column from the groups table (created with CNTLOUT =) with rows from the aggregation functions applied to the age column from the df dataset. The output from PROC SQL is displayed in Figure 4-12.

Group	Count	Mean	Max	Mean
0-25	11	20.63636	24	20.63636
26-50	2	30.5	32	30.5
51-75	0	.	.	.
Over 75	0	.	.	.

Figure 4-12. *Group By with Continuous Values*

Transform Based on Group Statistic

Up to this point, the GroupBy objects return DataFrames with fewer rows than the original DataFrame. This is to be expected since GroupBy objects are commonly used in aggregation operations. There are cases where you wish to apply a transformation based on group statistics and merge the transformed version with the original DataFrame. Calculating a z-score is an example illustrated in Listing 4-62.

Listing 4-62. Transform Based on GroupBy Statistic

```
>>> z = df.groupby('District').transform(lambda x: (x - x.mean()) / x.std())
>>> z.columns
Index(['Before', 'After', 'Age'], dtype='object')
>>>
```

```
>>> z = z.rename \
...      (columns = {'Before' : 'Z_Bfr',
...                  'After'  : 'Z_Aft',
...                  'Age'    : 'Z_Age',
...                 })
>>> df1 = pd.concat([df, z], axis=1)
>>> pd.options.display.float_format = '{:,.2f}'.format
>>> print(df1[['Name', 'Before', 'Z_Bfr', 'After', 'Z_Aft', 'Age',
    'Z_Age']].head(6))
      Name  Before  Z_Bfr  After  Z_Aft  Age  Z_Age
0   Patton      17  -0.68     27  -0.64   22  -0.24
1   Joyner      13  -0.77     22  -0.75   19  -0.94
2 Williams     111   1.39    121   1.42   29   1.41
3    Jurat      51   0.07     55  -0.03   22  -0.24
4     Aden      71  -0.08     70  -0.71   17  -1.08
5   Tanner     113   0.89    122   1.24   32   1.32
```

The logic to compute the z-score is accomplished by creating the z DataFrame with a GroupBy object using the syntax

```
z = df.groupby('District').transform(lambda x: (x - x.mean()) / x.std())
```

In this example, a lambda expression is used to create an anonymous or in-line function defining the z-score calculation. Like the def expression, this expression creates a function, but does not provide it a name. Hence, it is known as an anonymous function.

The transform() function computes the z-score for rows within each group using the group's computed mean and standard deviation. The transform() function returns a DataFrame the same shape as the input DataFrame making it useful for combining the two together.

Because pandas allows the same name for multiple columns, the rename attribute is applied to the z DataFrame passing a Python Dictionary of key:value pairs where the key is the old column name and the value is the new column name. The syntax

```
df1 = pd.concat([df, z], axis = 1)
```

creates the df1 DataFrame by concatenating the df and z DataFrames along the columns with the axis = 1 argument. We cover the details for pandas concatenation and joins in Chapter 5, "Data Management."

Listing 4-63 illustrates the same logic in SAS. PROC SUMMARY is called to create the intermediate variables used for calculating the z-scores. PROC SORT is called to sort the df dataset and the z_out dataset produced by PROC SUMMARY using the variable district as the sort key.

Listing 4-63. Transform Based on By Group Statistic

```
4 proc summary nway data = df;
5    class district;
6    var pre post age;
7    output out=z_out (drop = _TYPE_ _FREQ_)
8       mean(age)   = age_mean
9       mean(pre)   = pre_mean
10      mean(post)  = post_mean
11      std(age)    = age_std
12      std(pre)    = pre_std
13      std(post)   = post_std;
NOTE: There were 13 observations read from the dataset WORK.DF.
NOTE: The dataset WORK.Z_OUT has 3 observations and 7 variables.

14 proc sort data = df presorted;
15    by district;
16
NOTE: Sort order of input dataset has been verified.
NOTE: There were 13 observations read from the dataset WORK.DF.

17 proc sort data = z_out presorted;
18    by district;
19
NOTE: Sort order of input dataset has been verified.
NOTE: There were 3 observations read from the dataset WORK.Z_OUT.
20 data z_df (drop = age_mean pre_mean post_mean
21                   age_std pre_std post_std);
22    merge df
23           z_out;
24    by district;
25
```

```
26 z_pre  = (pre - pre_mean)   / pre_std;
27 z_post = (post - post_mean) / post_std;
28 z_age  = (age - age_mean)   / age_std;
29 format z_pre z_post z_age 8.2;
30
NOTE: There were 13 observations read from the dataset WORK.DF.
NOTE: There were 3 observations read from the dataset WORK.Z_OUT.
NOTE: The dataset WORK.Z_DF has 13 observations and 9 variables.
31 proc print data=z_df(obs=6) noobs;
32    var name pre z_pre post z_post age z_age;
33 run;
NOTE: There were 6 observations read from the dataset WORK.Z_DF.
```

The final step uses a Data Step to merge the df and z_out datasets on the district sort key and performs the z-score calculations. The intermediate variables from the z_out dataset are dropped with a DROP list. Figure 4-13 displays the output produced by PROC PRINT.

name	pre	z_pre	post	z_post	age	z_age
Patton	17	-0.68	27	-0.64	22	-0.24
Joyner	13	-0.77	22	-0.75	19	-0.94
Williams	111	1.39	121	1.42	29	1.41
Jurat	51	0.07	55	-0.03	22	-0.24
Aden	71	-0.08	70	-0.71	17	-1.08
Tanner	113	0.89	122	1.24	32	1.32

Figure 4-13. *Transformations with BY Group Statistics*

Pivot

pandas provide the pivot_table() function to create spreadsheet-style pivot tables. The pivot_table() function enables aggregation of data values across row and column dimensions. As we will see shortly, this function not only provides a multi-dimensional view of your data, but it turns out to be a convenient method to apply a MultiIndex to a DataFrame.

Begin by using `read_csv()` method to read detailed sales transaction data collected between 2016 and 2017 in Listing 4-64. This input data is transaction details referred to as stacked, or long format. There is one row per transaction.

Notice the `read_csv()` method uses the parameter `na_filter = False`. Without calling this argument, the `Territory` column does not include rows with the value "NA". In our case, "NA" denotes the value of North America and not missing values. Later in Chapter 6, "pandas Readers and Writers," we explore numerous arguments to the `read_csv()` function in detail.

Listing 4-64. Pivot Table Basics

```
>>> url = "https://raw.githubusercontent.com/RandyBetancourt/
PythonForSASUsers/master/data/Sales_Detail.csv"
>>> df2 = pd.read_csv(url, na_filter = False)
>>> df2.info()
<class 'pandas.core.frame.DataFrame'>
RangeIndex: 2823 entries, 0 to 2822
Data columns (total 10 columns):
OrderNum      2823 non-null int64
Quantity      2823 non-null int64
Amount        2823 non-null float64
Status        2823 non-null object
ProductLine   2823 non-null object
Country       2823 non-null object
Territory     2823 non-null object
SalesAssoc    2823 non-null object
Manager       2823 non-null object
Year          2823 non-null int64
dtypes: float64(1), int64(3), object(6)
memory usage: 220.6+ KB
>>>
>>> df2.pivot_table(index =  ['Year', 'ProductLine'],
...                 columns = ['Territory'],
...                  values = ['Amount'])
                Amount
```

Territory	APAC	EMEA	NA
Year ProductLine			
2016 Classic Cars	3,523.60	4,099.44	4,217.20
Motorcycles	3,749.53	3,309.57	3,298.12
Planes	3,067.60	3,214.70	3,018.64
Ships	nan	3,189.14	2,827.89
Trains	1,681.35	2,708.73	2,573.10
Trucks	3,681.24	3,709.23	3,778.57
Vintage Cars	2,915.15	2,927.97	3,020.52
2017 Classic Cars	3,649.29	4,062.57	3,996.12
Motorcycles	2,675.38	3,736.90	3,649.07
Planes	2,914.59	3,047.34	3,645.51
Ships	2,079.88	3,030.86	3,067.40
Trains	nan	3,344.41	2,924.96
Trucks	3,695.36	4,344.76	3,326.99
Vintage Cars	3,399.04	2,998.96	3,662.24

In order to appreciate the flexibility afforded by the pivot_table() function, the script includes output from info() method indicating the DataFrame has 2823 rows and 10 columns.

In this example, the pivot_table() function uses three arguments:

- index: Containing a Python list of columns forming row labels, with Year as the outer level and ProductLine as the inner level.

- columns: Containing a Python list of columns acting as keys to GroupBy on the pivot table columns. Unique values from the columns argument make up the columns in the pivot tables. In this example, the Territory column has values "APAC", "EMEA", and "NA" (for North America) with each value as the pivot table's columns.

- values: The column or Python list of columns to aggregate, in this example, the Amount column. The default aggregation method is np.mean.

Notice how row labels are formed using the Year column values as the outer level and ProductLine as the inner level. In other words the index argument to pivot_table() function creates either an index if one column is specified or a MultiIndex object if more than one column is specified. The same is true for the columns = argument.

Let's improve the pivot table created in Listing 4-64. Notice in that report NAN's have been returned indicating missing values. Further, we want to replace the default np.mean aggregation method for all columns by summing the values from the Quantity column. Finally, we can add row and column totals to get sub-totals and a grand total. These features are illustrated in Listing 4-65.

Listing 4-65. Pivot Table Improvements

```
pd.pivot_table(df2,values    = ['Amount', 'Quantity'],
               columns    = 'Territory',
               index      = ['Year', 'ProductLine'],
               fill_value = 0,
               aggfunc    = {'Amount'   : np.mean,
                             'Quantity' : np.sum},
                             margins=True)
```

The argument fill_value = 0 replaces the NaN's in the original output with zeros. The aggfunc() function passes a Python Dictionary to associate column names (key) with a corresponding aggregation method (value). In this example, the Amount column is aggregated using np.mean and the Quantity column is aggregated using np.sum. Figure 4-14 shows improvements to the pivot table.

		Amount				Quantity			
	Territory	APAC	EMEA	NA	All	APAC	EMEA	NA	All
Year	ProductLine								
2016	**Classic Cars**	3,523.60	4,099.44	4,217.20	4,106.95	842	9152	5673	15667
	Motorcycles	3,749.53	3,309.57	3,298.12	3,361.02	683	2265	2105	5053
	Planes	3,067.60	3,214.70	3,018.64	3,122.07	419	2106	1582	4107
	Ships	0.00	3,189.14	2,827.89	3,080.08	0	2664	1075	3739
	Trains	1,681.35	2,708.73	2,573.10	2,638.75	33	846	409	1288
	Trucks	3,681.24	3,709.23	3,778.57	3,733.73	252	2974	1901	5127
	Vintage Cars	2,915.15	2,927.97	3,020.52	2,965.11	1022	4523	4300	9845
2017	**Classic Cars**	3,649.29	4,062.57	3,996.12	4,005.96	1484	10433	6408	18325
	Motorcycles	2,675.38	3,736.90	3,649.07	3,655.50	193	3401	3016	6610
	Planes	2,914.59	3,047.34	3,645.51	3,226.59	394	4015	2211	6620
	Ships	2,079.88	3,030.86	3,067.40	3,030.85	56	2526	1806	4388
	Trains	0.00	3,344.41	2,924.96	3,201.18	0	921	503	1424
	Trucks	3,695.36	4,344.76	3,326.99	3,758.49	926	2176	2548	5650
	Vintage Cars	3,399.04	2,998.96	3,662.24	3,289.03	1178	5631	4415	11224
All		3,376.12	3,556.57	3,586.65	3,553.89	7482	53633	37952	99067

Figure 4-14. *shows improvements to the pivot table*

The pivot_table() function syntax is easy to understand and provides a straightforward solution for a variety of analysis problems. Consider Listing 4-66.

Listing 4-66. Sales by Year Over Territory

```
pd.pivot_table(df2,values    = ['Amount'],
               columns    = ['Territory'],
               index      = ['Year', 'Status'],
               fill_value = 0,
               aggfunc    = (np.sum))
```

Figure 4-15 shows that the EMEA territory has a usually high amount of cancellations compared to the rest of the organization.

		Amount		
	Territory	APAC	EMEA	NA
Year	Status			
2016	Cancelled	$0.00	$48,710.92	$0.00
	Shipped	$326,991.61	$2,446,585.86	$1,713,727.25
2017	Cancelled	$0.00	$100,418.90	$45,357.66
	In Process	$43,971.43	$87,329.98	$13,428.55
	On Hold	$0.00	$26,260.21	$152,718.98
	Shipped	$375,158.79	$2,725,139.76	$1,926,828.95

Figure 4-15. *Pivot Table Year Status Over Territory*

To produce the same report with SAS requires multiple steps after the .csv file is read with PROC IMPORT. The task is to summarize the amount variable and transpose the territory variable's unique values into variables. The steps are

1. Sort the sales_detail dataset created with PROC IMPORT by the territory variable.

2. Summarize the sales_detail dataset by territory for the amount variable with PROC SUMMARY. Output summary as sales_sum dataset.

3. Sort the sales_sum dataset by the variables year and status.

4. Transpose the sales_sum dataset on the territory variable (ID) by year and status with PROC TRANSPOSE. Create a transposed dataset called sales_trans.

5. Print the sales_trans dataset using the SAS-supplied dollar13.2 format.

Listing 4-67 illustrates this logic.

Listing 4-67. SAS Year Status Over Territory

```
4   filename git_csv temp;
5   proc http
6       url="https://raw.githubusercontent.com/RandyBetancourt/
        PythonForSASUsers/master/data/Sales_Detail.csv"
7       method="GET"
8       out=git_csv;
NOTE: 200 OK

9   proc import datafile = git_csv
10      dbms=csv
11      out=sales_detail
12      replace;
13 run;

NOTE: The dataset WORK.SALES_DETAIL has 2823 observations and 10 variables.

14 proc sort data=sales_detail;
15    by territory;
16 run;

NOTE: There were 2823 observations read from the dataset WORK.SALES_DETAIL.

17 proc summary data=sales_detail nway;
18    by territory;
19    class year status;
20    var amount;
21    output out=sales_sum (drop = _TYPE_ _FREQ_)
22        sum(amount)    = amount_sum;
23 run;

NOTE: There were 2823 observations read from the dataset WORK.SALES_DETAIL.
NOTE: The dataset WORK.SALES_SUM has 14 observations and 4 variables.
```

```
24 proc sort data=sales_sum;
25    by year status;
26 run;
```

NOTE: There were 14 observations read from the dataset WORK.SALES_SUM.
NOTE: The dataset WORK.SALES_SUM has 14 observations and 4 variables.

```
27 proc transpose data = sales_sum
28                  out = sales_trans(drop=_name_);
29                  id territory;
30 by year status;
31 run;
```

NOTE: There were 14 observations read from the dataset WORK.SALES_SUM.
NOTE: The dataset WORK.SALES_TRANS has 6 observations and 5 variables.

```
32 proc print data=sales_trans;
33    var apac emea na ;
34    id status year;
35 format apac emea na dollar13.2;
36 run;
```

The output from PROC PRINT is displayed in Figure 4-16.

Status	Year	APAC	EMEA	NA
Cancelled	2016	.	$48,710.92	.
Shipped	2016	$326,991.61	$2,446,585.86	$1,713,727.25
Cancelled	2017	.	$100,418.90	$45,357.66
In Process	2017	$43,971.43	$87,329.98	$13,428.55
On Hold	2017	.	$26,260.21	$152,718.98
Shipped	2017	$375,158.79	$2,725,139.76	$1,926,828.95

Figure 4-16. *SAS Transpose on Territory*

The key to creating this report is the call to PROC TRANSPOSE. The territory values in the detail dataset, sales_detail, are row-oriented. The ID statement maps the unique values for the territory variable into variables on the sales_trans output dataset. And because the summarizations are by the variables status and year, the call to PROC TRANSPOSE is also BY status and year.

Summary

In this chapter we discussed the role of indexing and hierarchical indexing as a means for providing labels for DataFrame rows and columns. We introduced the three indexers along with slicers to return subsets from a DataFrame:

1. [ ] operator

2. loc() indexer for slicing along rows and columns using labels

3. iloc() indexer for slicing along rows and columns based on a value position along an index

We examined how to apply a range of methods to the subset DataFrames to perform common data manipulation methods for analysis.

We provided a detailed discussion on the GroupBy object for split-apply-combine operations. We also provided a general introduction to pivot tables. Together these examples lay the foundation for Chapter 5, "Data Management," where we examine joining DataFrames through concatenation and merging methods.

CHAPTER 5

Data Management

In this chapter we discuss common data management tasks beginning with combining DataFrames. Other tasks discussed include sorting, finding duplicate values, drawing samples, and transposing. Every analysis task requires data to be organized into a specific form before the data is used to render meaningful results. Data often comes from multiple sources with a range of different formats. This requires you to logically relate and organize data to fit the analysis task. In fact, most of the effort for any data analysis is "wrangling" data to shape it appropriately.

pandas have two main facilities for combining DataFrames with various types of set logic and relational/algebraic capabilities for join/merge operations. The `concat()` method performs row-wise or column-wise concatenation operations and performs union and intersection set logic on DataFrames. The examples explored in this chapter are analogous to the SAS Data Step `SET` statement and `PROC APPEND`.

The `merge()` method offers an SQL-like interface for performing DataFrame join/merge operations. The SAS `MERGE` statement and `PROC SQL` are the analogs used to introduce the `merge()` method.

The `merge()` method is like the SAS match-merge operation. And since data is rarely tidy, we also explore cases where key columns are inferred as well as handling key columns having different names followed by merges with missing key values.

Start by constructing the `left` and `right` DataFrames illustrated in Listing 5-1. In this example, the DataFrames use the `ID` column as a common key.

Listing 5-1. Build Left and Right DataFrames

```
>>> import pandas as pd
>>> url_l = "https://raw.githubusercontent.com/RandyBetancourt/
PythonForSASUsers/master/data/Left.csv"
>>> left = pd.read_csv(url_l)
>>> url_r = "https://raw.githubusercontent.com/RandyBetancourt/
PythonForSASUsers/master/data/Right.csv"
```

© Randy Betancourt, Sarah Chen 2019
R. Betancourt and S. Chen, *Python for SAS Users*, https://doi.org/10.1007/978-1-4842-5001-3_5

```
>>> right = pd.read_csv(url_r)
>>>
>>> print(left)
      ID        Name Gender    Dept
0   929      Gunter      M     Mfg
1   446   Harbinger      M     Mfg
2   228      Benito      ·F     Mfg
3   299    Rudelich      M   Sales
4   442   Sirignano      F   Admin
5   321    Morrison      M   Sales
6   321    Morrison      M   Sales
7   882      Onieda      F   Admin
>>> print(right)
     ID   Salary
0   929   45,650
1   446   51,290
2   228   62,000
3   299   39,800
4   442   44,345
5   871   70,000
```

Notice the left DataFrame has '321' as a duplicate value in the ID column, making a many-to-one relationship between the DataFrames. Also notice how the right DataFrame has '871' as an ID value not found in the left DataFrame. These are the types of issues that may cause unexpected results when performing merge/join operations. These two DataFrames are used in several examples throughout this chapter.

Listing 5-2 builds the same input data into the left and right datasets in SAS. With the SAS examples, we explore the use of both Data Step and PROC SQL logic as analogs to the merge() and concat() methods for DataFrames.

Listing 5-2. Create Left and Right Datasets

```
4 data left;
5 infile datalines dlm=',';
6         length name $ 12 dept $ 5;
7         input name $
```

```
8               id
9               gender $
10              dept;
11 list;
12 datalines;

RULE:        ----+----1----+----2----+----3----+----4----+----5
13      Gunter,     929, M, Mfg
14      Harbinger, 446, M, Mfg
15      Benito,     228, F, Mfg
16      Rudelich,   299, M, Sales
17      Sirignano, 442, F, Admin
18      Morrison,   321, M, Sales
19      Morrison,   321, M, Sales
20      Oniedae,    882, F, Admin
NOTE: The dataset WORK.LEFT has 8 observations and 4 variables.
21 ;;;;
22
23 data right;
24    input id
25          salary;
26 list;
27 datalines;

RULE:        ----+----1----+----2----+----3----+----4----+----5
28         929 45650
29         446 51290
30         228 62000
31         299 39800
32         442 44345
33         871 70000
NOTE: The dataset WORK.RIGHT has 6 observations and 2 variables.

34 ;;;;
35
36 proc print data=left;
```

NOTE: There were 8 observations read from the dataset WORK.LEFT.

37 proc print data=right;
38 run;

Figure 5-1 uses PROC PRINT to display the left dataset.

Obs	name	dept	id	gender
1	Gunter	Mfg	929	M
2	Harbinger	Mfg	446	M
3	Benito	Mfg	228	F
4	Rudelich	Sales	299	M
5	Sirignano	Admin	442	F
6	Morrison	Sales	321	M
7	Morrison	Sales	321	M
8	Oniedae	Admin	882	F

Figure 5-1. *Left Dataset*

Figure 5-2 uses PROC PRINT to display the right dataset.

Obs	id	salary
1	929	45650
2	446	51290
3	228	62000
4	299	39800
5	442	44345
6	871	70000

Figure 5-2. *Right Dataset*

SAS Sort/Merge

To begin, consider Listing 5-3, also referred to as match-merge. This program is a common pattern for match-merging two SAS datasets containing a common key. In this example, both the left and right SAS datasets are sorted by the id variable enabling SAS By Group processing. After sorting, the match-merge joins the datasets by the id variable.

Experienced SQL users know the results from this match-merge are the same as a FULL OUTER join in PROC SQL in cases where the table relationships are one-to-one or many-to-one. In cases where the table relationships are many-to-many, the results from the Data Step and PROC SQL differ. The many-to-many use cases for SAS and pandas are detailed in Appendix B at the end of the book. For the remainder of this chapter, our examples deal with one-to-one or one-to-many join relationships represented by the left and right DataFrames and datasets created in Listing 5-1 and Listing 5-2.

Listing 5-3 combines observations from the left and right datasets into a single observation in the new merge_lr dataset according to the values for the id variable found in both datasets.

Listing 5-3. SAS Sort/Merge

```
4 proc sort data=left;
5     by id;
6 run;

NOTE: There were 8 observations read from the dataset WORK.LEFT.
NOTE: The dataset WORK.LEFT has 8 observations and 4 variables.

7 proc sort data=right;
8     by id;
9 run;

NOTE: There were 6 observations read from the dataset WORK.RIGHT.
NOTE: The dataset WORK.RIGHT has 6 observations and 2 variables.

10 data merge_lr;
11    merge left
12          right;
13    by id;
14 run;
```

NOTE: There were 8 observations read from the dataset WORK.LEFT.
NOTE: There were 6 observations read from the dataset WORK.RIGHT.
NOTE: The dataset WORK.MERGE_LR has 9 observations and 5 variables.

```
15 proc print data=merge_lr;
16    id id;
17 run;
```

NOTE: There were 9 observations read from the dataset WORK.MERGE_LR.

Figure 5-3 uses PROC PRINT to display the resulting merge_lr dataset.

id	name	dept	gender	salary
228	Benito	Mfg	F	62000
299	Rudelich	Sales	M	39800
321	Morrison	Sales	M	.
321	Morrison	Sales	M	.
442	Sirignano	Admin	F	44345
446	Harbinger	Mfg	M	51290
871				70000
882	Oniedae	Admin	F	.
929	Gunter	Mfg	M	45650

Figure 5-3. *Results from SAS Sort/Merge*

To introduce the pandas merge() method, consider Listing 5-4. Using a single Data Step, the program creates seven output datasets. Each of the joins illustrates the following operations:

INNER JOIN

RIGHT JOIN

LEFT JOIN

OUTER JOIN

LEFT JOIN with no matched keys

RIGHT JOIN with no matched keys

OUTER JOIN with no matched keys

Listing 5-4. Create Seven Output Datasets

```
4 data inner
5       right
6       left
7       outer
8       nomatch_l
9       nomatch_r
10      nomatch;
11
12 merge left(in=l)
13       right(in=r);
14 by id;
15
16 if (l=1 and r=1) then output inner; *Inner Join;
17
18 if r = 1 then output right; * Right Join;
19
20 if l = 1 then output left;  * Left Join;
21
21 if (l=1 or r=1) then output outer; *Full Outer Join;
23
24 if (l=1 and r=0) then output nomatch_l;
25
26 if (l=0 and r=1) then output nomatch_r;
27
28 if (l=0 or r=0) then output nomatch;
29
30 run;
```

NOTE: There were 8 observations read from the dataset WORK.LEFT.
NOTE: There were 6 observations read from the dataset WORK.RIGHT.
NOTE: The dataset WORK.INNER has 6 observations and 5 variables.

```
NOTE: The dataset WORK.RIGHT has 6 observations and 5 variables.
NOTE: The dataset WORK.LEFT has 8 observations and 5 variables.
NOTE: The dataset WORK.OUTER has 9 observations and 5 variables.
NOTE: The dataset WORK.NOMATCH_L has 3 observations and 5 variables.
NOTE: The dataset WORK.NOMATCH_R has 1 observations and 5 variables.
NOTE: The dataset WORK.NOMATCH has 4 observations and 5 variables.
```

Each of these seven join/merge operations is explored in detail along with their pandas counterpart operations.

Inner Join

An INNER JOIN selects only those rows whose key values are found in both tables. Another way to say this is the intersection of matched key values. The SAS Data Step for an INNER JOIN is shown in Listing 5-5. The id column in both datasets must have matching values to be included in the result set.

Listing 5-5. Data Step INNER JOIN

```
4  data inner;
5  merge left(in=l)
6        right(in=r);
7  by id;
8
9  if (l=1 and r=1) then output;
10 run;
```

```
NOTE: There were 8 observations read from the dataset WORK.LEFT.
NOTE: There were 6 observations read from the dataset WORK.RIGHT.
NOTE: The dataset WORK.INNER has 5 observations and 5 variables.
```

The dataset IN= option creates Boolean variables to indicate which dataset contributes values to the current observation being read. The IF statement applies a truth test selecting only those observations where the id variable has matched values in both the left **and** right datasets.

With the SAS example as a template, we illustrate the pandas merge() method. The merge() method signature is

```
pd.merge(left, right, how='inner', on=None, left_on=None,
         right_on=None,
         left_index=False, right_index=False, sort=False
         suffixes=('_x', '_y'), copy=True, indicator=False,
         validate=None)
```

Listing 5-6 uses the on='ID' argument to indicate the ID column is a key column found in both DataFrames. It turns out the on='ID' argument is not needed in this example, since the merge() method detects the presence of a column labeled ID in both DataFrames and automatically asserts them as the key column. The how='inner' argument performs an INNER JOIN, which is the default. The sort= argument is set to False. Not surprisingly, merge() operations on large DataFrames gain substantial performance improvements by not having to return rows in sorted order.

Listing 5-6. pandas INNER JOIN

```
>>> inner = pd.merge(left, right, on='ID', how='inner', sort=False)
>>> print(inner)
    ID       Name Gender   Dept  Salary
0  929     Gunter      M    Mfg  45,650
1  446  Harbinger      M    Mfg  51,290
2  228     Benito      F    Mfg  62,000
3  299   Rudelich      M  Sales  39,800
4  442  Sirignano      F  Admin  44,345
```

Listing 5-7 illustrates the PROC SQL query for an INNER JOIN.

Listing 5-7. PROC SQL INNER JOIN

```
4 proc sql;
5    select *
6 from left
7     ,right
8 where left.id = right.id;
9 quit;
```

An alternative syntax uses the PROC SQL keywords INNER JOIN. The join predicate, l.id = r.id, must be true to be included in the result set.

```
proc sql;
select *
   from left as l
inner join
   right as r
on l.id = r.id;
quit;
```

Figure 5-4 displays the result set from PROC SQL.

name	dept	id	gender	id	salary
Gunter	Mfg	929	M	929	45650
Harbinger	Mfg	446	M	446	51290
Benito	Mfg	228	F	228	62000
Rudelich	Sales	299	M	299	39800
Sirignano	Admin	442	F	442	44345

Figure 5-4. *PROC SQL INNER JOIN Results*

Right Join

A RIGHT JOIN returns all observations from the right dataset along with any observations from the left dataset where the id variable has a match with the id variable in the right dataset. In this case, all observations from the right dataset are returned along with any observations in the left dataset with id values matching in the right dataset.

The SAS Data Step equivalent for a RIGHT JOIN is illustrated in Listing 5-8.

Listing 5-8. Data Step RIGHT JOIN

```
4  data r_join;
5     merge left(in=l)
6           right(in=r);
```

```
7     by id;
8
9   if r=1 then output;
10  run;
```

NOTE: There were 8 observations read from the dataset WORK.LEFT.
NOTE: There were 6 observations read from the dataset WORK.RIGHT.
NOTE: The dataset WORK.R_JOIN has 6 observations and 5 variables.

The dataset IN= option creates Boolean variables to indicate whether the datasets contributed values to the current observation. The IF statement applies a truth test selecting all observations in the right table along with those observations in the left dataset where the id variable has matched values in the right dataset. In cases where there are observations in the right dataset with no matching id in the left dataset, these values are set to missing.

Listing 5-9 illustrates the compactness of the merge() method.

Listing 5-9. pandas RIGHT JOIN

```
>>> r_join = pd.merge(left, right, how='right', sort=True)
>>> print(r_join)
     ID        Name Gender   Dept  Salary
0   228      Benito      F    Mfg  62,000
1   299    Rudelich      M  Sales  39,800
2   442   Sirignano      F  Admin  44,345
3   446   Harbinger      M    Mfg  51,290
4   871         NaN    NaN    NaN  70,000
5   929      Gunter      M    Mfg  45,650
```

The merge() method automatically coalesces the ID column values from both DataFrames into a single column in the returned r_join DataFrame. In cases where there are rows in the right DataFrame with no matching id in the left DataFrame, these values are set to NaN's.

Listing 5-10 illustrates a RIGHT JOIN with PROC SQL.

Listing 5-10. PROC SQL RIGHT JOIN

```
4  proc sql;
5      select coalesce(left.id, right.id) as id
6             ,name
7             ,dept
8             ,gender
9             ,salary
10     from left
11  right join
12      right
13  on left.id = right.id;
14  quit;
```

The COALESCE function coerces the id columns from both tables to return a single column. Without the COALESCE function, the result set returns columns labeled ID from both the right and left tables with the ID column from the left table containing nulls for those rows with no matches found for the ID column from the right table.

Figure 5-5 displays the result set created from the RIGHT JOIN.

id	name	dept	gender	salary
228	Benito	Mfg	F	62000
299	Rudelich	Sales	M	39800
442	Sirignano	Admin	F	44345
446	Harbinger	Mfg	M	51290
871				70000
929	Gunter	Mfg	M	45650

Figure 5-5. *RIGHT JOIN Results*

As the output shows, all rows from the right table are returned and PROC SQL assigns missing values for rows in the right table having unmatched values for the id column in the left table.

Left Join

A LEFT JOIN returns all rows from the `left` dataset along with any rows from the `right` table where the join predicate is true. In this case, all rows from the `left` are returned along with any rows in the `right` with `id` values matching in the `left`. Listing 5-11 illustrates a LEFT JOIN.

Listing 5-11. Data Step LEFT JOIN

```
4   data l_join;
5   merge left(in=l)
6         right(in=r);
7   by id;
8
9   if l=1 then output;
10 run;
```

NOTE: There were 8 observations read from the dataset WORK.LEFT.
NOTE: There were 6 observations read from the dataset WORK.RIGHT.
NOTE: The dataset WORK.L_JOIN has 8 observations and 5 variables.

Listing 5-12 illustrates a LEFT JOIN on the `left` and `right` tables.

Listing 5-12. pandas LEFT JOIN

```
>>> l_join = pd.merge(left, right, how='left', sort=False)
>>> print(l_join)
    ID        Name Gender   Dept  Salary
0  929      Gunter      M    Mfg  45,650
1  446   Harbinger      M    Mfg  51,290
2  228      Benito      F    Mfg  62,000
3  299    Rudelich      M  Sales  39,800
4  442   Sirignano      F  Admin  44,345
5  321    Morrison      M  Sales     NaN
6  321    Morrison      M  Sales     NaN
7  882      Onieda      F  Admin     NaN
```

Like the pandas RIGHT JOIN example in Listing 5-9, the merge() method automatically coalesces the ID column values from both DataFrames into a single column in the returned l_join DataFrame. The output shows all rows from the left DataFrame are returned with the merge() method assigning NaN's for columns in the right DataFrame having unmatched values for the id column in the left DataFrame.

Listing 5-13 illustrates a LEFT JOIN with PROC SQL.

Listing 5-13. PROC SQL LEFT JOIN

```
4 proc sql;
5 select coalesce(left.id, right.id) as id
6            ,name
7            ,dept
8            ,gender
9            ,salary
10      from left
11 left join
12      right
13 on left.id = right.id;
14 quit;
```

Similar to Listing 5-10, this example uses the COALESCE function to coerce the id columns from both tables to return a single column. Figure 5-6 displays the PROC SQL output.

id	name	dept	gender	salary
228	Benito	Mfg	F	62000
299	Rudelich	Sales	M	39800
321	Morrison	Sales	M	.
321	Morrison	Sales	M	.
442	Sirignano	Admin	F	44345
446	Harbinger	Mfg	M	51290
882	Oniedae	Admin	F	.
929	Gunter	Mfg	M	45650

Figure 5-6. *LEFT JOIN Results*

Outer Join

Earlier we stated the SAS Sort/Merge returns the same result set as those from PROC SQL OUTER JOINs in cases where the table relationships are either one-to-one or one-to-many. The results from this example are the same as the SAS Sort/Merge results. See Listing 5-3 for the Data Step source program.

Listing 5-14 illustrates uses of the how='outer' argument to select all rows from the left and right tables to perform an OUTER JOIN.

Listing 5-14. pandas OUTER JOIN

```
>>> merge_lr = pd.merge(left, right, on='ID', how='outer', sort=True)
>>> print(merge_lr)
     ID        Name  Gender    Dept   Salary
0   228      Benito       F     Mfg   62,000
1   299    Rudelich       M   Sales   39,800
2   321    Morrison       M   Sales      NaN
3   321    Morrison       M   Sales      NaN
4   442   Sirignano       F   Admin   44,345
5   446   Harbinger       M     Mfg   51,290
6   871         NaN     NaN     NaN   70,000
7   882      Onieda       F   Admin      NaN
8   929      Gunter       M     Mfg   45,650
```

Listing 5-15 illustrates a PROC SQL OUTER JOIN.

Listing 5-15. PROC SQL OUTER JOIN

```
4  proc sql;
5     select coalesce(left.id, right.id)
6            ,name
7            ,dept
8            ,salary
9        from left
10 full join
11        right
12 on left.id=right.id;
13 quit;
```

All rows from the `left` and `right` tables are returned. In cases where there are no matched values for the `id` variable, the values are set to missing.

Figure 5-7 displays the result set from an OUTER JOIN on the `left` and `right` tables with `PROC SQL`.

	name	dept	salary
228	Benito	Mfg	62000
299	Rudelich	Sales	39800
321	Morrison	Sales	.
321	Morrison	Sales	.
442	Sirignano	Admin	44345
446	Harbinger	Mfg	51290
871			70000
882	Oniedae	Admin	.
929	Gunter	Mfg	45650

Figure 5-7. *PROC SQL OUTER JOIN*

Right Join Unmatched Keys

Up to this point, the examples are based on finding matching key values in the data to be joined. The next three examples illustrate joining data where keys are not matched.

Every SQL join is either a Cartesian product join or a subset of a Cartesian product join. In cases involving unmatched key values, a form of WHERE processing is required. Together, the SAS Data Step with its IN= and associated IF processing logic is a common pattern for this type of filtering. PROC SQL with a WHERE clause is used as well.

The next three examples illustrate the `indicator=` argument for the pandas `merge()` method as an analog to the SAS IN= dataset option. For pandas, the filtering process utilizes a Boolean comparison based on the `indicator=` value.

Consider Listing 5-16.

Listing 5-16. Data Step Unmatched Keys in Right

```
4   data r_join_nmk;
5   merge left(in=l)
6           right(in=r);
7   by id;
8
9   if (l=0 and r=1) then output;
10  run;
```

```
NOTE: There were 8 observations read from the dataset WORK.LEFT.
NOTE: There were 6 observations read from the dataset WORK.RIGHT.
NOTE: The dataset WORK.R_JOIN_NMK has 1 observations and 5 variables.
```

The statement

```
if (l=0 and r=1) then output;
```

behaves as a WHERE filter matching on the id column in both datasets resulting in rows from the right dataset with no matched values in the left dataset.

To perform a RIGHT JOIN on unmatched keys on DataFrames, use the indicator= argument to the merge() method. This argument adds a column to the output DataFrame with the default name _merge as an indicator for the source of each row. Their returned values are

```
left_only
right_only
both
```

By applying a Boolean filter to the indicator= values, we replicate the behaviors for the SAS IN= dataset option for merge operations. Consider Listing 5-17.

Listing 5-17. pandas RIGHT JOIN Unmatched Keys

```
>>> nomatch_r = pd.merge(left, right, on='ID', how='outer', sort=False,
indicator='in_col')
>>> print('\n',
...       nomatch_r,
...       '\n')
```

	ID	Name	Gender	Dept	Salary	in_col
0	929	Gunter	M	Mfg	45,650	both
1	446	Harbinger	M	Mfg	51,290	both
2	228	Benito	F	Mfg	62,000	both
3	299	Rudelich	M	Sales	39,800	both
4	442	Sirignano	F	Admin	44,345	both
5	321	Morrison	M	Sales	NaN	left_only
6	321	Morrison	M	Sales	NaN	left_only
7	882	Onieda	F	Admin	NaN	left_only
8	871	NaN	NaN	NaN	70,000	right_only

```
>>> nomatch_r[(nomatch_r['in_col'] == 'right_only')]
```

	ID	Name	Gender	Dept	Salary	in_col
8	871	NaN	NaN	NaN	70,000	right_only

The indicator= argument adds the in_col column to the nomatch_r DataFrame in this example. We print the nomatch_r DataFrame as an intermediate step to display values for the in_col column added by the indicator= argument.

The Boolean expression

```
nomatch_r[(nomatch_r['in_col'] == 'right_only')]
```

is a subsetting operation to create the nomatch_r DataFrame with the Boolean test

```
(nomatch_r['in_col'] == 'right_only')
```

selecting rows where the in_col column value is 'right_only'.

The SAS analog to Listing 5-17 example is generated by simply adding a WHERE filter to the example from Listing 5-10. This is illustrated in Listing 5-18.

Listing 5-18. PROC SQL RIGHT JOIN Unmatched Keys

```
4  proc sql;
5     select coalesce(left.id, right.id) as id
6              ,name
7              ,dept
8              ,gender
9              ,salary
10
```

```
11   from left
12        right join right on left.ID = right.ID
13   where left.ID is NULL;
14   quit;
```

The WHERE clause returns those rows from the right table having no matching id values in the left table. Columns returned from the left table are set to missing.

Figure 5-8 displays the result set.

id	name	dept	gender	salary
871				70000

Figure 5-8. *PROC SQL RIGHT JOIN No Matched Keys*

Left Join Unmatched Keys

To find the unmatched key values in the left table, consider Listing 5-19.

Listing 5-19. Data Step Unmatched Keys in Left

```
4    data l_join_nmk;
5    merge left(in=l)
6           right(in=r);
7    by id;
8
9    if (l=1 and r=0) then output;
10   run;
```

```
NOTE: There were 8 observations read from the dataset WORK.LEFT.
NOTE: There were 6 observations read from the dataset WORK.RIGHT.
NOTE: The dataset WORK.L_JOIN_NMK has 3 observations and 5 variables.
```

The statement

```
 if (l=1 and r=0) then output;
```

is the reverse from Listing 5-16. The IF statement behaves like a WHERE filter matching on the id column in both datasets resulting in just the observations from the left dataset having no matched id values in the right dataset.

Finding the unmatched key values in the left DataFrame is illustrated in Listing 5-20. Notice the call to the merge() method is the same as illustrated in Listing 5-17; however, in this case, we create the nomatch_l DataFrame and the subsequent filtering logic is different.

Listing 5-20. pandas LEFT JOIN Unmatched Keys

```
>>> nomatch_l = pd.merge(left, right, on='ID', how='outer', sort=False,
indicator='in_col')
>>> nomatch_l = nomatch_l[(nomatch_l['in_col'] == 'left_only')]
>>>
>>> print('\n',
...          nomatch_l,
...          '\n')

     ID     Name Gender   Dept Salary    in_col
5   321  Morrison      M  Sales    NaN  left_only
6   321  Morrison      M  Sales    NaN  left_only
7   882    Onieda      F  Admin    NaN  left_only
```

The statement

```
nomatch_l = nomatch_l[(nomatch_l['in_col'] == 'left_only')]
```

is the subsetting logic to create the nomatch_l DataFrame with the Boolean test

```
(nomatch_l['in_col'] == 'left_only')
```

selecting rows where the in_col column value is 'left_only'.

The same result set is generated by simply adding a WHERE filter to the example from Listing 5-13. This is illustrated in Listing 5-21.

Listing 5-21. PROC SQL LEFT JOIN on Unmatched Keys

```
4 proc sql;
5 select coalesce(left.id, right.id) as id
6            ,name
7            ,dept
8            ,gender
9            ,salary
10      from left
```

```
11 left join
12     right
13 on left.id = right.id
14 where right.id is null;
15 quit;
```

The WHERE clause returns those rows from the left table having no matching id values in the right table. Columns returned from the right table are set to missing.

Figure 5-9 displays the result set.

id	name	dept	gender	salary
321	Morrison	Sales	M	.
321	Morrison	Sales	M	.
882	Oniedae	Admin	F	.

Figure 5-9. *PROC SQL LEFT JOIN on Unmatched Keys*

Outer Join Unmatched Keys

An OUTER JOIN on unmatched keys returns rows from each dataset with unmatched keys in the other dataset. To find the unmatched key values in the left **or** right dataset, consider Listing 5-22.

Listing 5-22. Data Step OUTER JOIN Unmatched Keys in Both

```
4   data outer_nomatch_both;
5       merge left (in=l)
6             right (in=r);
7       by id;
8
9   if (l=0 or r=0) then output;
10 run;
```

NOTE: There were 8 observations read from the dataset WORK.LEFT.
NOTE: There were 6 observations read from the dataset WORK.RIGHT.
NOTE: The dataset WORK.OUTER_NOMATCH_BOTH has 4 observations and 5 variables.

The statement

```
if (l=0 or r=0) then output;
```

behaves like a WHERE filter matching on the id column in both datasets returning rows from the left dataset with no matched values in the right dataset **or** rows from the right dataset with no matched values in the left dataset.

To find unmatched keys in both DataFrames requires an OUTER JOIN with a corresponding filter identifying the null or missing values. Consider Listing 5-23.

Listing 5-23. pandas OUTER JOIN Unmatched Keys in Both

```
>>> nomatch_both = pd.merge(left, right, on='ID', how='outer', sort=False,
indicator='in_col')
>>> print('\n',
...        nomatch_both,
...        '\n')
```

	ID	Name	Gender	Dept	Salary	in_col
0	929	Gunter	M	Mfg	45,650	both
1	446	Harbinger	M	Mfg	51,290	both
2	228	Benito	F	Mfg	62,000	both
3	299	Rudelich	M	Sales	39,800	both
4	442	Sirignano	F	Admin	44,345	both
5	321	Morrison	M	Sales	NaN	left_only
6	321	Morrison	M	Sales	NaN	left_only
7	882	Onieda	F	Admin	NaN	left_only
8	871	NaN	NaN	NaN	70,000	right_only

```
>>>
>>> nomatch_both[(nomatch_both['in_col'] == 'right_only') |
...              (nomatch_both['in_col'] == 'left_only')]
```

	ID	Name	Gender	Dept	Salary	in_col
5	321	Morrison	M	Sales	NaN	left_only
6	321	Morrison	M	Sales	NaN	left_only
7	882	Onieda	F	Admin	NaN	left_only
8	871	NaN	NaN	NaN	70,000	right_only

The nomatch_both DataFrame holds the rows resulting from the OUTER JOIN. The indicator= argument adds the in_col column to the DataFrame containing values subject to a Boolean test for identifying the null values.

The statement

```
nomatch_both[(nomatch_both['in_col'] == 'right_only') |
            (nomatch_both['in_col'] == 'left_only')]
```

is the filtering logic to create the nomatch_both DataFrame with the Boolean test

```
(nomatch_both['in_col'] == 'right_only') |
(nomatch_both['in_col'] == 'left_only')
```

selecting rows where the in_col column value is 'left_only' **or** where the in_col column value is 'right_only'.

An alternative Boolean expression that is more Pythonic is

```
nomatch_both = nomatch_both[nomatch_both["in_col"] != 'both']
```

selecting those rows where the in_col column value is **not** 'both'.

Listing 5-24 illustrates finding the unmatched key values in both the right and left tables.

Listing 5-24. PROC SQL OUTER JOIN Unmatched Keys in Both

```
4 proc sql;
5    select coalesce(left.id, right.id)
6           ,name
7           ,dept
8           ,salary
9      from left
10 full join
11     right
12 on left.id=right.id
13 where left.id ne right.id;
14 quit;
```

The WHERE clause returns rows from the left table having no matching id values in the right table **and** rows from the right table having no matching id values in the left table. Figure 5-10 displays the PROC SQL output.

	name	dept	salary
321	Morrison	Sales	.
321	Morrison	Sales	.
871			70000
882	Oniedae	Admin	.

Figure 5-10. OUTER JOIN Unmatched Keys Found in Both Tables

Validate Keys

As a part of any data management tasks, one must understand the relationships among tables being joined or merged. For example, the results one expects from joining may not be correct if tables believed to have unique key values turn out to have non-unique key values instead. Fortunately, both the pandas library and SAS have methods to detect and enforce join key uniqueness if this is a requirement. Consider Listing 5-25.

Listing 5-25. pandas Validate 1:1 Relationship

```
>>> dups = pd.merge(left, right, on='ID', how='outer', sort=False,
validate="one_to_one" )
pandas.errors.MergeError: Merge keys are not unique in left dataset; not a
one-to-one merge
```

In this example, the validate= argument determines if the merge is of a specified type of relationship. The valid values for validate= are

- one_to_one or 1:1: Check if keys are unique in both the left and right DataFrames.

- one_to_many or 1:m: Check if keys are unique in the left Dataframe.

- many_to_one or m:1: Check if keys are unique in the right DataFrame.

- many_to_many or m:m: Allowed, but does not result in a check.

The default value is None. In this example, validate="one_to_one" raises a pandas.errors.MergeError and reports the merge key, ID, in the left Dataframe is not unique.

Joining on an Index

Recall in Chapter 4, "Indexing and GroupBy," we detailed the use of indexes as row labels for DataFrames. The pandas library implements the join() method to combine columns from two differently indexed DataFrames into a single DataFrame. It turns out the join() method is a convenience for calling the merge() method in those cases where a DataFrame lacks an index (other than the default RangeIndex) or where key columns have different names.

Consider Listing 5-26. In this example, the left and right DataFrames use an index to label the rows.

Listing 5-26. LEFT JOIN on Indexed DataFrames

```
>>> import pandas as pd
>>> left = pd.DataFrame(
...     { 'Style'  :  ['S1', 'S2', 'S3', 'S4'],
...        'Size'   :  ['SM', 'MD', 'LG', 'XL']},
...        index =    ['01', '02', '03', '05'])
>>> right = pd.DataFrame(
...     { 'Color' :  ['Red', 'Blue', 'Cyan', 'Pink'],
...        'Brand' :  ['X', 'Y', 'Z', 'J']},
...        index =    ['01', '02', '03', '04'])
>>> print(left)
   Style Size
01   S1   SM
02   S2   MD
03   S3   LG
05   S4   XL
>>> print(right)
   Color Brand
01  Red    X
02  Blue   Y
03  Cyan   Z
04  Pink   J
>>>
```

```
>>> df1 = left.join(right, how='left')
>>> print(df1)
   Style Size Color Brand
01    S1   SM   Red     X
02    S2   MD  Blue     Y
03    S3   LG  Cyan     Z
05    S4   XL   NaN   NaN
```

This example creates the left DataFrame with a Python list of values assigning the values '01', '02', '03, and '05' as the row labels. Similarly, the right DataFrame is created with an index for row labels, '01' to '04'. The df1 DataFrame is created by calling the join() method which joins either on an index (as in this case) or on a designated key column.

In this example, the call to the join() method performs the default LEFT JOIN with the how='left' argument.

The indexes from both columns are preserved on the new df1 DataFrame as a function of the type of join called. Observe how the print() function displays the index column as row labels in the df1 DataFrame.

We can appreciate how the join() method is a convenience for the merge() method by reducing the amount of typing needed, since the corresponding syntax needed to produce the same results is

```
df1 = left.merge(right, how='left', left_index=True, right_index=True)
```

The join() method provisions four joining methods:

- Left: Uses the calling DataFrame's index, or a key column, if specified. This is the default join() method.

- Right: Uses the other DataFrame's index.

- Outer: Returns union of calling DataFrame's index with the other DataFrame index and sorts the index.

- Inner: Returns intersection of calling DataFrame's index with the other DataFrame index and preserves the order of the calling DataFrame index.

Consider Listing 5-27.

Listing 5-27. OUTER JOIN on Indexed DataFrames

```
>>> df2 = left.join(right, how='outer')
>>> print(df2)
   Style Size Color Brand
01    S1   SM   Red     X
02    S2   MD  Blue     Y
03    S3   LG  Cyan     Z
04   NaN  NaN  Pink     J
05    S4   XL   NaN   NaN
```

The how='outer' argument enables an OUTER JOIN.

An INNER JOIN operation on the indexed DataFrames is illustrated in Listing 5-28.

Listing 5-28. INNER JOIN on Index DataFrames

```
>>> df3 = left.join(right, how='inner')
>>> print(df3)
   Style Size Color Brand
01    S1   SM   Red     X
02    S2   MD  Blue     Y
03    S3   LG  Cyan     Z
```

In both Listing 5-27 and Listing 5-28, the indexes labeling the rows are the join keys and remain a part of the joined DataFrames.

Join Key Column with an Index

In those cases where a DataFrame is not indexed, use the on= argument to identify the key column used in a join operation. Observe in Listing 5-29 that the left Dataframe does not have an index and the right DataFrame does.

Listing 5-29. OUTER JOIN Key Column with Index

```
>>> left = pd.DataFrame(
...     {'Style'  : ['S1', 'S2', 'S3', 'S4'],
...      'Size'   : ['SM', 'MD', 'LG', 'XL'],
...      'Key'    : ['01', '02', '03', '05']})
```

```
>>> right = pd.DataFrame(
...     {'Color' :  ['Red', 'Blue', 'Cyan', 'Pink'],
...      'Brand' :  ['X', 'Y', 'Z', 'J']},
...       index =  ['01', '02', '03', '04'])
>>> print(left)
  Style Size Key
0    S1   SM  01
1    S2   MD  02
2    S3   LG  03
3    S4   XL  05
>>> print(right)
   Color Brand
01   Red     X
02  Blue     Y
03  Cyan     Z
04  Pink     J
>>>
>>> df4 = left.join(right, on='Key', how='outer')
>>> print(df4)
  Style Size Key Color Brand
0    S1   SM  01   Red     X
1    S2   MD  02  Blue     Y
2    S3   LG  03  Cyan     Z
3    S4   XL  05   NaN   NaN
3   NaN  NaN  04  Pink     J
```

The on= argument identifies the column called Key in the right DataFrame as the join key used with the index on the left DataFrame as the join key.

As pointed out previously, the join() method is a convenience for calling the merge() method to join an indexed DataFrame with a non-indexed DataFrame. The same result set from Listing 5-29 is generated with Listing 5-30.

Listing 5-30. Merge Key Column with an Index

```
>>> df5 = pd.merge(left, right, left_on='Key', how='outer', right_
index=True)
>>>
```

```
>>> print(df5)
   Style Size Key Color Brand
0    S1   SM   01   Red     X
1    S2   MD   02  Blue     Y
2    S3   LG   03  Cyan     Z
3    S4   XL   05   NaN   NaN
3   NaN  NaN   04  Pink     J
```

In this example, the how='outer' argument calls for an OUTER JOIN using the left_on='Key' argument to designate the join key on the left Dataframe. The right_index=True argument designates the index as the join key on the right DataFrame.

Update

Update operations are used in cases where there is a master table containing original data values. Transaction datasets are typically shaped the same as the master datasets containing new values for updating the master dataset. In the case of SAS, an observation from the transaction dataset that does not correspond to any observations in the master dataset becomes a new observation. Begin by observing the behavior of the SAS UPDATE statement in Listing 5-31.

Listing 5-31. SAS Update

```
4 data master;
5    input ID salary;
6 list;
7 datalines;

RULE:        ----+----1----+----2----+----3----+----4----+----
8            023 45650
9            088 55350
10           099 55100
11           111 61625
NOTE: The dataset WORK.MASTER has 4 observations and 2 variables.
12 ;;;;
13
14 data trans;
```

```
15 infile datalines dlm=',';
16 input ID
17        salary
18        bonus;
19 list;
20  datalines;

RULE:         ----+----1----+----2----+----3----+----4----+----
21            023, 45650, 2000
22            088, 61000,
23            099, 59100,
24            111, 61625, 3000
25            121, 50000,

NOTE: The dataset WORK.TRANS has 5 observations and 3 variables.
26 ;;;;
27 data new_pay;
28    update master(rename=(salary = old_salary))
29    trans (rename=(salary = new_salary));
30 by id;
31 run;

NOTE: There were 4 observations read from the dataset WORK.MASTER.
NOTE: There were 5 observations read from the dataset WORK.TRANS.
NOTE: The dataset WORK.NEW_PAY has 5 observations and 4 variables.
32
33 proc print data=new_pay;
34    id ID;
35 run;
```

The SAS UPDATE statement creates the new_pay dataset by applying transaction values from the transact dataset to the master dataset. A BY variable is required. Because the ID values are read in sorted order on input, a call to PROC SORT is not needed in this example.

All non-missing values for variables in the transact dataset replace the corresponding values in the master dataset. A RENAME statement is used to rename the salary variable in order to display the effects of the UPDATE operation. The resulting new_pay dataset is displayed in Figure 5-11.

ID	old_salary	new_salary	bonus
23	45650	45650	2000
88	55350	61000	.
99	55100	59100	.
111	61625	61625	3000
121	.	50000	.

Figure 5-11. *SAS Update Results*

In this example, the master dataset does not contain a bonus variable. Since the transact dataset contains a bonus variable, it is applied to the new_pay dataset.

The pandas update() method is used to modify DataFrame values using non-NA values from another DataFrame. In contrast to SAS, the update() method performs an in-place update to the calling DataFrame, in our case the master DataFrame. The SAS UPDATE statement forces the creation of a new dataset and does not modify the master dataset. To understand these difference, consider Listing 5-32.

Listing 5-32. DataFrame update() Method

```
>>> import numpy as np
>>> master = pd.DataFrame({'ID': ['023', '088', '099', '111'],
...            'Salary': [45650, 55350, 55100, 61625]})
>>> trans = pd.DataFrame({'ID': ['023', '088', '099', '111', '121'],
...          'Salary': [45650, 61000, 59100, 61625, 50000],
...          'Bonus': [2000, np.NaN , np.NaN, 3000, np.NaN]})
>>> print(master)
    ID  Salary
0  023   45650
1  088   55350
2  099   55100
3  111   61625
>>> print(trans)
```

```
    ID  Salary   Bonus
0  023   45650  2000.0
1  088   61000     NaN
2  099   59100     NaN
3  111   61625  3000.0
4  121   50000     NaN
>>> master.update(trans)
>>> print(master)
    ID  Salary
0  023   45650
1  088   61000
2  099   59100
3  111   61625
```

The master DataFrame calls the update() method using the trans DataFrame to update non-NA values using values in the trans DataFrame. The default join operation for the update() method is a LEFT JOIN which explains why row ID 121 is not in the updated master DataFrame. This row exists only in the trans DataFrame. This is also the explanation for why the Bonus column in the trans DataFrame is not a part of the update to the master DataFrame.

An alternate approach is attempting a call to the DataFrame update() method with the how= argument set to outer. Unfortunately, this raises the NotImplementedError: Only left join is supported error illustrated in Listing 5-33. (In order to run this example, copy and paste the code for defining the left and right DataFrame from Listing 5-32.) Remember, the update() method performs an in-place update.

Listing 5-33. DataFrame update() OUTER JOIN

```
>>> master.update(trans, join='outer')
NotImplementedError: Only left join is supported
```

The correct alternative is to call the merge() method as illustrated in Listing 5-34.

Listing 5-34. DataFrame Update Using merge() Method

```
>>> master = pd.DataFrame({'ID2': ['023', '088', '099', '111'],
...            'Salary2': [45650 , 55350, 55100, 61625]})
>>> trans = pd.DataFrame({'ID2': ['023' , '088', '099', '111', '121'],
...            'Salary2': [45650 , 61000, 59100, 61625, 50000],
```

```
...                      'Bonus2': [2000 , np.NaN, np.NaN, 3000, np.NaN]})
>>> df6 = pd.merge(master, trans,
...                     on='ID2', how='outer',
...                     suffixes=('_Old','_Updated' ))
>>> print(df6)
   ID2  Salary2_Old  Salary2_Updated  Bonus2
0  023       45650.0            45650  2000.0
1  088       55350.0            61000     NaN
2  099       55100.0            59100     NaN
3  111       61625.0            61625  3000.0
4  121           NaN            50000     NaN
```

The on='ID2' argument uses the ID column common to the master and trans
DataFrame as join keys. The how='outer' argument performs an OUTER JOIN
and suffixes=('_Old','_Updated') adds a suffix to like-named columns in both
DataFrames to disambiguate the DataFrame column contribution.

Conditional Update

There are cases when updates need to be applied conditionally. SAS users are
accustomed to thinking in terms of IF/THEN/ELSE logic for conditional updates. To help
understand how this logic works with pandas, we use two examples. The first example
defines a Python function to calculate tax rates conditionally on the Salary2_Updated
column in the df6 DataFrame. This example will look familiar to SAS users. It uses row
iteration with if/else logic to calculate the new Taxes column.

The second approach is a better performing method of using the loc() indexer to
apply calculated values to the DataFrame.

Begin with Listing 5-35. Our first step is to copy the df6 DataFrame, created in
Listing 5-34, to one called df7.

Listing 5-35. Conditional DataFrame Column Update with a Function

```
>>> #copy df6 to df7 to be used in second example
... df7 = df6.copy()
>>> print(df6)
```

```
    ID2  Salary2_Old  Salary2_Updated  Bonus2
0   023        45650.0            45650  2000.0
1   088        55350.0            61000     NaN
2   099        55100.0            59100     NaN
3   111        61625.0            61625  3000.0
4   121            NaN            50000     NaN
>>> def calc_taxes(row):
...     if row['Salary2_Updated'] <= 50000:
...         val = row['Salary2_Updated'] * .125
...     else:
...         val = row['Salary2_Updated'] * .175
...     return val
...
>>> df6['Taxes'] = df6.apply(calc_taxes, axis=1)
>>> print(df6)
    ID2  Salary2_Old  Salary2_Updated  Bonus2       Taxes
0   023        45650.0            45650  2000.0    5706.250
1   088        55350.0            61000     NaN   10675.000
2   099        55100.0            59100     NaN   10342.500
3   111        61625.0            61625  3000.0   10784.375
4   121            NaN            50000     NaN    6250.000
```

This example defines the calc_taxes function to be applied iterating over the DataFrame rows. The row variable is local to the function definition and returns the val object value when called. The function contains two conditions, if and else. If you need to cascade a Series of if statements, then use the elif keyword following the first if statement.

The if and else statements define the Taxes column calculated at a 12.5% rate when the Salary2_Updated value is less than or equal to $50,000. Otherwise the tax rate is 17.5%.

The statement

```
df6['Taxes'] = df6.apply(calc_taxes, axis=1)
```

creates the Taxes column in the df6 DataFrame by calling the apply function with the calc_taxes function and the axis=1 argument indicates the function is applied along the column.

The second approach for conditional update uses the .loc indexer illustrated in Listing 5-36.

Listing 5-36. Conditional DataFrame Update with loc() Indexer

```
>>> df7.loc[df7['Salary2_Updated'] <= 50000, 'Taxes'] = df7.Salary2_Updated
* .125
>>> df7.loc[df7['Salary2_Updated'] >  50000, 'Taxes'] = df7.Salary2_Updated
* .175
>>> print(df7)
     ID Salary2_Old Salary2_Updated  Bonus2      Taxes
0   023     45650.0           45650  2000.0   5706.250
1   088     55350.0           61000     NaN  10675.000
2   099     55100.0           59100     NaN  10342.500
3   111     61625.0           61625  3000.0  10784.375
4   121         NaN           50000     NaN   6250.000
```

There are two conditions: 12.5% tax rate on the Salary2_Updated column less than or equal to $50,000 is

```
df7.loc[df7['Salary2_Updated'] <=50000, 'Taxes'] = df7.Salary2_Updated * .125
```

One way to read this statement is to consider the syntax to the left of the comma (,) similar to a WHERE clause. The df7 DataFrame calls the loc() indexer to find the condition df7['Salary2_Updated'] less than or equal to $50,000. To the right of the comma is the assignment when the condition is True; the value for the Taxes column (which is created on the DataFrame) is calculated at a rate of 12.5% of the value found in the Salary2_Updated column.

The second condition, 17.5% tax rate on the Salary2_Updated column greater than $50,000

```
df7.loc[df7['Salary2_Updated'] >50000, 'Taxes'] = df7.Salary2_Updated * .175
```

works in a similar fashion.

Specifically, the loc() indexer creates a Boolean mask which is used to index the DataFrame and return those rows meeting the logical condition. This is illustrated in Listing 5-37. For the logical condition, df7['Salary2_Updated'] <= 50000, only when the Boolean mask returns True is the value multiplied by .125. Likewise for the logical condition, df7['Salary2_Updated'] > 50000, is the value multiplied by 17.5.

Listing 5-37. Boolean Mask for Logical Conditions

```
>>> nl = '\n'
>>>
>>> print(nl,
...         "Boolean Mask for 'Salary2_Updated' <= 50000",
...         nl,
...         df7['Salary2_Updated'] <= 50000,
...         nl,
...         "Boolean Mask for 'Salary2_Updated' > 50000",
...         nl,
...     df7['Salary2_Updated'] > 50000)

Boolean Mask for 'Salary2_Updated' <= 50000
0    True
1    False
2    False
3    False
4    True
Name: Salary2_Updated, dtype: bool
Boolean Mask for 'Salary2_Updated' > 50000
0    False
1    True
2    True
3    True
4    False
Name: Salary2_Updated, dtype: bool
```

A conditional update with a SAS Data Step is illustrated in Listing 5-38.

Listing 5-38. SAS Conditional Update

```
4 data calc_taxes;
5    set new_pay;
6    if new_salary <= 50000 then
7       taxes = new_salary * .125;
8    else taxes = new_salary * .175;
9 run;
```

NOTE: There were 5 observations read from the dataset WORK.NEW_PAY.
NOTE: The dataset WORK.CALC_TAXES has 5 observations and 5 variables.

```
10 proc print data=calc_taxes;
11    id ID;
12 run;
```

The SAS IF/ELSE statement is similar to the Python function defining the calc_taxes function in Listing 5-35.

Figure 5-12 uses PROC PRINT to display the newly created taxes variable.

ID	old_salary	new_salary	bonus	taxes
23	45650	45650	2000	5706.25
88	55350	61000	.	10675.00
99	55100	59100	.	10342.50
111	61625	61625	3000	10784.38
121	.	50000	.	6250.00

Figure 5-12. *SAS Conditional Update*

Concatenation

The pandas library implements a concat() method similar in behavior to the SAS SET statement. It is used to "glue" DataFrames together both on a row-oriented basis and on a column-oriented basis, like the SAS MERGE statement. Here we examine its behavior as an analog to the SAS SET statement.

The concat() method signature is

```
pd.concat(objs, axis=0, join='outer', join_axes=None,
          ignore_index=False, keys=None, levels=None,
          names=None, verify_integrity=False,
          sort=None, copy=True)
```

Begin by creating the example DataFrames shown in Listing 5-39.

Listing 5-39. DataFrames for concat() Method

```
>>> loc1 = pd.DataFrame({'Onhand': [21, 79, 33, 81],
...                       'Price': [17.99, 9.99, 21.00, .99]},
...                       index = ['A0', 'A1', 'A2', 'A3'])
>>>
>>> loc2 = pd.DataFrame({'Onhand': [12, 33, 233, 45],
...                       'Price': [21.99, 18.00, .19, 23.99]},
...                       index = ['A4', 'A5', 'A6', 'A7'])
>>>
>>> loc3 = pd.DataFrame({'Onhand': [37, 50, 13, 88],
...                       'Price': [9.99, 5.00, 22.19, 3.99]},
...                       index = ['A8', 'A9', 'A10', 'A11'])
>>> frames = [loc1, loc2, loc3]
>>> all = pd.concat(frames)
>>> print(all)
      Onhand  Price
A0        21  17.99
A1        79   9.99
A2        33  21.00
A3        81   0.99
A4        12  21.99
A5        33  18.00
A6       233   0.19
A7        45  23.99
A8        37   9.99
A9        50   5.00
A10       13  22.19
A11       88   3.99
```

This example uses the DataFrame() method to create the three DataFrames, loc1, loc2, and loc3. The objects are placed into a Python list and assigned to the frames object with the syntax

```
frames = [loc1, loc2, loc3]
```

The three DataFrames are concatenated by calling the concat() method using the syntax

all = pd.concat(frames)

creating the output all DataFrame.

The analog SAS program is shown in Listing 5-40. It creates the three SAS datasets, loc1, loc2, and loc3, and uses the SET statement to concatenate them together producing the all dataset.

Listing 5-40. SAS SET Statement

```
4 data loc1;
5 length id $ 3;
6 input id $
7       onhand
8       price;
9 list;
10 datalines;
```

```
RULE:         ----+----1----+----2----+----3----+----4----+----
12            A0 21 17.19
13            A1 79 9.99
14            A2 33 21
15            A3 81 .99
NOTE: The dataset WORK.LOC1 has 4 observations and 3 variables.
16  ;;;;
17 data loc2;
18 length id $ 3;
19   input id $
20       onhand
21       price;
22 list;
23 datalines;
```

```
RULE:         ----+----1----+----2----+----3----+----4----+----
24            A4 12 21.99
25            A5 33 18
26            A6 233 .19
27            A7 45 23.99
```

215

```
NOTE: The dataset WORK.LOC2 has 4 observations and 3 variables.
28  ;;;;
29  data loc3;
30  length id $ 3;
31  input id $
32          onhand
34          price;
35  list;
36  datalines;

RULE:          ----+----1----+----2----+----3----+----4----+----
37          A8 37 9.99
38          A9 50 5
39          A10 13 22.19
40          A11 88 3.99
NOTE: The dataset WORK.LOC3 has 4 observations and 3 variables.
41 ;;;;
42 data all;
43
44    set loc1
45         loc2
46         loc3;
47  run;

NOTE: There were 4 observations read from the dataset WORK.LOC1.
NOTE: There were 4 observations read from the dataset WORK.LOC2.
NOTE: There were 4 observations read from the dataset WORK.LOC3.
NOTE: The dataset WORK.ALL has 12 observations and 3 variables.

48 proc print data=all;
49    run;
```

The PROC SQL UNION ALL set operator is an alternative to the SAS SET statement for creating the all table. This example is illustrated in Listing 5-41.

Listing 5-41. PROC SQL UNION ALL

```
4 proc sql;
5    create table all as
6 select * from loc1
7    union all
8 select * from loc2
9    union all
10 select * from loc3;
NOTE: Table WORK.ALL created, with 12 rows and 3 columns.

11
12   select * from all;
13   quit;
```

The PROC SQL output is displayed in Figure 5-13.

id	onhand	price
A0	21	17.19
A1	79	9.99
A2	33	21
A3	81	0.99
A4	12	21.99
A5	33	18
A6	233	0.19
A7	45	23.99
A8	37	9.99
A9	50	5
A10	13	22.19
A11	88	3.99

Figure 5-13. *PROC SQL Creating ALL Table*

The concat() method is able to construct a hierarchical index by providing the keys= argument to form the outermost level. Listing 5-42 illustrates this feature.

Listing 5-42. Hierarchical Index from concat() Method

```
>>> all = pd.concat(frames, keys=['Loc1', 'Loc2', 'Loc3'])
>>> print(all)
           Onhand  Price
Loc1 A0        21  17.99
     A1        79   9.99
     A2        33  21.00
     A3        81   0.99
Loc2 A4        12  21.99
     A5        33  18.00
     A6       233   0.19
     A7        45  23.99
Loc3 A8        37   9.99
     A9        50   5.00
     A10       13  22.19
     A11       88   3.99
>>> all.loc['Loc3']
     Onhand  Price
A8       37   9.99
A9       50   5.00
A10      13  22.19
A11      88   3.99
```

With the hierarchical index in place, we can easily identify subsets using the loc() indexer discussed in Chapter 4, "Indexing and GroupBy." In this example, the loc() indexer slices those rows belonging to the original loc3 DataFrame.

The IN= dataset option enables the ability to uniquely identify observations contributed by a specific SAS dataset as illustrated in Listing 5-43.

Listing 5-43. SET Statement Using IN=

```
4 data all;
5 length id $ 3;
```

```
6     set loc1 (in=l1)
7           loc2 (in=l2)
8           loc3 (in=l3);
9   if l1 then location = 'Loc1';
10  if l2 then location = 'Loc2';
11  if l3 then location = 'Loc3';
12  run;
```

```
NOTE: There were 4 observations read from the dataset WORK.LOC1.
NOTE: There were 4 observations read from the dataset WORK.LOC2.
NOTE: There were 4 observations read from the dataset WORK.LOC3.
NOTE: The dataset WORK.ALL has 12 observations and 4 variables.
13
14  proc print data = all(where=(location='Loc3'));
15      id id;
16      var onhand price;
17  run;
```

The IF statements create the location variable by using the IN= dataset option by identifying which dataset contributed observations. To identify those observations contributed from the loc3 dataset, apply the WHERE= filter. In this example, WHERE=(location='Loc3') is applied when calling PROC PRINT. The results are displayed in Figure 5-14.

id	onhand	price
A8	37	9.99
A9	50	5.00
A10	13	22.19
A11	88	3.99

Figure 5-14. *SET with IN= Option*

Similar to SAS PROC APPEND, the pandas library provisions an append() method. Consider Listing 5-44. This method is a convenience for calling the concat() method. The append() method syntax is likely a more natural syntax for SAS users.

Listing 5-44. pandas append() Method

```
>>> all_parts = loc1.append([loc2, loc3])
>>> print(all_parts)
      Onhand  Price
A0        21  17.99
A1        79   9.99
A2        33  21.00
A3        81   0.99
A4        12  21.99
A5        33  18.00
A6       233   0.19
A7        45  23.99
A8        37   9.99
A9        50   5.00
A10       13  22.19
A11       88   3.99
```

DataFrame loc1 calls the append() method to append the loc2 and loc3 DataFrames. For this example, the equivalent syntax using the concat() method is

```
all_parts = pd.concat([loc1, loc2, loc3], join='outer')
```

SAS uses PROC APPEND to append observations from a dataset to a base dataset as illustrated in Listing 5-45.

Listing 5-45. SAS PROC APPEND

```
4 proc append base = loc1
5               data = loc2;
6 run;

NOTE: Appending WORK.LOC2 to WORK.LOC1.
NOTE: There were 4 observations read from the dataset WORK.LOC2.
NOTE: 4 observations added.
NOTE: The dataset WORK.LOC1 has 8 observations and 3 variables.

7 proc append base = loc1
8               data = loc3;
```

```
NOTE: Appending WORK.LOC3 to WORK.LOC1.
NOTE: There were 4 observations read from the dataset WORK.LOC3.
NOTE: 4 observations added.
NOTE: The dataset WORK.LOC1 has 12 observations and 3 variables.
```

```
9  proc print data=loc1;
10 run;
```

In cases where more than one dataset is being appended, multiple calls to PROC APPEND are needed. In some cases, appending is a better performance choice over the SET statement when appending smaller datasets to a larger dataset. PROC APPEND avoids reading observations in the BASE= dataset by positioning the record pointer at the end of the BASE= dataset. Observations from the DATA= dataset are applied to the end of the BASE= dataset. Figure 5-15 displays the loc1 dataset after the append operations.

Obs	id	onhand	price
1	A0	21	17.19
2	A1	79	9.99
3	A2	33	21.00
4	A3	81	0.99
5	A4	12	21.99
6	A5	33	18.00
7	A6	233	0.19
8	A7	45	23.99
9	A8	37	9.99
10	A9	50	5.00
11	A10	13	22.19
12	A11	88	3.99

Figure 5-15. *PROC APPEND Results*

Finding Column Min and Max Values

A common task is finding the minimum and maximum values *in* a column. The pandas max() and min() methods return the minimum and maximum column values, respectively. This is illustrated in Listing 5-46.

Listing 5-46. Return DataFrame Column Min and Max

```
>>> all_parts['Price'].max()
23.99
>>> all_parts['Price'].min()
0.19
>>> all_parts[all_parts['Price']==all_parts['Price'].max()]
    Onhand  Price
A7      45  23.99
```

The first two lines of the script return the maximum and minimum values for the Price column in the all_parts Dataframe. The line in the script returns the row for the maximum value of Price using the [ ] indexer followed by the Boolean comparison.

Listing 5-47 illustrates the same logic with PROC SQL.

Listing 5-47. Return Dataset Column Min and Max

```
4 proc sql;
5 select min(price) as Price_min
6      , max(price) as Price_max
7 from loc1;
8 quit;
```

Figure 5-16 displays the PROC SQL result set.

Price_min	Price_max
0.19	23.99

Figure 5-16. *Returned Column Min and Max*

Sorting

Both the pandas library and SAS provide sort methods and options for controlling how values are sorted. Examine Listing 5-48. It creates the df DataFrame and calls the sort_ values attribute with a Python list of column names indicating a multi-key sort.

Listing 5-48. pandas sort_values Attribute

```
>>> df = pd.DataFrame({'ID': ['A0', 'A1', 'A2', 'A3', 'A4', '5A', '5B'],
...                     'Age': [21, 79, 33, 81, np.NaN, 33, 33],
...                     'Rank': [1, 2, 3, 3, 4, 5, 6]})
>>> print(df)
   ID   Age  Rank
0  A0  21.0     1
1  A1  79.0     2
2  A2  33.0     3
3  A3  81.0     3
4  A4   NaN     4
5  5A  33.0     5
6  5B  33.0     6
>>> df.sort_values(by=['Age', 'Rank'])
   ID   Age  Rank
0  A0  21.0     1
2  A2  33.0     3
5  5A  33.0     5
6  5B  33.0     6
1  A1  79.0     2
3  A3  81.0     3
4  A4   NaN     4
```

Both the sort_values attribute and PROC SORT use ascending as the default sort order. Listing 5-49 is the analog illustrating a call to PROC SORT using a multi-key sort. Of course, the same dataset can be generated with PROC SQL and an ORDER BY statement.

Listing 5-49. SAS PROC SORT

```
4   data df;
5   length id $ 2;
6   input id $
7           age
8           rank;
9   list;
10  datalines;

RULE:          ----+----1----+----2----+----3----+----4----+----
11             A0 21 1
12             A1 79 2
13             A2 33 3
14             A3 81 3
15             A4 .  4
16             5A 33 5
17             5B 33 6
NOTE: The dataset WORK.DF has 7 observations and 3 variables.
18  ;;;;
19
20 proc sort data = df;
21    by age rank;
22 run;

NOTE: There were 7 observations read from the dataset WORK.DF.

23 proc print data = df;
24    id id;
25 run;
```

Figure 5-17 displays the results of the sort operation.

id	age	rank
A4	.	4
A0	21	1
A2	33	3
5A	33	5
5B	33	6
A1	79	2
A3	81	3

Figure 5-17. *PROC SORT Results*

PROC SORT sorts missing values as the smallest numeric value. The default behavior for pandas sort_values attribute is to sort NaN's as the largest numeric values. The sort_values attribute has the na_position= argument which uses values of 'first' or 'last' for placing NaN's at the beginning or the end, respectively, of a DataFrame.

Listing 5-50 illustrates overriding the default behavior of 'last' with 'first' with the sort_values attribute.

Listing 5-50. Sort NaN's to Beginning of DataFrame

```
>>> df.sort_values(by=['Age', 'Rank'], na_position='first')
    ID   Age  Rank
4   A4   NaN    4
0   A0  21.0    1
2   A2  33.0    3
5   5A  33.0    5
6   5B  33.0    6
1   A1  79.0    2
3   A3  81.0    3
```

The behaviors between sort_values attribute and PROC SORT differ with respect to where the sort occurs. By default, the sort_values attribute returns a new DataFrame with the inplace= argument set to False. By contrast, PROC SORT sorts the dataset in place unless an output dataset is specified with the OUT= option.

For a multi-key sort using the sort_values attribute, the ascending or descending sort order is specified with the ascending= argument using True or False for the same number of values listed with the by= argument. Take, for example, Listing 5-51.

Listing 5-51. Multi-key Sort Ascending and Descending

```
>>> df.sort_values(by=['Age', 'Rank'], na_position='first', ascending =
(True, False))
     ID   Age  Rank
4   A4    NaN    4
0   A0   21.0    1
6   5B   33.0    6
5   5A   33.0    5
2   A2   33.0    3
1   A1   79.0    2
3   A3   81.0    3
```

In this example, the Age column is sorted by ascending value and the Rank column is sorted by descending value.

PROC SQL uses the keyword DESCENDING following a column name to indicate a descending sort order used with ORDER BY. Listing 5-52 illustrates the DESCENDING keyword to alter the default sort order.

Listing 5-52. PROC SQL ORDER BY

```
4 proc sql;
5    select * from df
6 order by age, rank descending;
7 quit;
```

The results from PROC SQL with a multi-key sort is displayed in Figure 5-18.

id	age	rank
A4	.	4
A0	21	1
5B	33	6
5A	33	5
A2	33	3
A1	79	2
A3	81	3

Figure 5-18. *PROC SQL Multi-key ORDER BY*

Finding Duplicates

In some cases data entry errors lead to duplicate data values or non-unique key values or duplicate rows. In Listing 5-25, we discuss validating the join relationship among tables. The validation argument for the merge() method validates whether a join is of a particular type. This raises the question on how to find and remove duplicate key values.

Consider Listing 5-53. This example illustrates how to find duplicate key values using the duplicated attribute.

Listing 5-53. Find DataFrame Duplicate Keys

```
>> print(df)
   ID   Age  Rank
0  A0  21.0    1
1  A1  79.0    2
2  A2  33.0    3
3  A3  81.0    3
4  A4   NaN    4
5  5A  33.0    5
6  5B  33.0    6
>>> dup_mask = df.duplicated('Age', keep='first')
>>> df_dups = df.loc[dup_mask]
>>> print(df_dups)
```

```
    ID  Age  Rank
5   5A  33.0    5
6   5B  33.0    6
```

The duplicated attribute returns Booleans indicating duplicate rows and, in this case, limited to duplicate values in the Age column. By default, the duplicated attribute applies to all DataFrame columns. In other words, the default behavior is to identify duplicate rows.

The statement

```
dup_mask = df.duplicated('Age', keep='first')
```

defines a Boolean mask using the keep='first' argument for the duplicated attribute. The keep= argument has the following three values:

- first: Mark duplicates as True except for the first occurrence.

- last: Mark duplicates as False except for the last occurrence.

- False: Mark all duplicates as True.

The statement

```
df_dups = df.loc[dup_mask]
```

creates the df_dups DataFrame containing the duplicate values for the Age column. This form of conditional slicing is covered in detail in Chapter 4, "Indexing and GroupBy," in the section "Conditional Slicing."

Dropping Duplicates

The drop_duplicates attribute returns a de-duplicated DataFrame based on its argument values. This feature is illustrated in Listing 5-54.

Listing 5-54. Drop Duplicate Column Values

```
>> print(df)
    ID  Age   Rank
0   A0  21.0     1
1   A1  79.0     2
2   A2  33.0     3
```

```
3  A3  81.0      3
4  A4  NaN       4
5  5A  33.0      5
6  5B  33.0      6
>>> df_deduped = df.drop_duplicates('Age', keep = 'first')
>>> print(df_deduped)
   ID  Age  Rank
0  A0  21.0    1
1  A1  79.0    2
2  A2  33.0    3
3  A3  81.0    3
4  A4  NaN     4
```

The keep= argument has the same values and behavior as the keep= argument for the duplicated attribute.

Similarly, with SAS, the NODUPKEY and NODUPRECS options for PROC SORT are used to detect and remove duplicate values. The NODUPKEY option removes observations with duplicate BY values. This is analogous to the drop_duplicates attribute with a column argument.

The PROC SORT NODUPRECORDS is analogous to the drop_duplicates attribute with the keep= argument set to False. In each case, duplicate observations or rows, if found, are eliminated.

Consider Listing 5-55. This example replicates the logic for Listing 5-53 and Listing 5-54.

Listing 5-55. SAS Find and Drop Duplicates

```
4 proc sort data = df nodupkey
5    out = df_deduped
6    dupout = df_dups;
7    by age;
8
9 run;
NOTE: There were 7 observations read from the dataset WORK.DF.
NOTE: 2 observations with duplicate key values were deleted.
NOTE: The dataset WORK.DF_DEDUPED has 5 observations and 3 variables.
NOTE: The dataset WORK.DF_DUPS has 2 observations and 3 variables.
```

```
10 proc print data = df;
11    id id;
12 run;
```

NOTE: There were 7 observations read from the dataset WORK.DF.

```
13 proc print data = df_dups;
14    id id;
15 run;
```

NOTE: There were 2 observations read from the dataset WORK.DF_DUPS.

```
16 proc print data = df_deduped;
17    id id;
18 run;
```
NOTE: There were 5 observations read from the dataset WORK.DF_DEDUPED.

In this example, the OUT= dataset option creates the df_deduped dataset dropping the duplicate values for the age variable found in the df dataset. Without the OUT= option, PROC SORT does an in-place sort overwriting the df dataset. The NODUPKEY option removes observations with duplicate BY values for the age variable. The DUPOUT= option identifies the output dataset to output the duplicate values.

Figure 5-19 uses PROC PRINT to display the original dataset with duplicate age values.

id	age	rank
A0	21	1
A1	79	2
A2	33	3
A3	81	3
A4	.	4
5A	33	5
5B	33	6

Figure 5-19. *Original df Dataset*

Figure 5-20 uses PROC PRINT to display the duplicate observations found using the NODUPKEY option that are written to the df_dups dataset using the DUPOUT= option.

id	age	rank
5A	33	5
5B	33	6

Figure 5-20. *Duplicate Age Observations*

Figure 5-21 uses PROC PRINT to display the de-duplicated dataset df_deduped.

id	age	rank
A4	.	4
A0	21	1
A2	33	3
A1	79	2
A3	81	3

Figure 5-21. *Deduped Observations*

Sampling

Sampling is often a requirement in data analysis. The idea is to select a sample from a population and, by analyzing the sample, draw inferences about the population. In a simple random sample without replacement process every row has an equal chance of being selected. Once selected, the observation cannot be chosen again. Listing 5-56 illustrates this concept.

Listing 5-56. Simple Random Sample from a DataFrame

```
>>> np.random.seed(987654)
>>> df = pd.DataFrame({'value': np .random.randn(360)},
...       index=pd.date_range('1970-01-01', freq='M', periods=360))
```

```
>>> print(df.head(5))
                value
1970-01-31 -0.280936
1970-02-28 -1.292098
1970-03-31 -0.881673
1970-04-30  0.518407
1970-05-31  1.829087
>>>
>>> samp1 = df.sample(n= 100, replace=False)
>>> samp1.head(5)
                value
1993-10-31 -0.471982
1998-04-30 -0.906632
1980-09-30 -0.313441
1986-07-31 -0.872584
1975-01-31  0.237037
>>> print(samp1.shape)
(100, 1)
```

The df DataFrame is constructed using the numpy `random.randn` random number generator to generate 360 values into the value column with a standard normal distribution. The samp1 DataFrame is created by drawing a sample by calling the sample attribute along with the n= argument to set the number of rows to be drawn without replacement. The replace= argument is False by default to sample without replacement.

The same logic for a simple random sample without replacement is illustrated in Listing 5-57.

Listing 5-57. Simple Random Sample from a Dataset

```
4  data df;
5  do date = '01Jan1970'd to '31Dec2000'd by 31;
6     value = rand('NORMAL');
7     output;
8  end;
9  format date yymmdd10.;
10 run;
```

NOTE: The dataset WORK.DF has 366 observations and 2 variables.

```
11 data samp1 (drop = k n);
12 retain k 100 n;
13 if _n_ = 1 then n = total;
14   set df nobs=total;
15
16  if ranuni(654321) <= k/n then do;
17     output;
18        k = k -1;
19     end;
20 n = n -1;
21
22 if k = 0 then stop;
23 run;
```

NOTE: There were 360 observations read from the dataset WORK.DF.
NOTE: The dataset WORK.SAMP1 has 100 observations and 2 variables.

```
24 proc print data = samp1 (obs=5);
25     id date;
26     var value;
27 run;
```

The df dataset is generated using a DO/END block. The values assigned to the value variable are randomly generated from the standard normal distribution.

The samp1 dataset is created by reading the df dataset and retaining the k variable to the desired sample size of 100. The total variable holds the value for the number of observations read from the input df dataset using the NOBS= dataset option on the SET statement. When the first observation is read from the df dataset, the n variable is assigned the value from the total variable.

The IF-THEN/DO block is based on the logic that each observation in the input dataset has an equal probability of k/n (100/360) of being selected as the first observation in the sample. The values for the k and n variables are decremented by one to reach the desired sample size. If a random number from the RANUNI function is less than or equal to k/n, then the observation is included in the sample. The iteration stops when k, which began with a retained value of 100, decrements to zero (0).

The pandas `sample` attribute uses the `frac=` argument to include a portion, for example, 30% of the rows to be included in the sample. This capability is illustrated in Listing 5-58.

Listing 5-58. Proportional Sample from a DataFrame with Replacement

```
>>> samp2 = df.sample(frac=.3, replace=True)
>>> print(samp2.head(5))
                value
1971-05-31  0.639097
1997-10-31  1.779798
1971-07-31  1.578456
1981-12-31  2.114340
1980-11-30  0.293887
>>> print(samp2.shape)
(108, 1)
```

The `replace=True` argument indicates the sample is drawn with replacement.

Convert Types

There are occasions when a value is assigned to a DataFrame column that is not appropriate for a desired operation. For example, date values may have been read as strings or numeric values are read as strings.

pandas provisions the attribute to convert types. This feature is illustrated in Listing 5-59. The DataFrame `dtypes` attribute returns the column's type.

Listing 5-59. Converting Types

```
>>> df8 = pd.DataFrame({'String': ['2', '4', '6', '8'],
...                     'Ints'   : [1, 3, 5, 7]})
>>> df8.dtypes
String    object
Ints       int64
dtype: object
>>> df8['String'] = df8['String'].astype(float)
>>> df8['Ints']   = df8['Ints'].astype(object)
```

```
>>> df8.dtypes
String     float64
Ints        object
dtype: object
```

In this example, DataFrame `df8` contains two columns, `String` and `Ints`, with types of `object` and `int64`, respectively. After the calls to the `astype` attribute, the `String` and `Ints` columns have data types `float64` and `object`, respectively. The "Column Types" section in Chapter 3, "pandas Library," provides more details for the common pandas types.

Rename Columns

Listing 5-60 illustrates calling the DataFrame rename attribute to rename column labels.

Listing 5-60. Rename Columns

```
>>> df8.rename(columns={"String": "String_to_Float",
...                     "Ints": "Ints_to_Object"},
... inplace=True)
>>> print(df8)
   String_to_Float Ints_to_Object
0              2.0              1
1              4.0              3
2              6.0              5
3              8.0              7
```

The DataFrame `rename` attribute accepts the Dictionary key:value pairs where the key is the existing column name and the value is the new name. The default value for the `inplace=` argument is `False`.

Map Column Values

Mapping column values is similar to the function provided by PROC FORMAT. Mapping allows translation of DataFrame column values into associated values as illustrated in Listing 5-61.

Listing 5-61. Mapping Column Values

```
>>> dow = pd.DataFrame({"Day_Num":[1,2,3,4,5,6,7]})
>>> dow_map={1:'Sunday',
...          2:'Monday',
...          3:'Tuesday',
...          4:'Wednesday',
...          5:'Thursday',
...          6:'Friday',
...          7:'Saturday'
...          }
>>>
>>> dow["Day_Name"] = dow["Day_Num"].map(dow_map)
>>> print(dow)
   Day_Num   Day_Name
0        1     Sunday
1        2     Monday
2        3    Tuesday
3        4  Wednesday
4        5   Thursday
5        6     Friday
6        7   Saturday
```

The dow DataFrame is constructed with the Day_Num column having values 1 through 7. dow_map defines a Dictionary of key:value pairs where the keys are equivalent to the values on the Day_Num column. The Dictionary values are the values to be mapped to these keys, in this case, names for the week day. The statement

```
dow["Day_Name"] = dow["Day_Num"].map(dow_map)
```

creates the Day_Name column in the dow DataFrame by calling the map attribute with the dow_map Dictionary for the Day_Num column.

Transpose

Transposing creates a DataFrame by restructuring the values in a DataFrame, transposing columns into row. By default a DataFrame is transposed in place. In most cases, an output DataFrame is created with an assignment statement. Creating a new DataFrame by transposing an existing DataFrame is shown in Listing 5-62.

Listing 5-62. Transpose a DataFrame

```
>>> uni = {'School'   :  ['NCSU',   'UNC',          'Duke'],
...         'Mascot'   :  ['Wolf',   'Ram',          'Devil'],
...         'Students' :  [22751,     31981,          19610],
...         'City'     :  ['Raleigh', 'Chapel Hill', 'Durham']}
>>> df_uni = pd.DataFrame(data=uni)
>>> print (df_uni)
  School Mascot  Students          City
0   NCSU   Wolf     22751       Raleigh
1    UNC    Ram     31981   Chapel Hill
2   Duke  Devil     19610        Durham
>>> df_uni.dtypes
School        object
Mascot        object
Students       int64
City          object
dtype: object
>>>
>>> t_df_uni = df_uni.T
>>> print(t_df_uni)
                 0            1        2
School        NCSU          UNC     Duke
Mascot        Wolf          Ram    Devil
Students     22751        31981    19610
City       Raleigh  Chapel Hill   Durham
```

```
>>> t_df_uni.dtypes
0      object
1      object
2      object
dtype: object
>>>
>>> t_df_uni[0]
School           NCSU
Mascot           Wolf
Students        22751
City          Raleigh
Name: 0, dtype: object
```

The example begins by defining the Dictionary uni. The statement

```
df_uni = pd.DataFrame(data=uni)
```

uses the uni Dictionary to create the df_uni DataFrame.

The call to create the transposed DataFrame and create the output t_df_uni
DataFrame is the statement

```
t_df_uni = df_uni.T
```

In cases where the DataFrame has mixed data types, such as this one, the transposed
DataFrame columns are returned as object (string) types. The Students column in the
original df_uni DataFrame is int64. The columns 0–2 in the transposed DataFrame are
object data types.

The [ ] indexer is used to return column 0 in this example.

Listing 5-63 illustrates transposing a SAS dataset.

Listing 5-63. SAS Transpose

```
4 data df_uni;
5 infile datalines dlm=',';
6          length school $ 4
7                 mascot $ 5
8                 city $ 11;
9          input school $
10                mascot $
```

```
11              students
12              city $;
13  list;
14  datalines;
RULE:           ----+----1----+----2----+----3----+----4----+----5
2922            NCSU, Wolf, 22751, Raleigh
2923            UNC, Ram, 31981, Chapel Hill
2924            Duke, Devil, 19610, Durham
```
NOTE: The dataset WORK.DF_UNI has 3 observations and 4 variables.

```
15  ;;;;
16
17 proc print data = df_uni;
18    id school;
19 run;
```

NOTE: There were 3 observations read from the dataset WORK.DF_UNI.

```
20
21 proc transpose data = df_uni
22               out = t_df_uni;
23 var school mascot students city;
24 run;
```

NOTE: Numeric variables in the input dataset will be converted to character in the output dataset.
NOTE: There were 3 observations read from the dataset WORK.DF_UNI.
NOTE: The dataset WORK.T_DF_UNI has 4 observations and 4 variables.
```
25
26 proc print data = t_df_uni;
27    run;
```

NOTE: There were 4 observations read from the dataset WORK.T_DF_UNI.
```
28
29 proc sql;
30    select name
31         , type
```

```
32      from dictionary.columns
33 where libname='WORK' and memname='T_DF_UNI';
34 quit;
```

The call to PROC TRANSPOSE transposes the input dataset df_uni and creates the transposed t_df_uni dataset using the OUT= option. Observe the note in the SAS log

```
Numeric variables in the input dataset will be converted to character in
the output dataset.
```

The note indicates numerics, in this case, the student variable, are converted to characters. The PROC SQL code queries the SAS DICTIONARY table COLUMNS to display the column names and data types for the transposed t_df_uni dataset.

Figure 5-22 uses PROC PRINT to display the input dataset. Figure 5-23 uses PROC PRINT to display the transposed dataset. Figure 5-24 displays the PROC SQL results from the DICTIONARY.COLUMNS table.

school	mascot	city	students
NCSU	Wolf	Raleigh	22751
UNC	Ram	Chapel Hill	31981
Duke	Devil	Durham	19610

Figure 5-22. Input Dataset to Transpose

Obs	_NAME_	COL1	COL2	COL3
1	school	NCSU	UNC	Duke
2	mascot	Wolf	Ram	Devil
3	students	22751	31981	19610
4	city	Raleigh	Chapel Hill	Durham

Figure 5-23. Output Dataset from Transpose

Column Name	Column Type
NAME	char
COL1	char
COL2	char
COL3	char

Figure 5-24. *Transposed Dataset Variable Types*

Summary

In this chapter, we examined a variety of essential data management tasks needed to reshape and organize data. The primary focus was to enable an understanding of joining/merging and reshaping DataFrames. These principles set the stage for the next chapter's topic, "pandas Readers and Writers."

CHAPTER 6

pandas Readers and Writers

In this chapter we discuss methods for reading data from a range of input data sources such as comma-separated values (.csv) files, database tables, JSON, and other sources of input to create DataFrames. The pandas readers are a collection of input/output methods for writing and loading values into DataFrames. These input/output methods are analogous to the family of SAS/Access Software used by SAS to read data values into SAS datasets and write SAS datasets into target output formats.

The pandas main facility for input and output to DataFrames are the readers like `read_csv()`, `read_json()` and `read_sql_table()`, among others, which we cover in detail. These readers use similar syntax. The first argument is the path or location to the target which can be fully qualified filenames, relative filenames (relative to the current working directory executing Python), database tables, URLs (including HTTPS, SFTP, and S3 access methods), and so on. In many cases, the defaults for the readers' arguments are enough for read/write operations.

The reader methods have arguments to specify:

- Input and output locations

- Column and index location and names

- Parsing rules for handling incoming data

- Missing data rules

- Datetime handling

- Quoting rules

- Compression and file formats

- Error handling

243

© Randy Betancourt, Sarah Chen 2019
R. Betancourt and S. Chen, *Python for SAS Users*, https://doi.org/10.1007/978-1-4842-5001-3_6

We start by examining a Series of use cases for reading .csv files beginning with simple examples followed by additional examples combining various arguments to enable a more complex set of parsing rules.

Reading .csv Files

Consider Listing 6-1.

Listing 6-1. Basic .csv Read

```
>>> import pandas as pd
>>> url = "https://raw.githubusercontent.com/RandyBetancourt/
PythonForSASUsers/master/data/messy_input.csv"
>>> df1 = pd.read_csv(url, skiprows=2)
>>> print(df1)
     ID       Date   Amount  Quantity   Status Unnamed: 5
0    42  16-Oct-17  $23.99     123.0   Closed     Jansen
1  7731  15-Jan-17  $49.99       NaN  Pending        Rho
2  8843   9-Mar-17     129      45.0      NaN      Gupta
3  3013  12-Feb-17              15.0  Pending   Harrison
4  4431   1-Jul-17  $99.99       1.0   Closed       Yang
>>> print(df1.dtypes)
ID              int64
Date           object
Amount         object
Quantity      float64
Status         object
Unnamed: 5     object
dtype: object
```

In this example, the call to the read_csv() reader uses two arguments. The URL object holds the string value for the input location to be read followed by the skiprows= argument. As you can see from Figure 6-1, the column headers are on row 3.

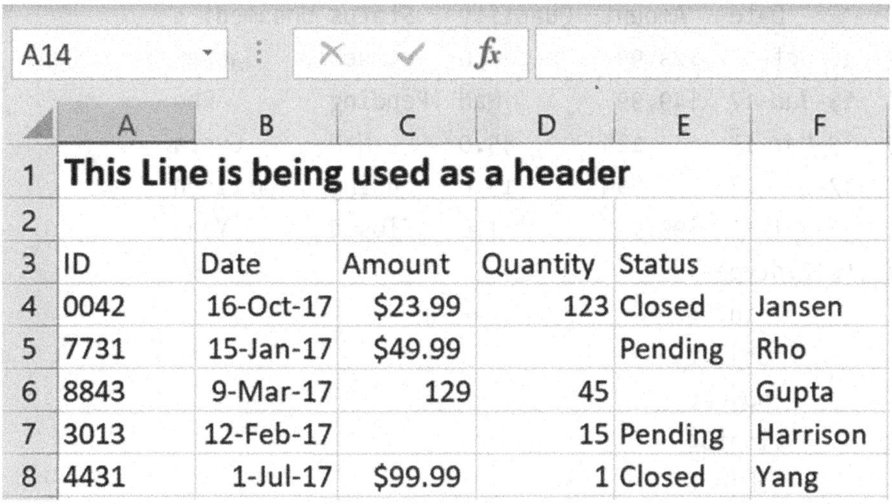

	A	B	C	D	E	F
1	This Line is being used as a header					
2						
3	ID	Date	Amount	Quantity	Status	
4	0042	16-Oct-17	$23.99	123	Closed	Jansen
5	7731	15-Jan-17	$49.99		Pending	Rho
6	8843	9-Mar-17	129	45		Gupta
7	3013	12-Feb-17		15	Pending	Harrison
8	4431	1-Jul-17	$99.99	1	Closed	Yang

Figure 6-1. *.csv File Input*

Also observe how the ID values for column "A" are left aligned which is the default for character strings in Excel. Column "F" is missing its header label and there are several missing values.

Listing 6-1 displays the column types. These types are inferred from the input data read from the .csv file. The `read_csv()` reader in this example maps the `ID` column to an `int64` type despite the fact that these values are stored as strings in the .csv file. In subsequent examples we will see how to explicitly control type mappings when reading values into DataFrames or unloading values from DataFrames.

Listing 6-1 displays the type for the `Date` column as object indicating these values are stored in the `df1` DataFrame as strings.

The `read_csv()` reader provisions the `na_values=` argument to define how missing values are handled on input. The `na_values=` argument allows the definition of any value to represent missing for both character and numeric column types. This feature is illustrated in Listing 6-2.

Listing 6-2. Setting na_values for read_csv()

```
>>> miss = {'Amount' : [' ', 'NA']}
>>> df2 = pd.read_csv(url, skiprows=2, na_values=miss)
>>> print(df2)
```

```
      ID       Date    Amount  Quantity   Status Unnamed: 5
0     42  16-Oct-17   $23.99     123.0    Closed     Jansen
1   7731  15-Jan-17   $49.99       NaN   Pending        Rho
2   8843   9-Mar-17      129      45.0       NaN      Gupta
3   3013  12-Feb-17      NaN      15.0   Pending   Harrison
4   4431   1-Jul-17   $99.99       1.0    Closed       Yang
>>> print(df2.dtypes)
ID              int64
Date           object
Amount         object
Quantity      float64
Status         object
Unnamed: 5     object
dtype: object
>>>
>>> df1[3:4]
      ID       Date Amount  Quantity   Status Unnamed: 5
3   3013  12-Feb-17             15.0  Pending   Harrison
>>> df2[3:4]
      ID       Date Amount  Quantity   Status Unnamed: 5
3   3013  12-Feb-17    NaN    15.0  Pending   Harrison
```

In this example, the syntax

```
miss = {'Amount' : [' ', 'NA']}
```

creates the miss object as a Dictionary key:value pair where the key value Amount is the DataFrame column name followed by values blank (' ') and NA used to designate both as missing values. The parameter na_values= uses this miss Dictionary to map values to missing when they are encountered in the Amount column.

In contrast to Listing 6-1, the value for the Amount column on row 3 in the df1 DataFrame is blank

```
>>> df1[3:4]
      ID       Date Amount  Quantity   Status Unnamed: 5
3   3013  12-Feb-17             15.0  Pending   Harrison
```

whereas in Listing 6-2, the value for the Amount column on row 3 in the df2 Dataframe is NaN. These values are displayed with the row-slicing operations

```
>>> df2[3:4]
```

```
         ID       Date Amount  Quantity   Status Unnamed: 5
3      3013  12-Feb-17    NaN      15.0  Pending   Harrison
```

The read_csv() reader has two parameters to explicitly set column types: the dtype= and the converters= arguments. Both arguments accept Dictionary key:value pairs with the keys identifying the target column(s) and values that are functions converting the read values into their corresponding column types. The dtype= argument allows you to specify how to treat incoming values, for example, either as strings or numeric types. The converters= argument allows you to call a conversion function which in turn maps the data onto the desired column type based on the function's logic, for example, parsing a string value to be read as a datetime. The converters= argument takes precedence over the dtype= argument in the event both are used together.

Listing 6-3 illustrates using the dtype= argument to map the ID column type to object, in other words a sequence of characters.

Listing 6-3. Explicit Type Mapping for read_csv() Reader

```
>>> df3 = pd.read_csv(url, skiprows=2, na_values=miss, dtype={'ID' : object})
>>> print(df3)
         ID       Date  Amount  Quantity   Status Unnamed: 5
0      0042  16-Oct-17  $23.99     123.0   Closed     Jansen
1      7731  15-Jan-17  $49.99       NaN  Pending        Rho
2      8843   9-Mar-17     129      45.0      NaN      Gupta
3      3013  12-Feb-17     NaN      15.0  Pending   Harrison
4      4431   1-Jul-17  $99.99       1.0   Closed       Yang
>>> print(df3.dtypes)
ID              object
Date            object
Amount          object
Quantity       float64
Status          object
```

```
Unnamed: 5       object
dtype: object
>>>
>>> print(df2['ID'].dtype)
int64
>>> print(df3['ID'].dtype)
object
```

In this example, the ID column in the df3 DataFrame has a type of object compared to the ID column type in the df2 DataFrame which is int64.

The converters= argument permits a function to convert the incoming data with the function results determining the column's type. In this example, regardless of whether the incoming values for the ID column are numeric or character types, they are stored in the target DataFrame as strings.

To further illustrate this point, consider Listing 6-4. Here we define the strip_ sign() function to remove the dollar sign ($) from the incoming values for the Amount column. The converters= argument contains the Dictionary key:value pair with the key identifying the Amount column and the corresponding value naming the converter function, in this case, strip_sign.

Listing 6-4. read_csv() with convert=

```
>>> import math
>>>
>>> def strip_sign(x):
...           y = x.strip()
...           if not y:
...               return math.nan
...           else:
...               if y[0] == '$':
...                   return float(y[1:])
...               else:
...                   return float(y)
...
>>> df4 = pd.read_csv(url, skiprows=2, converters={'ID' : str, 'Amount':
strip_sign})
>>>
```

```
>>> print(df4,
... '\n', '\n',
... 'Amount dtype:', df4['Amount'].dtype)

      ID        Date   Amount   Quantity    Status Unnamed: 5
0   0042   16-Oct-17    23.99      123.0    Closed     Jansen
1   7731   15-Jan-17    49.99        NaN   Pending        Rho
2   8843    9-Mar-17   129.00       45.0       NaN      Gupta
3   3013   12-Feb-17      NaN       15.0   Pending   Harrison
4   4431    1-Jul-17    99.99        1.0    Closed       Yang

 Amount dtype: float64
```

The strip_sign() function returns a float or a NaN when the incoming value is missing. Because the strip_sign() function returns numeric values, the resulting type for the Amount column in the df4 DataFrame is float64.

Listing 6-5 illustrates mapping the ID column as a string and setting this column as the DataFrame index at the end of the read/parse operation. Chapter 4, "Indexing and GroupBy," contains details for working effectively with DataFrame indexes.

Listing 6-5. read_csv() set_index Attribute

```
>>> df5 = pd.read_csv(url, skiprows=2, na_values=miss, converters={'ID' :
str}).set_index('ID')
>>> print(df5)
           Date    Amount   Quantity    Status Unnamed: 5
ID
0042   16-Oct-17   $23.99      123.0    Closed     Jansen
7731   15-Jan-17   $49.99        NaN   Pending        Rho
8843    9-Mar-17      129       45.0       NaN      Gupta
3013   12-Feb-17      NaN       15.0   Pending   Harrison
4431    1-Jul-17   $99.99        1.0    Closed       Yang
>>> print(df5.dtypes)
Date             object
Amount           object
Quantity        float64
Status           object
```

```
Unnamed: 5      object
dtype: object
>>>
>>> df5.loc['0042']
Date               16-Oct-17
Amount                $23.99
Quantity                 123
Status                Closed
Unnamed: 5            Jansen
Name: 0042, dtype: object
```

With the ID column as the index, rows can be sliced with their labeled values:

```
df5.loc['0042']
```

```
Date               16-Oct-17
Amount                $23.99
Quantity                 123
Status                Closed
Unnamed: 5            Jansen
Name: 0042, dtype: object
```

Date Handling in .csv Files

A common requirement for reading data input is preserving date and datetime values rather than treating the values as strings. This can be done via the `converters=` argument, but there are special built-in converters. The `read_csv()` reader has specialized parameters for datetime handling. In most cases, the default datetime parser simply needs to know which column or list of columns compose the input date or datetime values. In those cases where date or datetime values are non-standard, the `parse_dates=` argument accepts a defined function to handle custom date and datetime formatting instructions.

Listing 6-6 illustrates the `parse_dates=` argument for the `read_csv()` method.

Listing 6-6. Parsing Dates with parse_dates=

```
>>> miss = {'Amount' : [' ', 'NA']}
>>> df5 = pd.read_csv(url, skiprows=2, na_values=miss, converters={'ID' :
str}).set_index('ID')
>>>
>>> df6 = pd.read_csv(url, skiprows=2, na_values=miss, converters={'ID' :
str}, parse_dates=['Date']).set_index('ID')
>>> print(df6)
          Date   Amount  Quantity   Status Unnamed: 5
ID
0042 2017-10-16  $23.99     123.0   Closed     Jansen
7731 2017-01-15  $49.99       NaN  Pending        Rho
8843 2017-03-09     129      45.0      NaN      Gupta
3013 2017-02-12     NaN      15.0  Pending   Harrison
4431 2017-07-01  $99.99       1.0   Closed       Yang
>>>
>>> print(df6.dtypes)
Date           datetime64[ns]
Amount                 object
Quantity              float64
Status                 object
Unnamed: 5             object
dtype: object
>>>
>>> print(df5['Date'].dtype)
object
>>> print(df6['Date'].dtype)
datetime64[ns]
```

The parse_dates= parameter accepts a Python list of column names, in this case, the Date column. In Listing 6-5, the Date column in the df5 DataFrame has the default object type as shown:

```
>>> print(df5['Date'].dtype)
object
```

In contrast, with this example, the Date column is now mapped as a datetime64 column type as a result of using the parse_dates= argument.

```
>>> print(df6['Date'].dtype)
datetime64[ns]
```

Chapter 7, "Date and Time," covers the details on date and datetime types and how they are manipulated.

Listing 6-7 illustrates the ability to use custom labels for column headings.

Listing 6-7. Controlling Column Heading

```
>>> cols=['ID', 'Trans_Date', 'Amt', 'Quantity', 'Status', 'Name']
>>> df7 = pd.read_csv(url, skiprows=3, na_values=miss,
        converters={'ID' : str},
        parse_dates=['Trans_Date'], header=None, names=cols,
        usecols=[0, 1, 2, 3, 4, 5]).set_index('ID')
>>> print(df7)
      Trans_Date      Amt  Quantity   Status      Name
ID
0042 2017-10-16   $23.99     123.0   Closed    Jansen
7731 2017-01-15   $49.99       NaN  Pending       Rho
8843 2017-03-09      129      45.0      NaN     Gupta
3013 2017-02-12               15.0  Pending  Harrison
4431 2017-07-01   $99.99       1.0   Closed      Yang
>>> print(df7.dtypes)
Trans_Date    datetime64[ns]
Amt                   object
Quantity             float64
Status                object
Name                  object
dtype: object
```

The example begins by defining a Python list of column headings in the order in which they are read from the .csv file with the syntax

```
cols=['ID', 'Trans_Date', 'Amt', 'Quantity', 'Status', 'Name']
```

The names= argument accepts the cols object to label the DataFrame columns. You must set the header= argument to None to inform the reader not to use the column labels found in the .csv file. Next, the usecols= argument specifies the input columns to be read. Remember, Python uses a 0-based index for start positions, so the default column A in the .csv file maps to column 0 in the DataFrame, column B in the .csv file maps to column 1 in the DataFrame, and so on.

Finally, notice that since we are not reading the column labels found in the .csv file, the skiprows= argument is set to 3 for this example which is where we find the first line of data values (line 4 in the .csv file). Since Python uses a 0-based index as the start position, row 1 in the .csv file maps to row 0 in the DataFrame, row 2 in the .csv file maps to row 1 in the DataFrame, and so on.

Read .xls Files

As you might expect, pandas provides the read_excel() reader for reading Microsoft .xls files. The parameters and arguments for read_excel() reader are similar to the read_csv() reader.

Take a look at Listing 6-8.

Listing 6-8. Read .xls File into DataFrame

```
df8 = pd.read_excel('C:\\data\\messy_input.xlsx', sheet_name='Trans1',
skiprows=2, converters={'ID' : str}, parse_dates={'Date' :['Month', 'Day',
                    'Year']}, keep_date_col=True).set_index('ID')
print(df8)
print(df8.dtypes)
```

The results are rendered in Figure 6-2, executed in a Jupyter notebook. In order to execute this example, download the messy_input.xlsx file from

```
https://github.com/RandyBetancourt/PythonForSASUsers/blob/master/data/
messy_input.xlsx
```

and copy it into a location where you have read/write access on the local filesystem. In this example, we chose "C:\data\messy_input.xlsx".

	Date	Amount	Quantity	Status	Name	Year	Month	Day
ID								
0042	2017-10-16	23.99	123.0	Closed	Jansen	2017	10	16
7731	2017-01-15	49.99	NaN	Pending	Rho	2017	1	15
8843	2017-03-09	129	45.0	NaN	Gupta	2017	3	9
3013	2017-02-12		15.0	Pending	Harrison	2017	2	12
4431	2017-07-01	99.99	1.0	Closed	Yang	2017	7	1

```
Date              datetime64[ns]
Amount                    object
Quantity                 float64
Status                    object
Name                      object
Year                       int64
Month                      int64
Day                        int64
dtype: object
```

Figure 6-2. *Read .xls File DataFrame Output*

In this example, we use the parse_dates= parameter to define the Date column with the syntax

parse_dates={'Date' :['Month', 'Day', 'Year']}

parse_dates= argument accepts a Dictionary key:value pair where the key is the name of the output datetime DataFrame column being defined, in this case, Date. The Dictionary values name the input columns composing the constituent input columns for the Date column values. In this case, the Year, Month, and Day columns are parsed together to define the Date column.

We also illustrate keeping the Year, Month, and Day columns with the syntax

keep_date_col=True

The keep_date_col= argument determines the keep disposition for the columns used with the parse_dates= argument. In this case, Year, Month, and Day columns are kept on the df8 DataFrame.

It is not uncommon to read multiple Excel files together to form a single DataFrame. Listing 6-9 illustrates this use case.

Consider sales transactions for the month are stored in separate Excel files each with identical layouts. In this example, we introduce the glob module from the Python Standard Library. The glob module finds all the filenames matching a specified pattern based on the rules used by the Unix shell. This is useful when you need to search for filenames using string expressions and wildcard characters.

The three .xlsx files for this example are located at

```
https://github.com/RandyBetancourt/PythonForSASUsers/tree/master/data
```

and in this case are copied to the folder C:\data.

Listing 6-9. Appending Multiple .xls Files into a DataFrame

```
>>> import glob
>>> input = glob.glob('C:\\data\*_2*.xlsx')
>>> print(input)
['C:\\data\\February_2018.xlsx', 'C:\\data\\January_2018.xlsx', 'C:\\data\\
March_2018.xlsx']
>>>
>>> final = pd.DataFrame()
>>> for f in glob.glob('C:\\data\*_2*.xlsx'):
...      df = pd.read_excel(f, converters={'ID' : str}).set_index("ID")
...      final = final.append(df, ignore_index=False, sort=False)
...
>>> print(final)
      Amount  Quantity
ID
1042   99.89        21
3311   59.99        12
9846   12.99        25
2222   19.19       115
8931   79.99         2
0044  199.89        10
8731   49.99         2
7846  129.00        45
1111   89.19        15
2231   99.99         1
0002   79.89        43
2811   19.99        19
```

```
8468    112.99          25
3333    129.99          11
9318     69.99          12
```

The input object is defined by calling the glob module to search the filenames using the pattern

```
'C:\\data\*_2*.xlsx'
```

This call returns a Python list of filenames matching our pattern subsequently displayed by calling the first print() method. The files to append together are

```
['C:\\data\\February_2018.xlsx', 'C:\\data\\January_2018.xlsx', 'C:\\data\\
March_2018.xlsx']
```

In order to read these .xls files in a single operation, an empty DataFrame called final is defined with the syntax

```
final = pd.DataFrame()
```

Next a for loop calling the glob module is used to return the Python list of our input three files followed by the call to the read_excel() reader to read the current .xls file in the Python list into the df dataframe. Finally the panda .append attribute for the final DataFrame is called appending each df dataframe to the end of the final DataFrame. Also notice inside the for loop, the set_index() method is used to map the ID column as the DataFrame index.

An alternative to retrieving a Python list of fully qualified pathnames for this type of iterative processing is retrieving input filenames relative to the current working directory executing your Python session. This involves importing the os module from the Python Standard Library to first determine the location for the Python's current working directory followed by a call to change the current working directory to a new location. This operation is illustrated in Listing 6-10.

Listing 6-10. Absolute vs. Relative Filenames

```
>>> import os
>>>
>>> wd = os.getcwd()
>>> print (wd)
```

```
C:\Users\randy\Desktop\Py_Source
>>> os.chdir('C:\\data')
>>> wd = os.getcwd()
>>> print(wd)
C:\data
>>> csv_files = glob.glob('*.csv')
>>> print(csv_files)
['dataframe.csv', 'dataframe2.csv', 'Left.csv', 'messy_input.csv', 'Right.
csv', 'Sales_Detail.csv', 'School_Scores.csv', 'scores.csv', 'Tickets.csv']
```

The syntax

```
wd = os.getcwd()
```

creates the wd object holding the value for the location of the current working directory executing the Python session, in this case

```
C:\Users\randy\Desktop\Py_Source
```

The syntax

```
os.chdir('C:\\data')
```

calls the os.chdir attribute and changes the working directory for the current Python session to

```
C:\data
```

The call to the glob module uses *.csv as an argument to define the csv_files object holding a Python list of all the filenames in the current directory have the filename extension .csv.

A similar approach for reading and appending multiple .csv files with SAS is illustrated in Listing 6-11. The .csv files in this example can be downloaded from

```
https://github.com/RandyBetancourt/PythonForSASUsers/tree/master/data
```

The SAS FILENAME statement calls the FILENAME PIPE access method to return the fully qualified .csv files found in the directory

```
  c:\data
```

Listing 6-11. Appending Multiple .csv Files to a Dataset

```
1     filename tmp pipe 'dir "c:\data\*_2*.csv" /s/b';
2
3     data _null_;
4        infile tmp;
5        length file_name $ 128;
6        input file_name $;
7
8        length imported $500;
9        retain imported ' ';
10
11       imported = catx(' ',imported,cats('temp',put(_n_,best.)));
12       call symput('imported',strip(imported));
13
14       call execute('proc import datafile="'
15                    || strip(file_name)
16                    || '" out=temp'
17                    || strip(put(_n_,best.))
18                    || ' dbms=csv replace; run;'
19                   );
20    run;
```

```
NOTE: The infile TMP is:
      Unnamed Pipe Access Device,
      PROCESS=dir "c:\data\*_2*.csv" /s/b,RECFM=V,
      LRECL=32767

NOTE: 3 records were read from the infile TMP.
      The minimum record length was 22.
      The maximum record length was 25.

5 rows created in WORK.TEMP1 from c:\data\February_2018.csv.
5 rows created in WORK.TEMP2 from c:\data\January_2018.csv.
5 rows created in WORK.TEMP3 from c:\data\March_2018.csv.
```

```
94   data final;
95      set &imported;
96      format amount dollar8.2;
97   run;
```

NOTE: There were 5 observations read from the dataset WORK.TEMP1.
NOTE: There were 5 observations read from the dataset WORK.TEMP2.
NOTE: There were 5 observations read from the dataset WORK.TEMP3.
NOTE: The dataset WORK.FINAL has 15 observations and 3 variables.

The _NULL_ Data Step reads the list of filenames of the FILENAME PIPE statement and assigns these fully qualified filename values to the file_name variable. The CALL SYMPUT statement creates the Macro variable &imported. On each iteration of the Data Step, it concatenates the values "temp1", "temp2", and so on. This Macro variable value becomes the list of input datasets used on line 95 to create the output dataset final.

The syntax

```
call execute('proc import datafile="'
               || strip(file_name)
               || '" out=temp'
               || strip(put(_n_,best.))
               || ' dbms=csv replace; run;'
             );
```

builds the PROC IMPORT statement and corresponding options as a parameter to the CALL EXECUTE statement. The CALL EXECUTE statement executes the call to PROC IMPORT three times, one for each record read from the FILENAME PIPE statement.

Figure 6-3 uses PROC PRINT to display the contents of the final dataset.

Obs	ID	Amount	Quantity
1	1042	$99.89	21
2	3311	$59.99	12
3	9846	$12.99	25
4	2222	$19.19	115
5	8931	$79.99	2
6	44	$199.89	10
7	8731	$49.99	2
8	7846	$129.00	45
9	1111	$89.19	15
10	2231	$99.99	1
11	2	$79.89	43
12	2811	$19.99	19
13	8468	$112.99	25
14	3333	$129.99	11
15	9318	$69.99	12

Figure 6-3. *Final Dataset Output*

Write .csv Files

There are cases when you need to export the contents of a DataFrame to a .csv file or an .xls file. In those cases, use the to_csv() writer and the to_excel() writer. The to_csv() writer is illustrated in Listing 6-12.

Listing 6-12. Output DataFrame to .csv

```
>>> final.to_csv('C:\\data\\final.csv', header=True)
```

The writer does not return any information to the console to indicate the operation's success. Figure 6-4 displays the first five rows of the output file, in this case, C:\data\final.csv.

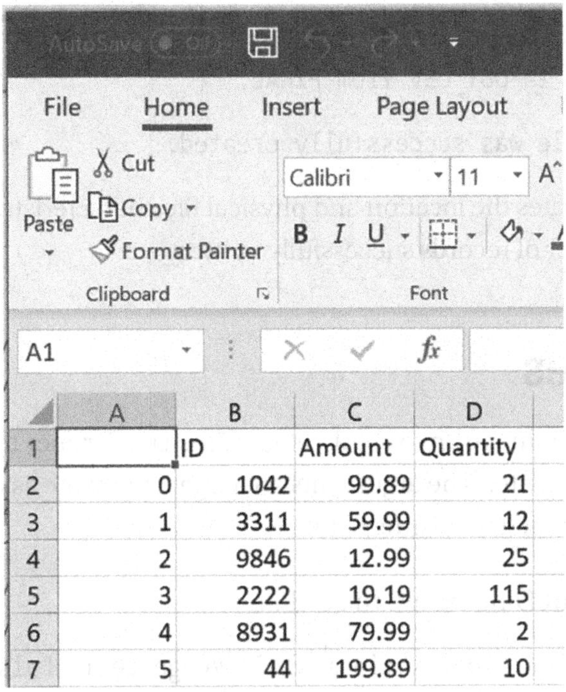

Figure 6-4. *Results from to_csv()*

Use PROC EXPORT to write the contents of a SAS dataset to a .csv file. This capability is illustrated in Listing 6-13.

Listing 6-13. Output SAS Dataset to .csv

```
4  filename out_csv "c:\data\final_ds.csv";
5  proc export data = final
6              outfile = out_csv
7              dbms = csv;
8  run;

NOTE: The file OUT_CSV is:
      Filename=c:\data\final_ds.csv,
      RECFM=V,LRECL=32767,File Size (bytes)=0,
      Last Modified=12Nov2018:10:13:47,
      Create Time=12Nov2018:10:13:47

NOTE: 16 records were written to the file OUT_CSV.
      The minimum record length was 11.
      The maximum record length was 18.
```

NOTE: There were 15 observations read from the dataset WORK.FINAL.

15 records created in OUT_CSV from FINAL.

NOTE: "OUT_CSV" file was successfully created.

The SAS log indicates the location and physical file characteristics of the output .csv along with the number of records successfully written.

Write .xls Files

You can write a DataFrame to an Excel sheet multiple DataFrames to a book of sheets, using the to_excel() writer. The arguments are largely the same as the to_csv() writer. This capability is illustrated in Listing 6-14.

Listing 6-14. Output DataFrame to .xls File

```
>>> final.to_excel('C:\\data\\final.xls', merge_cells=False)
```

The results from the to_excel() operation are displayed in Figure 6-5.

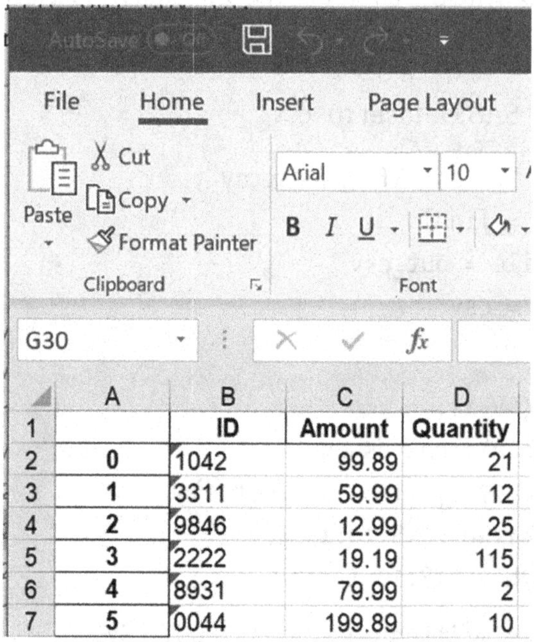

Figure 6-5. *Results from write_excel()*

There are multiple ways to output a SAS dataset to .xls files. PROC EXPORT provides a convenient approach; however, it limits the format control you can exert on the appearances of the output .xls file. Alternatively, if you want much finer control over the output format in Excel, then the ODS tagsets.ExcelXP can be used. Listing 6-15 illustrates calling tagsets.ExcelXP to write the contents of a SAS dataset to an Excel file.

Listing 6-15. Output Final Dataset to .xls

```
4 ods tagsets.ExcelXP
5     file="c:\data\final_ds.xls"
6     style=statistical
7     options(frozen_headers='1'
8                   embedded_titles='yes'
9                   default_column_width='18');
NOTE: Writing TAGSETS.EXCELXP Body file: c:\data\final_ds.xls
NOTE: This is the Excel XP tagset (Compatible with SAS 9.1.3 and above,
v1.131, 04/23/2015). Add
options(doc='help') to the ods statement for more information.
10
11 proc print data=final;
12 run;

NOTE: There were 15 observations read from the dataset WORK.FINAL.
NOTE: PROCEDURE PRINT used (Total process time):
      real time              0.08 seconds
      cpu time               0.01 seconds

13 ods tagsets.excelxp close;
14 run;
```

Note that if you are using SAS Display Manager to generate this example, you may need to disable the "View results as they are generated feature". This is found by going to the SAS Tools menu in Display Manager option and selecting Options ➤ Preferences and then selecting the Results tab. Uncheck the box labeled "View results as they are generated" as shown in Figure 6-6.

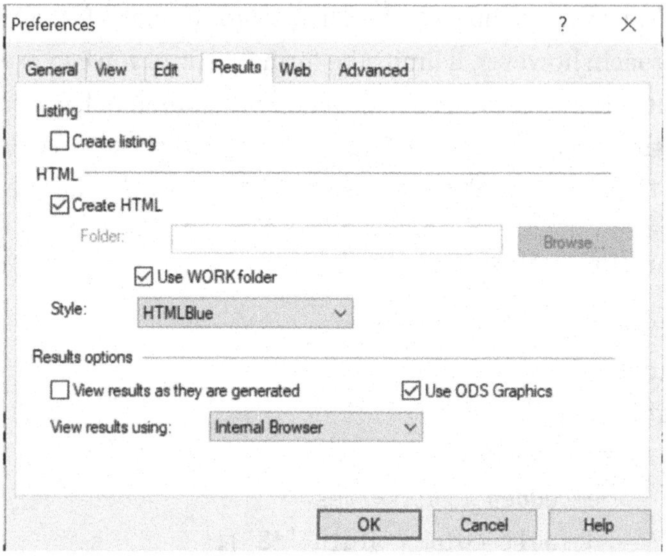

Figure 6-6. *SAS Preferences Menu*

Read JSON

JSON stands for JavaScript Object Notation and is a well-defined structure for exchanging data among different applications. JSON is designed to be read by humans and easily parsed by programs. It is relied upon to transmit data through RESTful web services and APIs.

The flexibility for calling a REST API to acquire data is illustrated in Listing 6-16. This example creates the jobs DataFrame by calling GitHub Jobs API over HTTPS using read_json() reader to return a set of posted positions along with a detailed job description.

Details on the GitHub Jobs API are at

https://jobs.github.com/api

Listing 6-16. panda Read JSON API

```
>>> jobs = pd.read_json("https://jobs.github.com/positions.
json?description=python")
>>> print(jobs.shape)
(41, 11)
>>> print(jobs.columns)
```

```
Index(['company', 'company_logo', 'company_url', 'created_at', 'description',
       'how_to_apply', 'id', 'location', 'title', 'type', 'url'],
      dtype='object')
>>> print(jobs[['company', 'location']].head(5))
                      company                    location
0                      Sesame            New York; Berlin
1                    BlueVine            Redwood City, Ca
2          New York University   New York, New York 10001
3       University of Cambridge                Cambridge, UK
4   Norwegian Block Exchange AS     Oslo, Norway or Remote
```

In this example, the read_json() reader makes a call over HTTPS to the GitHub Jobs API returning records where the position field contains the string 'Python'. At the time this script was executed, there were 41 job positions posted. This is shown by the call to the shape attribute showing 41 rows and 11 columns in the jobs DataFrame.

Similarly, SAS provides several different methods for reading JSON files. By far, the simplest method is to use the JSON LIBNAME access method, illustrated in Listing 6-17.

Listing 6-17. SAS Read JSON Access Method

```
4   filename response temp;
5
6   proc http
7     url="https://jobs.github.com/positions.json?description=python"
8     method= "GET"
9     out=response;
10  run;

NOTE: 200 OK

11
12  libname in_json JSON fileref=response;
NOTE: JSON data is only read once.  To read the JSON again, reassign the
JSON LIBNAME.
```

```
NOTE: Libref IN_JSON was successfully assigned as follows:
      Engine:        JSON
      Physical Name: C:\Users\randy\AppData\Local\Temp\SAS
      Temporary Files\_TD9088_RANDY-PC_\#LN00063
13  proc copy in=in_json
14              out=work;run;

NOTE: Copying IN_JSON.ALLDATA to WORK.ALLDATA (memtype=DATA).
NOTE: There were 462 observations read from the dataset IN_JSON.ALLDATA.
NOTE: The dataset WORK.ALLDATA has 462 observations and 4 variables.
NOTE: Copying IN_JSON.ROOT to WORK.ROOT (memtype=DATA).
NOTE: There were 42 observations read from the dataset IN_JSON.ROOT.
NOTE: The dataset WORK.ROOT has 42 observations and 12 variables.

15
16  proc print data=work.root (obs=5);
17      id company;
18      var location;
19  run;

NOTE: There were 5 observations read from the dataset WORK.ROOT.
```

Figure 6-7 uses PROC PRINT to display the first five observations read from the GitHub Jobs API.

company	location
Sesame	New York; Berlin
BlueVine	Redwood City, Ca
New York University	New York, New York 10001
University of Cambridge	Cambridge, UK
Norwegian Block Exchange AS	Oslo, Norway or Remote

Figure 6-7. *SAS Read of JSON Records*

The SAS program has three steps in order to load the JSON records into a SAS dataset. They are

1. Call `PROC HTTP` to fetch the records with the query:

    `https://jobs.github.com/positions.json?description=python`

2. Along with a `GET` to return the records to the SAS session. The `OUT=response` statement stores incoming records in a temporary file associated with the `response` FILEREF.

3. Copy the incoming `JSON.ROOT` and `JSON.ALLDATA` datasets to the `WORK` directory. Obviously, you can copy these datasets into a permanent SAS data library. The copy operation is needed since the JSON access method reads the incoming records only once.

4. Continue the processing logic to manipulate the `ROOT` dataset created by the `JSON LIBNAME` engine. In our case we simply call `PROC PRINT` to display the first five observations from the dataset.

In order to make this particular example work, the SAS session must be executed with an encoding of UTF-8. By default, SAS sessions executing under Windows use WLATIN1 encoding which can lead to transcoding errors when calling the `JSON LIBNAME` engine to read UTF-8 formatted records. Use the following `PROC OPTIONS` statement to determine the encoding method used by the SAS session:

```
proc options option=encoding; run;

  SAS (r) Proprietary Software Release 9.4   TS1M5

ENCODING=UTF-8     Specifies the default character-set encoding for the SAS
session.
```

Note that the encoding option can only be changed at SAS initialization time. This is generally controlled by the `sasv9.cfg` configuration file. The default location on Windows is

```
C:\Program Files\SASHome\SASFoundation\9.4\nls\en\sasv9.cfg
```

Write JSON

The pandas library provides the to_json() writer to write the contents of a DataFrame to a JSON file. This feature is illustrated in Listing 6-18.

Listing 6-18. Write DataFrame to JSON

```
>>> df8.drop(columns = ['Day', 'Month', 'Year'], inplace = True)
>>> df8.to_json("c:\\data\\df8_output.json", orient='records', lines=True)
```

The results of writing the df8 DataFrame to a JSON-formatted file is displayed in Figure 6-8.

```
1  {"Date":1508112000000,"Amount":23.99,"Quantity":123.0,"Status":"Closed","Name":"Jansen"}
2  {"Date":1484438400000,"Amount":49.99,"Quantity":null,"Status":"Pending","Name":"Rho"}
3  {"Date":1489017600000,"Amount":129,"Quantity":45.0,"Status":null,"Name":"Gupta"}
4  {"Date":1486857600000,"Amount":" ","Quantity":15.0,"Status":"Pending","Name":"Harrison"}
5  {"Date":1498867200000,"Amount":99.99,"Quantity":1.0,"Status":"Closed","Name":"Yang"}
```

Figure 6-8. *Write DataFrame to JSON*

In order to write a SAS dataset to a Series of JSON records, use PROC JSON as illustrated in Listing 6-19. PROC JSON was introduced with Base SAS release 9.4.

Listing 6-19. Output a SAS Dataset to JSON

```
4  proc json out='c:\data\sas_final.json' pretty
5                                          nosastags;
6      export final;
7  run;
```

The first two JSON records are displayed in Figure 6-9.

```
1  [
2      {
3          "ID": 1042,
4          "Amount": 99.89,
5          "Quantity": 21
6      },
7      {
8          "ID": 3311,
9          "Amount": 59.99,
10         "Quantity": 12
11     },
```

Figure 6-9. *Write SAS Dataset to JSON*

Read RDBMS Tables

Common input sources of data for analysis are relational database tables. The pandas. io.sql module provides a set of query wrappers to enable data retrieval while minimizing dependencies on RDBMS-specific APIs. Another way of saying this is, the clever folks who brought you pandas also figured out they can avoid re-inventing the wheel so they utilize a library called SQLAlchemy as an abstraction layer to the various databases needing to be read. This approach reduces the amount of database-dependent code pandas needed internally to read and write data using ODBC-compliant engines, which is to say, nearly all databases.

By using the SQLAlchemy library to read RDBMS tables (and queries), you pass SQLAlchemy Expression language constructs which are database-agnostic to the target database. This is analogous to PROC SQL's behavior of using general SAS SQL constructs which in turn are translated on your behalf for a specific database without you having to know the RDBMS SQL dialect.

In order to execute these Read RDBMS Table examples, you need three components to be set up. They are

1. The SQLAlchemy library

2. The appropriate RDBMS driver library, in our case, the pyodbc library

3. The appropriately configured Windows ODBC client connecting to a target database

The following examples use Microsoft SQL Server 2017 for Windows as the target RDBMS for reading and writing. With a little bit of effort, you can convert these examples to execute on a different RDBMS running either locally or remotely.

The SQLAlchemy library is a part of the Anaconda distribution described in Chapter 1, "Why Python?"

To confirm a version of the SQLAlchemy library is available, start a Python session and enter

```
>>> import sqlalchemy
>>> sqlalchemy.__version__
'1.2.7'
```

Notice the two consecutive underscores before and after the string version.

The second part of the setup is the client-side library, which is the pyodbc library in our case. To confirm a version of the pyodbc library is available, start a Python session and enter

```
>>> import pyodbc
>>> pyodbc.version
'4.0.23'
```

Our setup has both Python 3.6 and SQL Server 2017 executing on the same Windows 10 machine. If the SQL Server instance is running remotely, you will need to make the appropriate adjustments.

The third and final step is to configure an ODBC DSN to connect to the target RDBMS. In order to set up the appropriate ODBC client interface on Windows 10, launch the ODBC Data Source Administrator by going to the Windows Start Menu to click

Start ➤ Windows Administrative Tools ➤ ODBC Data Sources (64-bit) to launch the ODBC Data Source Administrator shown in Figure 6-10.

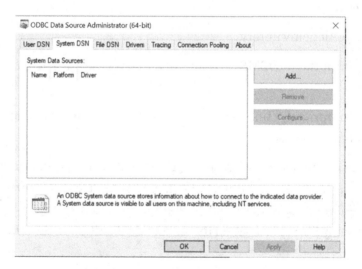

Figure 6-10. *ODBC Data Source Administrator*

If you are using Windows 7, navigate to Control Panel ➤ System and Security ➤ Administrative Tools and select Data Sources (ODBC). These examples illustrate the ODBC setup for Windows 10.

Make sure that the System DSN tab is selected and then click the Add... button to select the driver for the SQL Server Database. See Figure 6-11.

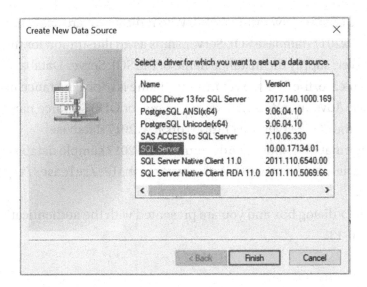

Figure 6-11. *Create New Data Source*

Press the Finish button which displays the Create a New Data Source to SQL Server dialog box presented in Figure 6-12.

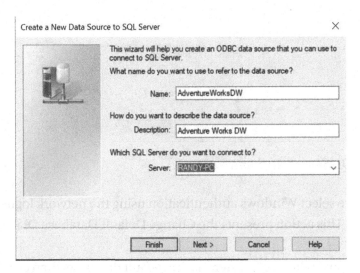

Figure 6-12. *Create a New Data Source to SQL Server*

For Name: we choose AdventureWorksDW to indicate we are using the AdventureWorksDW2017 database SQL Server ships as an illustration for their Analytical Services. For Server: supply the instance name of the SQL Server Database you want to connect to. In our case, the SQL Server instance name is a local instance named RANDY-PC. Notice we use AdventureWorksDW as the name for ODBC source name which in turn connects to the SQL Server AdventureWorksDW2017 database.

For more information about the AdventureWorks2017 sample databases, see

https://github.com/Microsoft/sql-server-samples/releases/tag/ adventureworks

Press the Next> dialog box and you are presented with the authentication dialog box shown in Figure 6-13.

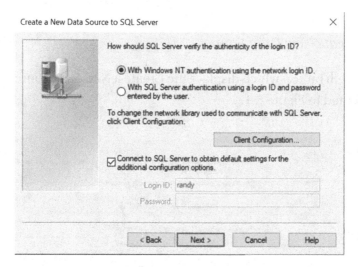

Figure 6-13. *SQL Server Authentication*

In our case, we select Windows authentication using the network login ID. Press the Next> dialog box. This action presents the Change Default Database Dialog menu shown in Figure 6-14.

If your dialog box indicates "master" as the default database, then check the box labeled "Change the default database to:" and select AdventureWorksDW2017, assuming it is available and your account has been granted read access.

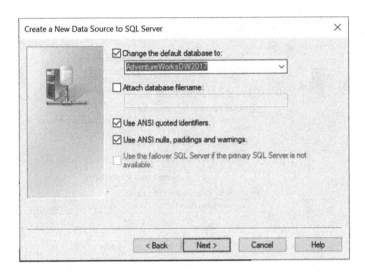

Figure 6-14. *Change Default Database*

Check the Change the default database tick box and supply the database name AdventureWorksDW2017. This is illustrated in Figure 6-15.

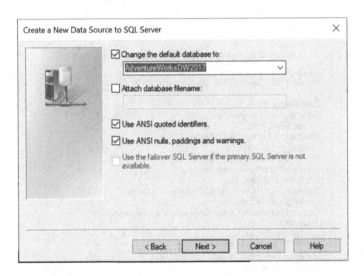

Figure 6-15. *Change the Default Database*

Press Finish> to be presented with the "Change the language of SQL Server messages to:" tick box. In our case, we chose to log the ODBC driver statistics. This is illustrated in Figure 6-16.

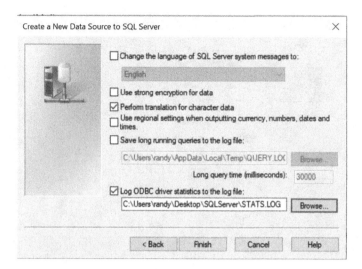

Figure 6-16. *Change SQL Server Language*

Press Finish> to be presented with the ODBC Data Source Configuration panel shown in Figure 6-17.

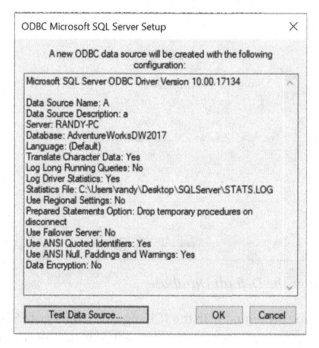

Figure 6-17. *Confirm Connection Details*

Press Test Data Source... box to test the ODBC Connection. You should see the Test Results dialog box shown in Figure 6-18.

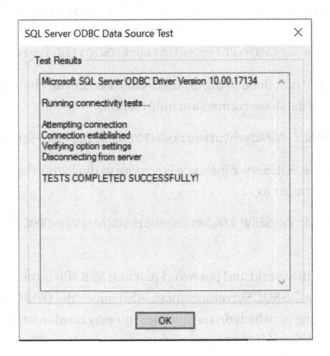

Figure 6-18. *Confirming Test Results*

In order to connect to the SQL Server AdventureWorksDW2017 database with SQLAlchemy, we use the create_engine function to create an engine object from the database URI. Database-specific information for the create_engine function and URI formatting is at

https://docs.sqlalchemy.org/en/latest/core/engines.html

You only need to create the engine once per database instance you are connecting to. The create_engine function containing the SQL Server Database URI is illustrated in Listing 6-20.

Listing 6-20. create_engine Function

```
>>> import pyodbc
>>> from sqlalchemy import create_engine, MetaData, Table, select
>>>
>>> ServerName = "RANDY-PC"
>>> Database = "AdventureWorksDW2017?driver=SQL+Server"
```

```
>>> TableName = "DimCustomer"
>>>
>>> engine = create_engine('mssql+pyodbc://' + ServerName + '/' + Database)
>>> print(engine)
Engine(mssql+pyodbc://RANDY-PC/AdventureWorksDW2017?driver=SQL Server)
```

The engine object is defined using tuples to concatenate the objects ServerName and Database to form the database connection information:

```
mssql+pyodbc://RANDY-PC/AdventureWorksDW2017?driver=SQL Server
```

In cases where the SQL Server instance is remote to the Python session, the engine object string will be similar to

```
mssql+pyodbc://USER:PW@SERVER/AdventureWorksDW?driver=ODBC+Driver+13+for+SQ
L+Server
```

where USER:PW are the userid and password pair and SERVER is the remote hostname or IP address running the SQL Server instances. Also notice the ODBC driver name could be different, depending on which driver you use. You may need to contact database administrator for additional information.

Once the engine object is correctly defined, use the read_sql_table() method to read all or subsets of database artifacts such as tables and views. Consider Listing 6-21, needing just two arguments: the target database table, in this case, DimCustomer table, and the engine object defining the connection string to the target database instance.

Listing 6-21. Basic Read with pd.read_sql_table

```
>>> import pandas as pd
>>> t0 = pd.read_sql_table('DimCustomer', engine)
>>> t0.info()
<class 'pandas.core.frame.DataFrame'>
RangeIndex: 18484 entries, 0 to 18483
Data columns (total 29 columns):
CustomerKey            18484 non-null int64
GeographyKey           18484 non-null int64
CustomerAlternateKey   18484 non-null object
Title                  101 non-null object
FirstName              18484 non-null object
```

```
MiddleName              10654 non-null object
LastName                18484 non-null object
NameStyle               18484 non-null bool
BirthDate               18484 non-null datetime64[ns]
MaritalStatus           18484 non-null object
Suffix                  3 non-null object
Gender                  18484 non-null object
EmailAddress            18484 non-null object
YearlyIncome            18484 non-null float64
TotalChildren           18484 non-null int64
NumberChildrenAtHome    18484 non-null int64
EnglishEducation        18484 non-null object
SpanishEducation        18484 non-null object
FrenchEducation         18484 non-null object
EnglishOccupation       18484 non-null object
SpanishOccupation       18484 non-null object
FrenchOccupation        18484 non-null object
HouseOwnerFlag          18484 non-null object
NumberCarsOwned         18484 non-null int64
AddressLine1            18484 non-null object
AddressLine2            312 non-null object
Phone                   18484 non-null object
DateFirstPurchase       18484 non-null datetime64[ns]
CommuteDistance         18484 non-null object
dtypes: bool(1), datetime64[ns](2), float64(1), int64(5), object(20)
memory usage: 4.0+ MB
```

The info attribute for the t0 DataFrame displays the names of all the columns read from the database table, the number of rows with non-null values, and the columns' corresponding types. For example, the BirthDate column is mapped to a datetime64 type. This indicates the BirthDate column can be used in datetime arithmetic expressions without needing cast it to datetime64 using the to_datetime() function.

If needed, the read_sql_table() reader accepts the parse_dates= argument to coerce date and datetime columns into a datetime64 type with

```
parse_dates={'BirthDate': {'format': '%Y-%m-%d'}}
```

using a nested Dictionary key:value pairs where the key is the name of the column followed by another Dictionary where the key is 'format' and the value is the date parsing instructions, known as format directives.

The to_datetime() function along with format directives is discussed in detail in Chapter 7, "Data and Time."

To return a subset of columns from a database table, use the columns= argument illustrated in Listing 6-22.

The call to the read_sql_table() method contains three arguments. The first argument is the target table, DimCustomer; the second argument is the engine object containing the connection information needed to access the SQL Server Database instance; and the third argument is columns= which forms the SELECT list that is ultimately executed as a T-SQL query on the SQL Server instance.

Listing 6-22. Returning Column Subset

```
>>> col_names = ['FirstName', 'LastName', 'BirthDate', 'Gender',
'YearlyIncome', 'CustomerKey']
>>> tbl = 'DimCustomer'
>>> t1 = pd.read_sql_table(tbl, engine, columns=col_names)
>>> t1.info()
<class 'pandas.core.frame.DataFrame'>
RangeIndex: 18484 entries, 0 to 18483
Data columns (total 6 columns):
FirstName        18484 non-null object
LastName         18484 non-null object
BirthDate        18484 non-null datetime64[ns]
Gender           18484 non-null object
YearlyIncome     18484 non-null float64
CustomerKey      18484 non-null int64
dtypes: datetime64[ns](1), float64(1), int64(1), object(3)
memory usage: 866.5+ KB
```

Use the index_col= argument to map an input column as the DataFrame index to create row labels. This feature is shown in Listing 6-23. This example extends Listing 6-22 by adding a fourth parameter, index_col=, for the call to read_sql_table reader().

Listing 6-23. Mapping Column to an Index

```
>>> t2 = pd.read_sql_table(tbl, engine, columns=col_names, index_
col='CustomerKey')
>>> print(t2[['FirstName', 'LastName', 'BirthDate']].head(5))
            FirstName LastName  BirthDate
CustomerKey
11000             Jon     Yang 1971-10-06
11001          Eugene    Huang 1976-05-10
11002           Ruben   Torres 1971-02-09
11003          Christy     Zhu 1973-08-14
11004       Elizabeth  Johnson 1979-08-05
>>> t2.index
Int64Index([11000, 11001, 11002, 11003, 11004, 11005, 11006, 11007, 11008,
11009,
. . .
29474, 29475, 29476, 29477, 29478, 29479, 29480, 29481, 29482,
29483],
dtype='int64', name='CustomerKey', length=18484)
```

Observe how the CustomerKey column read from the database is now the row label for the t2 DataFrame.

Query RDBMS Tables

As part of an analysis effort, we often need to construct SQL queries against the target dataset to return rows and columns to construct a DataFrame. Use the read_sql_query() reader to send an SQL query to the database and form a DataFrame from the returned result set. This feature is illustrated in Listing 6-24.

Listing 6-24. DataFrame from Query to RDBMS

```
>>> q1 = pd.read_sql_query('SELECT FirstName, LastName, Gender, BirthDate,
YearlyIncome '
...                        'FROM dbo.DimCustomer '
...                        'WHERE YearlyIncome > 50000; '
...                            , engine)
```

```
>>> print(q1[['FirstName', 'LastName', 'BirthDate']].tail(5))
      FirstName LastName    BirthDate
9853      Edgar    Perez  1964-05-17
9854      Alvin      Pal  1963-01-11
9855     Wesley    Huang  1971-02-10
9856      Roger    Zheng  1966-03-02
9857     Isaiah  Edwards  1971-03-11
```

In this example, the first argument to the read_sql_query() is a valid T-SQL query for SQL Server. This is followed by the engine object which holds the connection information to the database created previously. This call creates the q1 DataFrame. Notice how each line of the SQL query uses single quotes and a space before the close quote.

Listing 6-25 illustrates the SAS analog in Listing 6-22. This example has the same SELECT list as Listing 6-22. Use PROC PWENCODE to encode your password string to ensure your password string is not stored in clear text. Alternatively, you can assign your encoded password string to a SAS Macro variable with

```
proc pwencode in='YOUR_PASSWORD_HERE' out=pwtemp;
run;
```

This defines the Macro variable &pwtemp holding the encoded password string.

Listing 6-25. SAS ODBC Access to SQL Server

```
4    proc pwencode in=XXXXXXXXXXX;
5    run;

     {SAS002}XXXXXXXXXXXXXXXXXXXXXXXXXXXXXXXA2522

6    libname sqlsrvr odbc
7            uid=randy
8            pwd={SAS002}XXXXXXXXXXXXXXXXXXXXXXXXXXXXXXXA2522
9            datasrc=AdventureWorksDW
10           bulkload=yes;
NOTE: Libref SQLSRVR was successfully assigned as follows:
      Engine:         ODBC
      Physical Name: AdventureWorksDW
```

```
11 title1 "Default Informats and Formats";
12 proc sql;
13    create table customers as
14    select FirstName
15            ,LastName
16            ,BirthDate
17            ,Gender
18            ,YearlyIncome
19            ,CustomerKey
20         from sqlsrvr.DimCustomer;
NOTE: Table WORK.CUSTOMERS created, with 18484 rows and 6 columns.

21    select name
22            ,informat
23            ,format
24         from DICTIONARY.COLUMNS
25         where libname = 'WORK' &
26               memname = 'CUSTOMERS';
27 quit;
```

The second set of PROC SQL statements, lines 21–26, query the SAS-maintained table, DICTIONARY.COLUMNS, to return format and informat assignments to the WORK. CUSTOMERS columns. SAS formats and informats are analogous to column types, in that the informats direct how values are read on input and formats direct how values are written on output.

In this case, the incoming SQL Server table values for the BirthDate column are read using the SAS $10. informat treating the values as a 10-byte long character string. The output from PROC SQL is displayed in Figure 6-19.

Default Informats and Formats

Column Name	Column Informat	Column Format
FirstName	$50.	$50.
LastName	$50.	$50.
BirthDate	$10.	$10.
Gender	$1.	$1.
YearlyIncome	DOLLAR23.2	DOLLAR23.2
CustomerKey	11.	11.

Figure 6-19. *Customer Table Default Formats and Informats Assigned by SAS*

In order to utilize the incoming BirthDate variable with SAS datetime expressions, a subsequent Data Step is needed to copy the BirthDate variable values into a different variable formatted for datetime handling. Listing 6-26 illustrates copying the customers dataset and using the INPUT function to load the original character values for the BirthDate variable to a numeric variable and assign it a permanent format of YYMMDD10.

Unlike Python, existing SAS variables cannot be recast. To output the customers dataset with the BirthDate variable with a datetime format requires copying the dataset, renaming the incoming BirthDate variable to, in this case, dob, and assigning dob's values to the output BirthDate variable with the INPUT function.

Listing 6-26. Mapping BirthDate Variable to Datetime Variable

```
4   data customers(drop = dob);
5       set customers(rename=(BirthDate = dob));
6   length BirthDate 8;
7
8   BirthDate = input(dob,yymmdd10.);
9   format BirthDate yymmdd10.;
10  run;
```

```
NOTE: There were 18484 observations read from the dataset WORK.CUSTOMERS.
NOTE: The dataset WORK.CUSTOMERS has 18484 observations and 6 variables.
```

```
11   title1 "Modified Informats and Formats";
12   proc sql;
13      select name
14              ,informat
15              ,format
16         from DICTIONARY.COLUMNS
17         where libname = 'WORK' &
18              memname = 'CUSTOMERS';
19   quit;
```

Figure 6-20 uses PROC SQL to query the SAS DICTIONARY tables in order to display the informats and formats assigned to the modified customers dataset.

Modified Informats and Formats

Column Name	Column Informat	Column Format
FirstName	$50.	$50.
LastName	$50.	$50.
Gender	$1.	$1.
YearlyIncome	DOLLAR23.2	DOLLAR23.2
CustomerKey	11.	11.
BirthDate		YYMMDD10.

Figure 6-20. *Customer Dataset Modified Formats and Informats*

Not all SQL queries return a result set. Listing 6-27 illustrates using the sql.execute() function. This is useful for queries that do not return a result set such as CREATE TABLE, DROP, INSERT statements, and so on. The SQL statements are specific to the target RDBMS.

Listing 6-27. sql.execute() Statement

```
>>> from pandas.io import sql
>>> sql.execute('USE AdventureWorksDW2017; ', engine)
<sqlalchemy.engine.result.ResultProxy object at 0x0000020172E0DE80>
>>> sql.execute('DROP TABLE CustomerPy', engine)
```

```
<sqlalchemy.engine.result.ResultProxy object at 0x0000020172E0DDA0>
>>> sql.execute("CREATE TABLE CustomerPy (ID int,                    \
...              Name nvarchar(255),                                 \
...              StartDate date);", engine)
<sqlalchemy.engine.result.ResultProxy object at 0x0000020172E0D898>
```

In this case, the T-SQL syntax for SQL Server DROPs the CustomerPy table with

```
sql.execute('DROP TABLE CustomerPy', engine)
```

followed by a CREATE TABLE statement to define the CustomerPy table

```
sql.execute("CREATE TABLE CustomerPy (ID int,
             Name nvarchar(255),
             StartDate date);", engine)
```

Figure 6-21 displays the created SQL Server table, CustomerPy physical attributes created with the sql.execute() statement.

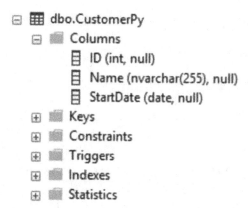

Figure 6-21. *sql.execute() Results*

Listing 6-28 illustrates the use of the SQL pass-thru facility as wrapper to pass T-SQL statements directly to SQL Server through the ODBC API. This example is the analog to Listing 6-27 for passing SQL to the database which does not return a result set.

Listing 6-28. SAS Pass-Thru to SQL Server

```
4  proc sql;
5     connect to odbc as sqlsrvr
6                  (dsn=AdventureWorksDW
```

```
7                        uid=randy
8                        password=
8!                   {SASOO2}XXXXXXXXXXXXXXXXXXXXXXXXXXXXXXA2522);
9
10      exec
11       (CREATE TABLE CustomerPy (ID int,
12                   Name nvarchar(255),
13                   StartDate date)) by sqlsrvr;
14
15    %put Note:  Return Code for SQL Server is: &sqlxrc;
Note:  Return Code for SQL Server is: 0
16    %put Note:  Return Message for SQL Server is: &sqlxmsg;
Note:  Return Message for SQL Server is:
17
18    select * from connection to sqlsrvr
19       (ODBC::SQLTables (,,"CustomerPy",));
20     disconnect from sqlsrvr;
21
22    %put Note:  Return Code for SQL Server is: &sqlxrc;
Note:  Return Code for SQL Server is: 0
23    %put Note:  Return Message for SQL Server is: &sqlxmsg;
Note:  Return Message for SQL Server is:
24    quit;
```

With SAS SQL Pass-Thru, any statement inside a parenthesized expression is passed directly to the database library API, in this case, ODBC.

```
(CREATE TABLE CustomerPy (ID int,
                  Name nvarchar(255),
                  StartDate date)
```

SAS/Access to ODBC supports calls to the ODBC::SQLAPI. This interface acts as an alternative method for querying the RDBMS catalog tables. In this example

```
select * from connection to sqlsrvr
     (ODBC::SQLTables (,,"CustomerPy",));
```

returns information about the created CustomerPy table. Figure 6-22 displays the query results.

TABLE_CAT	TABLE_SCHEM	TABLE_NAME	TABLE_TYPE	REMARKS
AdventureWorksDW2017	dbo	CustomerPy	TABLE	

Figure 6-22. *CustomerPy Attributes*

Read SAS Datasets

Organizations often have large numbers of permanent SAS datasets stored on the filesystem. pandas provide the read_sas() reader for creating DataFrames by reading permanent SAS datasets. Permanent SAS datasets are often referred to as .sas7bdat files (after the extension SAS uses to name dataset files on Windows and Unix filesystems). Listing 6-29 uses a Data Step to create the permanent out_data.to_df SAS dataset, where out_data maps to the filesystem location C:\data and to_df is the name of dataset, which is recognized by Windows as the file: C:\data\to_df.sas7bdat.

Listing 6-29. Create SAS Dataset for read_sas()

```
4 libname out_data 'c:\data';
NOTE: Libref OUT_DATA was successfully assigned as follows:
      Engine:        V9
      Physical Name: c:\data
5 data out_data.to_df;
6     length even_odd $ 4;
7     call streaminit(987650);
8     do datetime = '01Dec2018 00:00'dt to '02Dec2018 00:00'dt by 60;
9        amount = rand("Uniform", 50, 1200);
10       quantity = int(rand("Uniform", 1000, 5000));
12       if int(mod(quantity,2)) = 0 then even_odd = 'Even';
12           else even_odd = 'Odd';
13       output;
14    end;
15 format datetime datetime16.
16         amount dollar12.2
17         quantity comma10.;
18 run;
```

NOTE: The dataset OUT_DATA.TO_DF has 1441 observations and 4 variables.

```
19 proc contents data=out_data.to_df;
20 run;
```

```
21 proc print data=out_data.to_df(obs=5);
22 run;
```

NOTE: There were 5 observations read from the dataset OUT_DATA.TO_DF.

The SAS datetime variable is formatted as datetime constants; the amount variable is formatted to precede the value with a dollar sign ($) and the quantity variable to embed a comma (,) as part of its value. Figure 6-23 uses PROC CONTENTS to display the attribute information for the dataset. Notice that since we are using Windows, SAS dataset written to the filesystem uses wlatin1 encoding.

Data Set Name	OUT_DATA.TO_DF	Observations	1441
Member Type	DATA	Variables	4
Engine	V9	Indexes	0
Created	11/16/2018 10:25:25	Observation Length	32
Last Modified	11/16/2018 10:25:25	Deleted Observations	0
Protection		Compressed	NO
Data Set Type		Sorted	NO
Label			
Data Representation	WINDOWS_64		
Encoding	wlatin1 Western (Windows)		

Figure 6-23. *Attributes for OUT_DATA.TO_DF*

Figure 6-24 uses PROC PRINT to display the first five observations of the dataset.

Obs	even_odd	datetime	amount	quantity
1	Odd	01DEC18:00:00:00	$340.63	3,955
2	Even	01DEC18:00:01:00	$1,143.53	1,036
3	Even	01DEC18:00:02:00	$209.39	2,846
4	Even	01DEC18:00:03:00	$348.09	1,930
5	Even	01DEC18:00:04:00	$805.93	3,076

Figure 6-24. *Output for OUT_DATA.TO_DF*

With the OUT_DATA.TO_DF SAS dataset written to the filesystem, it can be used as input into the call to read_sas() reader to create a DataFrame. Listing 6-30 illustrates creating the from_sas DataFrame.

Listing 6-30. Create DataFrame from SAS Dataset

```
>>> from_sas = pd.read_sas("c:\\Data\\to_df.sas7bdat",
...                        format='SAS7BDAT',
...                        encoding = 'latin-1')
>>> from_sas.info()
<class 'pandas.core.frame.DataFrame'>
RangeIndex: 1441 entries, 0 to 1440
Data columns (total 4 columns):
even_odd    1441 non-null object
datetime    1441 non-null datetime64[ns]
amount      1441 non-null float64
quantity    1441 non-null float64
dtypes: datetime64[ns](1), float64(2), object(1)
memory usage: 45.1+ KB
>>> print(from_sas.head(5))
  even_odd            datetime       amount  quantity
0      Odd 2018-12-01 00:00:00   340.629296    3955.0
1     Even 2018-12-01 00:01:00  1143.526378    1036.0
```

2	Even 2018-12-01 00:02:00	209.394104	2846.0
3	Even 2018-12-01 00:03:00	348.086155	1930.0
4	Even 2018-12-01 00:04:00	805.929860	3076.0

The call to the read_sas() reader has as its first argument the full Windows's pathname to the OUT_DATA.TO_DF dataset (as it is known to SAS). The value for the second argument, format=, is SAS7BDAT. If the SAS dataset is in transport format, then this value is set to XPORT. The third argument, encoding=, is set to latin-1 to match the encoding for the to_df.sas7bdat dataset (as it is known to Windows).

The read_sas() reader issues a file lock for the target input in order to read the SAS dataset. This can cause file contention issues if you attempt to open the SAS dataset for output after executing the read_sas() reader. The SAS log will issue the following error:

```
ERROR: A lock is not available for OUT_DATA.TO_DF.DATA.
NOTE: The SAS System stopped processing this step because of errors.
WARNING: The dataset OUT_DATA.TO_DF was only partially opened and will not
be saved.
```

If this situation is encountered, ending the Python session used to call the read_sas() reader releases the file lock.

The pandas library does not provide a write_sas writer. In Chapter 8, "SASPy Module," we cover details for executing bi-directional interchange between panda DataFrames and SAS datasets using SAS Institute's open source SASPy Module.

Write RDBMS Tables

The pandas library provisions the ability to write DataFrames as RDBMS tables with the to_sql() writer. Consider Listing 6-31 which uses the from_sas DataFrame created in Listing 6-30. In this example, the from_sas DataFrame calls the to_sql() method attempting to create the SQLTableFromDF SQL Server table. This call returns an ODBC error indicating the to_sql() syntax is correct, but the underlying SQLAlchemy call to the ODBC API failed.

Listing 6-31. Write DataFrame to Table

```
>>> from_sas.to_sql('SQLTableFromDF', engine, if_exists='replace',
index=False)
pyodbc.ProgrammingError: ('42000', '[42000] [Microsoft][ODBC SQL Server
Driver][SQL Server]The incoming request has too many parameters. The server
supports a maximum of 2100 parameters. Reduce the number of parameters and
resend the request. (8003)
```

If you are using a different ODBC driver other than the SQLServer one used here, you may encounter a different error message indicating SQL inserts are rejected. Fortunately this error is easily eliminated by using the chunksize= argument for the to_sql() writer illustrated in Listing 6-32.

Listing 6-32. Chunk DataFrame Writes to Table

```
>>> from_sas.to_sql('SQLTableFromDF', engine, if_exists='replace',
chunksize=100, index=False)
```

The arguments to the to_sql() method call are

1. RDBMS target table to write, in this case, SQLTableFromDF.

2. The engine object containing the RDBMS connection string defined in Listing 6-20.

3. if_exists='replace' eliminates the need to explicitly DROP the target table if it already exists.

4. chunksize=100 which enables writes in increments of 100 rows to avoid size limitations when attempting to load larger DataFrames to an RDBMS table.

5. index=False does not define a primary key column when loading the DataFrame values into the RDBMS table.

Unlike SAS, when the to_sql() writer writes to the RDBMS table, it does not return messages or provide a return code to indicate success. Of course, we can send queries to the RDBMS to validate the existence of the SQLTableFromDF SQL Server table, which is the purpose of Listing 6-33.

Listing 6-33. Confirm to_sql() Writes

```
>>> confirm1 = pd.read_sql_query("SELECT column_name as 'COL_NAME', "
...             "data_type as 'Data_Type', "
...             "IS_NULLABLE as 'Nulls Valid' "
...             "FROM information_schema.columns "
...             "WHERE table_name = 'SQLTableFromDF' ", engine)
>>> print(confirm1)
   COL_NAME Data_Type Nulls Valid
0  even_odd   varchar         YES
1  datetime  datetime         YES
2    amount     float         YES
3  quantity     float         YES
```

Notice the quoting. Each physical line in the call to read_sql_query() reader requires double quotes. Single quotes are used to label column headings following the T-SQL AS keyword along with single quotes used in the T-SQL WHERE clause. The single quotes are passed to the RDBMS engine since they are a required element for a valid T-SQL query.

Figure 6-25 displays the output from SQL Server Management Studio execution of this query.

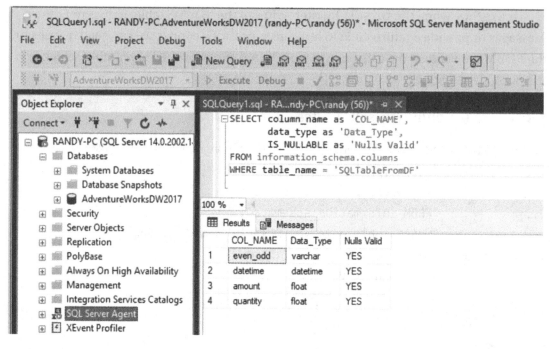

Figure 6-25. *SQL Server Table Write Confirmation*

In the case of Listing 6-32, there are no missing values in the from_sas DataFrame. Missing values between data formats can be challenging at times since each data format uses different sentinel values to indicate "missing".

In the case of a DataFrame, missing values can be NaN for float64s and NaT (for Not a Time) for datetime64 types. Consider Listing 6-34. The goal of this example is to load the resulting to_mssql DataFrame into an SQL Server table to ensure subsequent SQL queries properly handle these missing values.

Listing 6-34. Insert Missing Values into DataFrame

```
>>> import numpy as np
>>> from_sas.loc[from_sas['quantity'] < 2000, 'amount'] = np.NaN
>>> from_sas.loc[from_sas['quantity'] < 2000, 'datetime'] = np.NaN
>>>
>>> to_mssql = from_sas.copy()
>>>
>>> from_sas.isnull().sum()
even_odd        0
```

```
datetime     363
amount       363
quantity       0
dtype: int64
>>> print(to_mssql.head(5))
  even_odd            datetime      amount  quantity
0      Odd 2018-12-01 00:00:00  340.629296    3955.0
1     Even                 NaT         NaN    1036.0
2     Even 2018-12-01 00:02:00  209.394104    2846.0
3     Even                 NaT         NaN    1930.0
4     Even 2018-12-01 00:04:00  805.929860    3076.0
```

This example uses the loc() indexer to find rows meeting the logical condition for the quantity column value less than 2000. If found, the amount column and the datetime column values are set to np.NaN. For more details on using the loc() indexer to conditionally update values, see section "Conditional Updates" in Chapter 5, "Data Management."

In this example, notice the missing value for the datetime column whose type is datetime64 is NaT. In both cases the .isnull().sum() chained attributes indicate there are rows with missing values in the to_mssql DataFrame.

Consider Listing 6-35. In this example, we copy the from_sas DataFrame to the to_mssql DataFrame. This is followed by a call to the to_sql() writer to load the to_mssql DataFrame to the SQLTableFromDF2 SQL Server table.

Listing 6-35. Validate Reading Missing Values

```
>>> to_mssql = from_sas.copy()
>>>
>>> to_mssql.to_sql('SQLTableFromDF2', engine, if_exists='replace',
chunksize=100, index=False)
>>> confirm2 = pd.read_sql_query("SELECT TOP 5 * "
...                              "FROM SQLTableFromDF2 "
...                              "WHERE amount is NULL ", engine)
>>>
>>> print(confirm2)
  even_odd datetime amount  quantity
0     Even     None   None    1036.0
1     Even     None   None    1930.0
```

2	Odd	None	None	1677.0
3	Even	None	None	1352.0
4	Even	None	None	1876.0

The syntax

```
to_mssql.to_sql('SQLTableFromDF2', engine, if_exists='replace',
chunksize=100, index=False)
```

creates the `SQLTableFromDF2` SQL Server table. The syntax

```
confirm2 = pd.read_sql_query("SELECT TOP 5 * "
...                          "FROM SQLTableFromDF2 "
...                          "WHERE amount is NULL ", engine)
```

executes a T-SQL query returning the first five rows from the table using the T-SQL `WHERE` clause to create the `confirm2` DataFrame

```
WHERE amount is NULL
```

The call to the `print()` function for the `confirm2` DataFrame displays the values for the `datetime` and `amount` columns made the round trip from DataFrame to SQL Server Table back to a DataFrame maintaining the integrity of missing values between both data formats.

Summary

Data analysis tasks often require building a data processing pipeline to acquire and format data among a number of different data formats. This chapter provides the user with a solid grounding for acquiring data and loading them into a DataFrame using different panda readers as well as illustrates for writing DataFrame values to .csv, .xls, .sas7bdat, and RDBMS tables. By adding this know-how to one's skill set, it enables the user to build more elaborate scripts to tackle a range of data analysis tasks.

CHAPTER 7

Date and Time

Date and time data can be confusing because there are so many different formats that can mean the same or different values, depending on where we are and what we do. Date and time value handling are important in every field and can be critically important calculating durations, to GPS triangulation, your Uber ride, and whether you are able to schedule a meeting with colleagues in different parts of the world. Further, as we will see, languages like Python and SAS use different offsets for calendrical functions. Additional confusion often arises as a result of manipulating date and datetime values originating in the different time zone around the world.

Different Python modules define a variety of date and time objects and functions. In this chapter we start with Python's built-in `datetime` module. The topics covered here are

- `date`
- `time`
- `datetime`
- `timedelta`
- `tzinfo`

We will also briefly cover useful third-party date-related modules.

Date Object

The Python `date` object represents a value for dates composed of calendar year, month, and day based on the current Gregorian calendar. January 1 of year 1 is day 1, January 2 of year 1 is day 2, and so on. The range of Python date values ranges from January 1, 0001, to December 31, 9999. Internally the date object is composed of values for year, month, and day.

© Randy Betancourt, Sarah Chen 2019
R. Betancourt and S. Chen, *Python for SAS Users*, https://doi.org/10.1007/978-1-4842-5001-3_7

In contrast, SAS uses three counters for date, datetime, and time values. SAS date constants use the number of days from the offset of January 1, 1960, with the range of valid SAS date values of January 1, 1582, to December 31, 20,000. SAS datetime constants use the number of seconds from the offset of midnight, January 1, 1960. SAS time constants begin at midnight and increment to 86,400, the number of seconds in a day. SAS time constants have a resolution of 1 second.

Return Today's Date

We begin the discussion by reviewing both the Python and SAS today() functions to return the current local date. Begin with Listing 7-1.

Listing 7-1. Python today() Function

```
>>> from datetime import date
>>> now = date.today()
>>> print('\n', 'Today is:      ', now,
...        '\n', 'now Data Type:', type(now))

 Today is:       2019-01-06
 now Data Type: <class 'datetime.date'>
```

For Python, the now object is created by calling the today() function returning the current date that is printed using a default display format. Later in this chapter, we will examine how to alter the default display format. The now object is a datetime object. A Python datetime object is subject to date and time manipulation using both simple and complex methods. A Python date object is analogous to a SAS date constant.

Similarly, both Python and SAS expose numerous functions for manipulating date values. The SAS TODAY function behaves in the same manner as its Python counterpart, returning the current date. Listing 7-2 illustrates the same logic as Listing 7-1.

Listing 7-2. SAS TODAY Function

```
4 data _null_;
5    now = today();
6    put 'Today is: ' now yymmdd10.; ;
7 run;
```

OUTPUT:

Today is: 2019-01-06

Another difference between Python and SAS is Python displays date objects with a default format, whereas the SAS displays date constants as numeric values. SAS date constants must always be accompanied by either a SAS-supplied or user-supplied format to output values into a human-readable form. The default Python date format corresponds to the SAS-supplied yymmdd10.format.

The Python date object provides attributes such as .year, .month, and .day to return the year, month, and day values, respectively. These attributes return integer values. These attributes are similar to the SAS functions YEAR, MONTH, and DAY used to return the year, month, and day, respectively, from SAS date constants. See Listing 7-3.

Listing 7-3. Python Date Attributes

```
>>> from datetime import date
>>>
>>> nl    = '\n'
>>>
>>> d1    = date(1960, 1, 2)
>>> day   = d1.day
>>> month = d1.month
>>> year  = d1.year
>>>
>>> print(nl, 'd1:                ' , d1,
...        nl, 'd1 data type:     ' , type(d1),
...        nl, 'day:              ' , day,
...        nl, 'day data type:    ' , type(day),
...        nl, 'month:            ' , month,
...        nl, 'month data type:' , type(month),
...        nl, 'year:             ' , year,
...    nl, 'year data type: ' , type(year))

 d1:              1960-01-02
 d1 data type:    <class 'datetime.date'>
 day:             2
 day data type:   <class 'int'>
```

```
month:                  1
month data type: <class 'int'>
year:                   1960
year data type:  <class 'int'>
```

The d1 object is a date object created by calling the date() constructor. The rules for the date() constructor are all arguments are required and values are integers, and they must be in the following ranges:

- 1 <= year <= 9999

- 1 <= month <= 12

- 1 <= day <= number of valid days in the given month and year

Listing 7-4 illustrates the .min, .max, and .res attributes for the earliest, latest, and resolution for a Python date object, respectively.

Listing 7-4. Python Date Range

```
>>> import datetime
>>>
>>> nl       = '\n'
>>>
>>> early_dt = datetime.date.min
>>> late_dt  = datetime.date.max
>>> res      = datetime.date.resolution
>>>
>>> print(nl, 'Earliest Date:' ,early_dt,
...      nl, 'Latest Date:'    ,late_dt,
...      nl, 'Resolution:'     ,res)

 Earliest Date: 0001-01-01
 Latest Date: 9999-12-31
 Resolution: 1 day, 0:00:00
```

The analog to Listing 7-4 is the SAS program shown in Listing 7-5. This program illustrates the YEAR, MONTH, and DAY functions. Recall SAS date constants are enclosed in quotes (similar to strings) with "D" or 'd' concatenated to the end of the value to indicate a literal date constant. The "data type" for a SAS date literal is numeric and represents an offset from January 1, 1960.

298

Listing 7-5. SAS Date Functions

```
4 data _null_;
5   d1    = '2jan1960'd;
6   day   = day(d1);
7   month = month(d1);
8   year  = year(d1);
9
10 put 'Day:     ' day   /
12      'Month: ' month /
13      'Year:  ' year;
14   run;
```

OUTPUT:

```
Day:   2
Month: 1
Year:  1960
```

Date Manipulation

The Python date class permits the assignment of date values to objects which can be manipulated arithmetically. Consider Listing 7-6. Here we wish to determine the intervening number of days between two dates: January 2, 1960, and July 4, 2019.

Listing 7-6. Python Date Manipulation

```
>>> from datetime import date
>>>
>>> nl  = '\n'
>>>
>>> d1  = date(1960, 1, 2)
>>> d2  = date(2019, 7, 4)
>>> dif = d2 - d1
>>>
>>> print(nl                 , d1,
...        nl                 , d2,
...        nl,
```

```
...        nl, 'Difference:'      , dif,
...        nl, 'dif data type:'   , type(dif))
```

```
1960-01-02
2019-07-04
```

```
Difference: 21733 days, 0:00:00
dif data type: <class 'datetime.timedelta'>
```

In this example, objects d1 and d2 are date objects formed by calling the date()
constructor. As date objects, d1 and d2 can be utilized in date arithmetic such as
calculating an interval between two dates. The resulting dif object is a Timedelta which
we explore later in the chapter. In this case, there are 21,733 days between the two dates.

Listing 7-7 is the analog to Listing 7-6. Given SAS date constants are offsets from
January 1, 1960, they can be used in simple date arithmetic.

Listing 7-7. SAS Date Manipulation

```
4 data _null_;
5   d1  =  '2jan1960'd;
6   d2  =  '4jul2019'd;
7   dif =  d2 - d1;
8
9  put d1  yymmdd10.  /
10      d2  yymmdd10.  /
11      dif 'days';
12 run;
```

OUTPUT:

```
1960-01-02
2019-07-04
21733 days
```

In this example, SAS variables d1 and d2 are assigned arbitrary date literal constants.
The dif variable returns the number of days between these two dates.

Like any language, multiple methods can be used to solve a given problem. As an
example, consider Listing 7-8 which is an alternative for determining the number of
intervening days between two dates, similar to Listing 7-6.

This example introduces the `toordinal()` method to create the d1 and d2 objects, as integers returned from the method call and used to calculate intervening days between two dates.

Listing 7-8. Python toordinal() Function

```
>>> from datetime import date
>>>
>>> nl  = '\n'
>>>
>>> d1  = date(1960, 1, 2).toordinal()
>>> d2  = date(2019, 7, 4).toordinal()
>>> dif = d2 - d1
>>>
>>> print(nl, 'Ordinal for 02Jan1960:' ,d1,
...          nl, 'Ordinal for 07Jul2019:' ,d2,
...          nl, 'Difference in Days:'    ,dif)

 Ordinal for 02Jan1960: 715511
 Ordinal for 07Jul2019: 737244
 Difference in Days: 21733
```

The `toordinal()` method returns the ordinal value for January 2, 1960, and assigns it to the d1 object. Likewise, the `toordinal()` method returns the ordinal for July 4, 2019, and assigns it to the d2 object. The `dif` object is assigned the difference between the d1 and d2 object. The result is the number of days between these two dates. Unlike Listing 7-6, the type for the `dif` object is an int rather than returning a Timedelta.

Python provisions methods to parse date objects and return constituent components. Consider Listing 7-9. In this example, the dow1 object is assigned the integer value returned by calling the `weekday()` function, in this case, returning the integer value, 2. The `weekday()` function uses a zero-based (0) index where zero (0) represents Monday, one (1) represents Tuesday, and so on.

Listing 7-9. Python weekday() Function

```
>>> from datetime import datetime, date
>>>
>>> nl     = '\n'
```

```
>>>
>>> d1      = datetime(year=2019, month =12, day=25)
>>> dow1    = d1.weekday()
>>>
>>> dow2    = d1.isoweekday()
>>> iso_cal = date(2019, 12, 25).isocalendar()
>>>
>>> print(nl, 'Day of Week:'       ,dow1,
...         nl, 'ISO Day of Week:' ,dow2,
...         nl, 'ISO Calendar:'    ,iso_cal)

Day of Week: 2
ISO Day of Week: 3
ISO Calendar: (2019, 52, 3)
```

Where the dow1 object calls the weekday() function, in contrast, the dow2 object calls the isoweekday() function returning integers where integer value one (1) represents Monday and 7 represents Sunday.

Illustrated in this example is the .isocalendar attribute which parses the d1 date object to return a three-tuple value for the ISO year, ISO week number, and ISO day of the week.

The analog SAS program is shown in Listing 7-10.

Listing 7-10. SAS WEEKDAY and WEEK Functions

```
4  data _null_;
5     d1  = '25Dec2019'd;
6     dow = weekday(d1);
7     week1 = week(d1, 'u');
8     week2 = week(d1, 'v');
9     year  = year(d1);
10
12 put 'Day of Week: ' dow /
13     'Week1: ' week1    /
14     'Week2: ' week2    /
15     'Year:  ' year;
16 run;
```

302

OUTPUT:
```
Day of Week: 4
Week1: 51
Week2: 52
Year:  2019
```

In this example, the call to SAS WEEKDAY function is assigned to the dow variable and returns the value 4. The WEEKDAY function uses one (1) to represent Sunday, two (2) to represent Monday, and so on.

The WEEK function returns an integer value between 1 and 53 indicating the week of the year. The week1 variable is assigned the value from the call to the WEEK function using the d1 variable as its first parameter followed by the optional 'u' descriptor. This descriptor is the default using Sunday to represent the first day of the week.

The week2 variable is assigned the value from the call to the WEEK function followed by the optional 'v' descriptor. This descriptor uses Monday to represent the first day of the week and includes January 4 and the first Thursday of the year for week 1. If the first Monday of January is the second, third, or fourth, then these days are considered belonging to the week of the preceding year.

While the WEEKDAY functions for both Python and SAS are useful, they are often more meaningful if the returned integer values are mapped to names for the week day. In the case of Python, we introduce the calendar module. Like the date module, the calendar module uses January 1, 0001, as day 1 and provides calendar date handling functions and enables formatting. By default, the firstweekday() function is returns zero (0) and maps to Monday.

Begin by considering how the calendar.day_name attribute works. Listing 7-11 illustrates the calendar.day_name as a Python list which can be interrogated by supplying integer values between 0 and 6 for the index.

Listing 7-11. Calendar.day_name Attribute

```
>>> import calendar
>>> list(calendar.day_name)
['Monday', 'Tuesday', 'Wednesday', 'Thursday', 'Friday', 'Saturday', 'Sunday']
>>>
>>> calendar.day_name[6]
'Sunday'
```

In this example, we supply an index value of 6 in order to return the string 'Sunday'.

303

Now that we have the calendar module available, we can use it in a manner similar to the way SAS formats map values into other representations.

Listing 7-12 illustrates this concept. The dow2 object is assigned the integer value returned by calling the calendar.weekday() function for December 25, 2019.

Listing 7-12. Python Return Week Day Name

```
>>> import calendar
>>>
>>> nl   = '\n'
>>>
>>> dow2 = calendar.weekday(2019, 12, 25)
>>> nod2 = calendar.day_name[dow2]
>>>
>>> print(nl, 'Day of Week:' , dow2,
...         nl, 'Name of Day:' , nod2)

 Day of Week: 2
 Name of Day: Wednesday
```

The dow2 object is used as the index to the calendar.day_name, returning the string 'Wednesday'. Recall that Python uses a zero-based index. In this case, 0 maps to Monday.

The analog SAS example is shown in Listing 7-13.

Listing 7-13. SAS Return Week Day Names

```
4 data _null_;
5    d2   = '25Dec2019'd;
6    dow2 = weekday(d2);
7    nod2 = put(d2, weekdate9.);
8
9  put 'Day of Week: ' dow2 /
10     'Name of Day: ' nod2;
11 run;
```

OUTPUT:

```
Day of Week: 4
Name of Day: Wednesday
```

In this example, the d2 variable is a date variable and supplied as the parameter to the WEEKDAY function returning the value 4. The WEEKDAY function returns an integer value where one (1) is Sunday, two (2) is Monday, and so on. The PUT function creates the nod2 variable by assigning the dow2 variable value of 4 as the first parameter along with the SAS-supplied WEEKDATE9. format as the second parameter. The nod2 variable holds the value 'Wednesday'.

The default Python weekday() function is a 0-based index mapped to Monday as the start of the week, while the SAS WEEKDAY function is a 1-based index mapped to Sunday as the start of the week.

Another common task with date arithmetic is calculating dates based on a duration. The Python replace() method offers a way to substitute the year, month, and day argument for a date object and return a modified date.

Consider Listing 7-14. In this example, we shift an arbitrary date back by six days.

Listing 7-14. Python Date replace() Method

```
>>> from datetime import datetime, date
>>> d1 = date(2018, 12, 31)
>>> if d1 == date(2018, 12, 31):
...     d2 = d1.replace(day=25)
...
>>> print('\n', 'Before replace():', d1,
...       '\n', 'After replace(): ', d2)

 Before replace(): 2018-12-31
 After replace():  2018-12-25
```

The replace() function replaces the day value of 31 with the new value 25, in effect shifting the d1 date object value back by six (6) days. The replace() method is useful for basic date arithmetic such as counting days to a future event.

Consider Listing 7-15. This example calculates the number of days from today's date to a future date. It also illustrates conditional logic for handling cases when the future date falls in the current year, or when the future date falls into the succeeding year.

Listing 7-15. Python Count Days Until Birthday

```
>>> today = date.today()
>>> birth_day = date(today.year, 1, 24)
>>>
```

```
>>> if birth_day < today:
...     birth_day = birth_day.replace(year=today.year + 1)
...
>>> days_until = abs(birth_day - today)
>>>
>>> print(nl, 'Birthday:'                ,birth_day,
...     nl, 'birth_day Data Type:'  ,type(birth_day), nl,
...     nl, 'Days until Next:'      ,days_until,
...     nl, 'days_until Data Type:' ,type(days_until))
```

```
Birthday: 2020-01-24
birth_day Data Type: <class 'datetime.date'>

Days until Next: 240 days, 0:00:00
days_until Data Type: <class 'datetime.timedelta'>
```

In this example, the first argument to the date() constructor is the today.year argument which returns the current year followed by the integer 1 to represent January, then followed by the integer 24 to represent the 24th day. The if condition tests whether the input birthdate occurs during the current year.

If the birthday has already occurred in the current year, the if condition is False and not executed. If the birthday has not occurred in the current year, then the condition is True, and the replace() method is called to increment the year argument to year + 1.

The statement

```
days_until = abs(birth_day - today)
```

calculates the number of days between the input birthdate and today's date.

The same logic is illustrated with SAS in Listing 7-16.

Listing 7-16. SAS Count Days Until Birthday

```
4    data _null_;
5
6    today = today();
7
8    birth_day = '24Jan19'd;
9
10   if birth_day < today then do;
```

```
11      next_birth_day = intnx('year', birth_day, 1, 'sameday');
12      days_until = abs(next_birth_day - today);
13      put 'Next birthday is: ' next_birth_day yymmdd10.;
14    end;
15
16    else do;
17      next_birth_day = birth_day;
18      put 'Next birthday is: ' next_birth_day yymmdd10.;
19      days_until = abs(next_birth_day - today);
20    end;
21
22      put days_until ' days';
23    run;
```

```
Next birthday is: 2020-01-24
240  days
```

The IF-THEN/DO-END block tests whether the input birthdate has occurred during the current year. If this evaluates true, we increment the birthday year by 1. This code block is like the replace() function in Listing 7-15. In SAS, incrementing or decrementing date values is accomplished using the INTNX function. In this case, the syntax

```
next_birth_day = intnx('year', birth_day, 1, 'sameday');
```

assigns to the next_birth_day variable a date constant returned from INTNX function with four parameters; they are

1. 'year' is the interval value, that is, increment the date value by year increments.

2. birth_day designates the start date.

3. 1 is the integer value to increment the start date, in this case, 1 year, since 'year' is the interval value. This parameter may be a negative value for decrementing from the start date.

4. 'SAMEDAY' which is an optional alignment parameter.

With the next_birth_day calculated in this section of the code, the number of days remaining can be calculated and assigned to the days_until variable.

In the other case, when the input birthdate is greater than the current date (the false condition for the IF-THEN/DO-END), the ELSE/DO-END condition is executed to calculate the days remaining.

Shifting Dates

Another useful set of Python functions for shifting dates by a given interval is the paired fromordinal() and toordinal() methods. The fromordinal() method returns a date object when supplied an integer in the range of allowable Python dates . The fromordinal() method returns the integer value from a Python date object. Both these methods are illustrated in Listing 7-17.

Listing 7-17. Python Date Shifted 1,001 Days

```
>>> from datetime import datetime, date
>>>
>>> nl     = '\n'
>>>
>>> d1     = date(2019, 1, 1)
>>> to_ord = d1.toordinal()
>>>
>>> inc    = to_ord + 1001
>>> d2     = date.fromordinal(inc)
>>>
>>> print(nl, 'd1 Original Date:'   , d1,
...       nl, 'd1 Data Type:'       , type(d1), nl,
...       nl, 'Shifted Date:'       , d2,
...       nl, 'd2 Data Type:'       , type(d2), nl,
...       nl, 'to_ord Object:'      , to_ord,
...       nl, 'to_ord Data Type:'   , type(to_ord))

 d1 Original Date: 2019-01-01
 d1 Data Type: <class 'datetime.date'>

 Shifted Date: 2021-09-28
 d2 Data Type: <class 'datetime.date'>

 to_ord Object: 737060
 to_ord Data Type: <class 'int'>
```

In this example, the date() constructor is called assigning the d1 datetime object a value of January 1, 2019. In order to determine the calendar date 1,001 days hence, the d1 datetime object calls the toordinal() method returning the number of days from the ordinal start date of January 1, 0001, and the date value for the d1 object assigning this value to the to_ord object. The to_ord object is then incremented by 1,001, and assigned to the inc object. Finally, the fromordinal() function is called with the inc object as an argument returning the incremented date to the d2 object.

The analog SAS program logic uses the INTNX function which increments date, time, or datetime values by a given interval and returns the incremented or decremented date, time, or datetime. See Listing 7-18.

Listing 7-18. SAS Date Shifted 1,001 Days

```
4 data _null_;
5    d1 = '01Jan2019'd;
6    d2 = intnx('day', d1, 1001);
7 put 'Original Date: ' d1 yymmdd10. /
8      'Shifted Date:  ' d2 yymmdd10.;
9 run;
```

OUTPUT:
```
Original Date: 2019-01-01
Shifted Date:  2021-09-28
```

Date Formatting

Now let's examine formatting for dates and times. Both SAS and Python have many date formats to suit most requirements. Python uses two methods for formatting datetime values, strftime() and strptime().

Python date, datetime, and time objects use the strftime() method to display datetime values by arranging a set of format directives to control the appearances of the output. Using the strftime() method to format a Python datetime object to control appearances is analogous to the way a SAS or user-defined format controls the appearances for displaying SAS datetime constants. The strftime() method also converts a Python datetime object to a string. This is analogous to using the SAS PUT function to convert a SAS datetime constant, which is numeric, to a character variable. The result from calling the strftime() method is a Python date-, time-, or datetime-formatted string.

Conversely, the strptime() method creates a datetime object from a string representing a datetime value using a corresponding format directive to control its appearances. This is analogous to using the SAS INPUT function and the associated informat to create a character variable from a SAS date constant. The result from calling the strptime() method is a Python datetime object.

A mnemonic for remembering the difference in their behaviors is

- strftime() is like string-format-time.

- strptime() is like string-parse-time.

Table 7-1 displays the common format directives used for controlling the output to display Python datetime values.

Seeing working examples helps explain these concepts further. Start with Listing 7-19. The example begins by calling the date() constructor to assign the date January 24, 2019, to the dt datetime object.

Listing 7-19. Calling strftime() and strptime() Methods

```
>>> from datetime import date, time, datetime
>>>
>>> nl          = '\n'
>>> dt          = date(2019, 1, 24)
>>>
>>> dt_str      = dt.strftime('%d%B%Y')
>>> dt_frm_str = datetime.strptime(dt_str, '%d%B%Y')
>>>
>>> fmt = '%A, %B %dth, %Y'
>>>
>>> print(nl, 'dt Object:'              , dt,
...        nl, 'dt Data Type:'          , type(dt),
...        nl,
...        nl, 'dt_str Object:'         , dt_str,
...        nl, 'dt_str Data Type:'      , type(dt_str),
...        nl,
...        nl, 'dt_frm_str Object:'     , dt_frm_str,
```

```
...       nl, 'dt_frm_str Data Type:'  , type(dt_frm_str),
...       nl,
...       nl, 'Display dt_frm_str as:' , dt_frm_str.strftime(fmt),
...       nl, "Using Format Directive, '%A, %B %dth, %Y'")

dt Object: 2019-01-24
dt Data Type: <class 'datetime.date'>

dt_str Object: 24January2019
dt_str Data Type: <class 'str'>

dt_frm_str Object: 2019-01-24 00:00:00
dt_frm_str Data Type: <class 'datetime.datetime'>

Display dt_frm_str as: Thursday, January 24th, 2019
Using Format Directive, '%A, %B %dth, %Y'
```

The syntax

```
dt_str = dt.strftime('%d%B%Y')
```

creates the dt_str string object by assigning it the dt datetime value using the format directive %d%B%Y indicating the string object will be displayed as 24January2019. In SAS, converting a datetime object to a string is analogous to using the PUT function, along with an associated format to convert a numeric variable to a character variable.

The syntax which is part of the print() function

```
dt_frm_str.strftime('%A, %B %dth, %Y')
```

displays the dt_frm_str string object as

```
Thursday, January 24th, 2019
```

We define fmt = '%A, %B %dth, %Y' which is used as an argument to the strftime() function

```
dt_frm_str.strftime(fmt)
```

In SAS, this is analogous to assigning a format to a variable to control its appearance. Also notice how arbitrary characters can be included as part of the format directive. In this case, %dth, uses the %d directive to display the day of the month as a zero-padded decimal followed by the characters th, to form the characters 24th,.

When converting Python datetime objects to strings using the strftime() method, the format directives behave similarly to SAS formats. And when converting strings to datetime objects using the strptime() method, the format directives behave similarly to SAS informats.

Table 7-1. *Common Python Datetime Format Directives*[1]

Directive	Meaning	Example
%a	Weekday abbreviated name	Sun, Mon, etc.
%A	Weekday full name	Sunday, Monday, etc.
%w	Weekday as a decimal, where 0 is Sunday	0, 1, ..., 6
%b	Month abbreviated name	Jan, Feb, ... Dec
%B	Month full name	January, February, etc.
%d	Day of month, zero-padded decimal	01, 02, ..., 31
%Y	Year with century, zero-padded decimal	00, 01, ..., 99
%j	Day of year, zero-padded decimal	001, 002, ..., 366
%H	Hour, 24 hours as zero-padded decimal	00, 01, ..., 23
%I	Hour, 12 hours as zero-padded decimal	01, 02, ..., 12
%p	AM or PM	AM, PM
%M	Minute as zero-padded decimal	00, 01, ..., 59
%S	Second as zero-padded decimal	00, 01, ..., 59
%c	Date and time	Tue Aug 16 21:30:00 1988

[1]https://docs.python.org/3/library/datetime.html#strftime-and-strptime-behavior

Dates to Strings

Consider Listing 7-20 which calls the `strftime()` method to convert Python date objects to strings.

Listing 7-20. Python Date Object to Strings

```
>>> from datetime import date, time, datetime, timedelta
>>>
>>> nl      = '\n'
>>> d3      = date(2019, 12, 25)
>>>
>>> dt_str3 = date.strftime(d3,'%y-%m-%d')
>>> dt_str4 = date.strftime(d3,'%Y-%m-%d')
>>> dt_str5 = date.strftime(d3,'%Y-%B-%d')
>>>
>>> print(nl, 'Date Object d3:'     , d3,
...        nl, 'd3 Data Type:'       , type(d3),
...        nl,
...        nl, 'dt_str3:'            , dt_str3,
...        nl, 'dt_str3 Data Type:' , type(dt_str3),
...        nl,
...        nl, 'dt_str4:'            , dt_str4,
...        nl, 'dt_str4 Data Type:' , type(dt_str4),
...        nl,
...        nl, 'dt_str5:'            , dt_str5,
...        nl, 'dt_str5 Data Type:' , type(dt_str5))

 Date Object d3: 2019-12-25
 d3 Data Type: <class 'datetime.date'>

 dt_str3: 19-12-25
 dt_str3 Data Type: <class 'str'>

 dt_str4: 2019-12-25
 dt_str4 Data Type: <class 'str'>

 dt_str5: 2019-December-25
 dt_str5 Data Type: <class 'str'>
```

There are multiple calls to the strftime() method to illustrate formatting a string returned from datetime object using the pattern

dt_str = date.strftime(dN, format_directive)

The d3 datetime object is created by calling the date() constructor to set its date to December 25, 2019. Subsequently, three datetime-formatted strings are returned by calling the strftime() method with differing format directives. The format directive is given as the second argument to the strftime() method call and is composed of directives listed in Table 7-1. While these examples use a hyphen (-) as the field separator, you may use any separator such as a percent sign (%), slashes (/), colons (:), blanks (ASCII 32), and so on as well as including any arbitrary characters. Format directives are enclosed in quotes.

The analog SAS program is illustrated in Listing 7-21. The d3 variable is assigned a date constant and the VTYPE function returns N to indicate this variable is a numeric. With the d3 variable as the first parameter to the PUT function calls, the program illustrates different SAS formats to render different output styles similar to the Python format directives used in Listing 7-20.

Listing 7-21. SAS Dates to Character Variable

```
4 data _null_;
5 length tmp_st $ 16;
6    d3         = '25Dec2019'd;
7    date_type = vtype(d3);
8
9    dt_str3 = put(d3,yymmdd8.);
10   ty_str3 = vtype(dt_str3);
11
12   dt_str4 = put(d3,yymmdd10.);
13   ty_str4 = vtype(dt_str4);
14
15   tmp_st  = strip(put(d3,worddatx.));
16   dt_str5 = translate(tmp_st,'-',' ');
17   ty_str5 = vtype(dt_str3);
18
19 put 'Date Variable d3:   ' d3 date9.   /
```

```
20      'd3 Date Type:      ' date_type //
21       'dt_str3:           ' dt_str3   /
22       'dt_str3 Data Type: ' ty_str3   //
23       'd2_str4:           ' dt_str4   /
24       'dt_str4 Data Type: ' ty_str4   //
25       'dt_str5:           ' dt_str5   /
26    'dt_str5 Data Type: ' ty_str5;
27 run;

Date Variable d3:   25DEC2019
d3 Date Type:       N

dt_str3:            19-12-25
dt_str3 Data Type: C

d2_str4:            2019-12-25
dt_str4 Data Type: C

dt_str5:            25-December-2019
dt_str5 Data Type: C
```

The PUT function is called to convert a numeric variable to a character variable. The PUT function returns a value using the format specified in the function call, in this case, the SAS-supplied YYMMDD8., YYMMDD10., and WORDDATX. formats. The VTYPE function returns the variable type, C for character and N for numeric.

Listing 7-22 illustrates calling the strftime() together with the format() function to dynamically format a string.

Listing 7-22. String Formatting with strftime() Method

```
>> from datetime import date
>>>
>>> d4 = date(2019, 12, 25)
>>>
>>> 'In 2019, Christmas is on day {0} and falls on {1}'.format(date.
strftime(d4, '%j'),date.strftime(d4, '%A'))
'In 2019, Christmas is on day 359 and falls on Wednesday'
```

The first positional parameter, {0}, to the format() function uses the directive

```
date.strftime(d4, '%j')
```

to return the day of the year as a decimal number. The second positional parameter, {1}, uses the directive

```
date.strftime(d4, '%A')
```

returning the week day full name.

Strings to Dates

Now let's do the reverse process and convert a Python string object to a datetime object. The strptime() method is used to return a datetime object from a string. This feature is illustrated in Listing 7-23.

Listing 7-23. Python Strings to Date Object

```
>>> from datetime import datetime, date
>>>
>>> nl     = '\n'
>>> in_fmt = '%Y-%m-%d'
>>>
>>> dt_str = '2019-01-01' ·
>>> d5 = datetime.strptime(dt_str, in_fmt )
>>>
>>> print(nl, 'dt_str String:'     , dt_str,
...        nl, 'dt_str Data Type:' , type(dt_str),
...        nl,
...        nl, 'd5 Date is:'        , d5,
...        nl, 'd5 Data Type:'      , type(d5))

 dt_str String: 2019-01-01
 dt_str Data Type: <class 'str'>

 d5 Date is: 2019-01-01 00:00:00
 d5 Data Type: <class 'datetime.datetime'>
```

The dt_str object is assigned the string '2019-01-01'. The d5 datetime object is assigned the results from calling

```
d5 = datetime.strptime(dt_str, '%Y-%m-%d')
```

where the first argument is the dt_str object and the second argument is the directive matching this string.

Recall the strptime() method returns a datetime object, even though we are supplying a date string and the associated directive. As the name suggests, a datetime object holds a value for both date and time and is discussed later in this chapter. Since we do not have a time portion defined, the resulting d5 datetime object is set to midnight.

Listing 7-24 is the analog to Listing 7-23 illustrating the conversion of a character variable used for strings representing date to a SAS date constant.

Listing 7-24. SAS Character Variable to Date

```
4 data _null_;
5     dt_str      = '2019-01-01';
6     d5          = input(dt_str,yymmdd10.);
7     dt_str_type = vtype(dt_str);
8     d5_type     = vtype(d5);
9
10 put 'Original String: ' dt_str /
11     'Data Type: ' dt_str_type //
12     'Date is: ' d5 yymmdd10.  /
13     'Data Type: ' d5_type ;
14   run;
```

OUTPUT:

```
Original String: 2019-01-01
Data Type: C

Date is: 2019-01-01
Data Type: N
```

In contrast to Listing 7-21, this example uses the INPUT function to map a date string assigned to the dt_str variable as a date constant. The VTYPE function returns the data type for the d5 and dt_str variables.

Time Object

For Python, a time object represents the local time of day, independent of any particular day, and is subject to changes based on the tzinfo object. The tzinfo object is discussed later in this chapter in the section on time zone. The time module uses an epoch start, or offset, from midnight on January 1, 1970. This fact is illustrated in Listing 7-25. Keep in mind that the datetime module also has methods and functions for handling time. We will see additional Python time handling techniques in the datetime object section later in this chapter.

Returning the Python epoch start is illustrated in Listing 7-25.

Listing 7-25. Python Time Epoch

```
>>> import time
>>> time.gmtime(0)
>>>
time.struct_time(tm_year=1970, tm_mon=1, tm_mday=1, tm_hour=0, tm_min=0,
tm_sec=0, tm_wday=3, tm_yday=1, tm_isdst=0)
```

The gmtime() function converts a time value expressed as the number of seconds, in this case, zero, to the Python struct_time object, in effect, passing a timestamp value of zero (0) to the gmtime() function. A struct_time object is returned containing a sequence of time and date values which can be accessed by an index value and attribute name. Think of the struct_time object as a data structure used by the time module to provide access to time-related components analogous to a SAS time value.

Once a struct_time object is created, it exposes an index and attributes to return time-related components similar to SAS functions used to return time-related components from a SAS time constant.

Table 7-2 displays the index and attribute names used to return constituent components of a time value.

Table 7-2. *Python struct_time Object*[2]

Index	Attribute	Values
0	tm_year	For example, 2018
1	tm_mon	1 for Jan, 2 for Feb, etc. 1–12
2	tm_mday	1 for first, 2 for second, etc. 1–31
3	tm_hour	0 for midnight, 1, 2, etc. 0–23
4	tm_min	0, 1, 2, …, 59
5	tm_sec	0, 1, 2, …, 59
6	tm_wday	0 for Monday, 1 for Tuesday, …, 6 for Sunday
7	tm_yday	1, 2, …, 366

Notice how the struct_time object returns a year, month, and date value. Python time values have a resolution to the microsecond, or one millionth of a second, whereas SAS time values have a resolution of 1 second. Also notice that tm_mon, tm_mday, and tm_day are one-based (1) indexes rather than the traditional zero-based (0) index.

Listing 7-26 illustrates returning constituent components composing the time value assigned to the t time object. This example calls the gmtime() function with a timestamp value of zero, like Listing 7-25.

Listing 7-26. Python struct_time Object

```
>>> import time
>>>
>>> nl = '\n'
>>> t  = time.gmtime(0)
>>>
>>> print(nl, 'Hour:          '  , t.tm_hour,
...       nl, 'Minute:        '  , t.tm_min,
...       nl, 'Second:        '  , t.tm_sec,
...       nl, 'Day of Month:'    , t.tm_mday,
```

---

[2]https://docs.python.org/3/library/time.html#time.struct_time

```
...          nl, 'Day of Week: '   , t.tm_wday,
...          nl, 'Day of Year: '   , t.tm_yday,
...          nl, 'Year:        '   , t[0])
```

```
Hour:           0
Minute:         0
Second:         0
Day of Month: 1
Day of Week:  3
Day of Year:  1
Year:           1970
```

Except for the year, attribute names are used to return the values from the struct_time object. The year value is returned using an index value of zero (0).

Listing 7-27 is the analog to the Python example in Listing 7-26. This example illustrates the SAS time offset as the number of seconds from midnight, January 1, 1960. It also illustrates several datetime functions to return constituent date and time components.

Listing 7-27. SAS Time Example

```
4   data _null_;
5     t  = '00:00:00't;
6     hr  = hour(t);
7     mn  = minute(t);
8     sc  = second(t);
9     mo  = month(t);
10    dy  = day(t);
11    yr  = year(t);
12
13 put "'00:00:00't is: " t datetime32. /
14      'Hour:            ' hr /
15      'Minute:          ' mn /
16      'Second:          ' sc /
17      'Day of Month: ' mo /
18      'Day of Week:  ' dy /
19      'Year:            ' yr;
20  run;
```

OUTPUT:

```
'00:00:00't is:            01JAN1960:00:00:00
Hour:          0
Minute:        0
Second:        0
Day of Month: 1
Day of Week:  1
Year:          1960
```

In this example, the SAS datetime offset of midnight, January 1, 1960, is assigned to the t variable. This variable is used as the argument to several SAS date and time functions to return constituent components for this time constant.

Time of Day

In some cases, the analysis we are performing needs to consider elapsed time with a start time independent of the current day. For this purpose, Python and SAS provision functions to return the current time of day. These functions make calls to the underlying OS to return time of day from the processor's clock. Later in this chapter, we will explore how to handle variations in reported time influenced by time zone considerations.

For now, let's consider the basics for obtaining the current time as shown in Listing 7-28. Recall that in Listing 7-25 we use the gmtime() function to create a struct_time object by supplying the number of seconds from the Python time offset, which is zero (0) in that case. In this example, we call the time.time() function without an argument to return the local time.

In Python, calling the time.time() function returns the current time of day as a timestamp, that is, the number of seconds from the Python time offset. In order to return the local time in a human-readable form, we need to embed the time.time() function call inside the localtime() function call. Observe in Listing 7-28 how the t_stamp object is assigned the value from the time.time() function and returns a float, which is the timestamp value. In order to create the struct_time object for time, we use the localtime() function with time.time() function as the argument.

Listing 7-28. Python Return Time of Day

```
>>> import time
>>>
>>> nl       = '\n'
>>> t_stamp = time.time()
>>>
>>> now      = time.localtime(time.time())
>>> dsp_now = time.asctime(now)
>>>
>>> print(nl, 't_stamp Object:'     , t_stamp,
...          nl, 't_stamp Data Type:' , type(t_stamp),
...          nl,
...          nl, 'now Object:'         , now,
...          nl,
...          nl, 'dsp_now Object:'     , dsp_now,
...          nl, 'dsp_now Data Type:' , type(dsp_now))

 t_stamp Object: 1548867370.6703455
 t_stamp Data Type: <class 'float'>

 now Object: time.struct_time(tm_year=2019, tm_mon=1, tm_mday=30,
tm_hour=11, tm_min=56, tm_sec=10, tm_wday=2, tm_yday=30, tm_isdst=0)

 dsp_now Object: Wed Jan 30 11:56:10 2019
 dsp_now Data Type: <class 'str'>
```

Specifically, the syntax

```
now = time.localtime(time.time())
```

creates the now object by calling the localtime() function using the time.time() as an argument, which returns today's timestamp to the localtime() function. The result is the struct.time object assigned to the now object.

The syntax

```
dsp_now = time.asctime(now)
```

converts the time.struct object (created by the localtime() function call) to a string displaying day of week, date, time, and year. The asctime() function converts the Python struct_time object into a string.

Listing 7-29 is the analog to Listing 7-28. It uses the SAS DATETIME function to return the current date and time.

Listing 7-29. SAS Return Time of Day

```
4  data _null_;
5
6     now = datetime();
7     dow = put(datepart(now), weekdate17.);
8     tm  = put(timepart(now), time9.);
9     yr  = year(datepart(now));
10    bl  = ' ';
11    all = cat(tranwrd(dow,',',' '), tm, bl, yr);
12
13 put 'all Variable: ' all;
14 run;

all Variable: Tue  Jan 15  2019 13:50:18 2019
```

The now variable is a time constant with a value from today's date and time. The PUT function converts this numeric variable to a character variable, in this case, using the DATEPART, TIMEPART, and YEAR functions returning constitute datetime components. The TRANWRD function strips the comma (,) following the week day name.

Time Formatting

Formatting time values follows the same pattern discussed earlier in the chapter for formatting date values using the same format directives used for date and datetime objects. Additionally, the strftime() method converts struct_time object into strings representing the constituent parts of time.

Conversely, the strptime() method creates a time object from a string representing time values by using a corresponding format directive to control its appearances. The result from calling the strptime() function is a datetime object whose output is controlled by the corresponding format directive.

It is often the case that time and datetime values need conversion to strings or we have strings representing time and datetime values which need conversion to time or datetime objects and variables. The next four examples illustrate these conversions along with formatting time and datetime examples.

Times to Strings

We begin with Listing 7-30 calling the `strftime()` function to convert a Python time object, specifically converting the `struct_time` object components to a string.

Listing 7-30. Python Time Object to Strings

```
>>> import time
>>>
>>> nl  = '\n'
>>>
>>> now = time.localtime(time.time())
>>> n1  = time.asctime(now)
>>>
>>> n2  = time.strftime("%Y/%m/%d %H:%M"       , now)
>>> n3  = time.strftime("%I:%M:%S %p"          , now)
>>> n4  = time.strftime("%Y-%m-%d %H:%M:%S %Z" , now)
>>>
>>> print(nl, 'Object now:' , now,
...          nl,
...          nl, 'Object n1:'  , n1,
...          nl, 'Object n2:'  , n2,
...          nl, 'Object n3:'  , n3,
...          nl, 'Object n4:'  , n4)
 Object now: time.struct_time(tm_year=2019, tm_mon=1, tm_mday=30,
tm_hour=12, tm_min=21, tm_sec=8, tm_wday=2, tm_yday=30, tm_isdst=0)

 Object n1: Wed Jan 30 12:21:08 2019
 Object n2: 2019/01/30 12:21
 Object n3: 12:21:08 PM
 Object n4: 2019-01-30 12:21:08 Eastern Standard Time
```

As we saw earlier, we acquire the local time of day by calling `time.time()` to return a timestamp which is then passed to the `localtime()` function to return a `struct_time` object. This is accomplished with the syntax

```
now = time.localtime(time.time())
```

The n1 object calls the `asctime()` function, which returns a string with a default format as

Tue Jan 15 15:48:28 2019

without the need to supply a format directive.

Objects n2, n3, and n4 display the same datetime with different format directives. Format directives are supplied as a single argument composed of the directives listed in Table 7-1, in this case, using different separators such as hyphens (-), slashes (/), and colons (:) and any arbitrary characters.

The corresponding SAS program is illustrated in Listing 7-31. The results are the creation of the n1, n2, n3, and n4 variables whose values are strings matching the n1, n2, n3, and n4 Python string objects in Listing 7-30.

Listing 7-31. SAS Time Constants to Strings

```
5 data _null_;
6
7    now = datetime();
8    dt  = put(datepart(now), weekdate17.);
9    tm  = put(timepart(now), time9.);
10   yr  = year(datepart(now));
11
12   bl  = ' ';
13   n1  = cat(tranwrd(dt,',',' '), tm, bl, yr);
14   n2  = cat(put(datepart(now), yymmdds10.), put(timepart(now), time6.));
15   n3  = put(timepart(now), timeampm11.);
16   n4  = cat(put(datepart(now), yymmddd10.), put(timepart(now), time6.),
bl, tzonename());
17
18 put 'Variable n1: ' n1 /
19     'Variable n2: ' n2 /
20     'Variable n3: ' n3 /
21     'Variable n4: ' n4;
22 run;
```

OUTPUT:

```
Variable n1: Wed  Jan 30  2019 12:27:24 2019
Variable n2: 2019/01/30 12:27
Variable n3: 12:27:24 PM
Variable n4: 2019-01-30 12:27 EST
```

This example calls the DATETIME function to return the current date and time similar to the Python time() function. The Python time() function returns the struct_time object, whereas the SAS TIME function returns a time constant, '12:34:56't, representing the number of seconds from midnight.

In order to replicate the results in Listing 7-30, this example uses different SAS functions such as DATEPART and TIMEPART to extract the constituent elements from the current date and time, respectively. The TZONENAME function is a relatively new function introduced with release 9.4, returning the time zone name, assuming this option is set. By default, this option is not set and is set using the OPTIONS statement. We provide further details for handling time zone later in this chapter.

Strings to Time

When you have strings representing date or time values, use the strptime() function to convert them to a Python time object. This feature is illustrated in Listing 7-32. Strictly speaking, this example converts a string representing a time value to the struct_time object.

Listing 7-32. Python Strings to Time Object

```
>>> import time
>>>
>>> nl  = '\n'
>>> t   = time.strptime("12:34:56 PM", "%I:%M:%S %p")
>>>
>>> hr  = t.tm_hour
>>> min = t.tm_min
>>> sec = t.tm_sec
>>>
```

```
>>> print(nl, 't Object:     '   , t,
...        nl, 't Data Type:'    , type(t),
...        nl,
...        nl, 'hr Object:    '   , hr,
...        nl, 'hr Data Type:'    , type(hr),
...        nl,
...        nl, 'min Object:   '   , min,
...        nl, 'min Data Type:'   , type(min),
...        nl,
...        nl, 'sec Object:   '   , sec,
...        nl, 'sec Data Type:'   , type(sec))
```

```
 t Object:     time.struct_time(tm_year=1900, tm_mon=1, tm_mday=1,
tm_hour=12, tm_min=34, tm_sec=56, tm_wday=0, tm_yday=1, tm_isdst=-1)
 t Data Type: <class 'time.struct_time'>
```

```
 hr Object:     12
 hr Data Type: <class 'int'>
```

```
 min Object:     34
 min Data Type: <class 'int'>
```

```
 sec Object:     56
 sec Data Type: <class 'int'>
```

The syntax

```
t = time.strptime("12:34:56 PM", "%I:%M:%S %p")
```

converts the string "12:34:56 PM" into a struct_time object called t. The attributes tm_hour, tm_min, and tm_sec attached to the t object return integer values representing the hour, minute, and seconds, respectively.

The analog SAS program is shown in Listing 7-33.

Listing 7-33. SAS Character Variable to Time Constant

```
4 data _null_;
5
6    t_str = '12:34:56';
7    t    = input(t_str,time9.);
```

```
8
9    hr    = hour(t);
10   hr_t  = vtype(hr);
11
12   min   = minute(t);
13   min_t = vtype(min);
14
15   sec   = second(t);
16   sec_t = vtype(sec);
17
18 put 't Variable:     ' t timeampm11. //
19     'hr Variable:    ' hr             /
20     'hr Data Type:   ' hr_t           //
21     'min Variable:   ' min            /
22     'min Data Type:  ' min_t          //
23     'sec Variable:   ' sec            /
24     'sec Data Type:  ' sec_t;
25 run;
```

```
t Variable:     12:34:56 PM

hr Variable:    12
hr Data Type:   N

min Variable:   34
min Data Type: N

sec Variable:   56
sec Data Type: N
```

In this example, the characters '12:34:56' are assigned to the t_str variable. The INPUT function maps this string as a numeric value assigned to the t variable, creating a SAS time constant. The HOUR, MINUTE, and SECOND functions return numerics representing the hour, minute, and second, respectively, from the t variable.

Datetime Object

The Python datetime module provides a set of functions and methods for creating, manipulating, and formatting datetime objects. These methods and functions behave similarly to those from the date and time modules discussed earlier. In contrast to the date and time modules, here we discuss the `datetime` object to facilitate the handling of date and time values as a single object. We should point out that the Python examples in the "Date Object" section of this chapter import the date module and the examples in the "Time Object" section import the time module. So naturally, in this section we import the datetime module.

Like a Python date object, the `datetime` object assumes the current Gregorian calendar extended in both directions, and like the `time` object, a `datetime` object assumes there are exactly 3600*24 seconds in every day.

Likewise, while SAS distinguishes between date and time constants, a SAS datetime constant provides a consistent method for handling a combined date and time value as a single constant.

The Python datetime module provides the `datetime()` constructor method where

> minyear <= year <= maxyear
>
> 1 <= month <= 12
>
> 1 <= day <= number of days in the given month and year
>
> 0 <= hour < 24
>
> 0 <= minute < 60
>
> 0 <= second < 60
>
> 0 <= microsecond < 1000000
>
> tzinfo = None

We begin with constructing a datetime object. The `datetime()` constructor method requires the year, month, and day arguments with the remaining arguments optional.

Listing 7-34 illustrates creating a datetime object with different constructor methods, each returning a datetime object. This example illustrates `datetime.datetime()`, `datetime.datetime.now()`, and `datetime.datetime.utcnow()` constructor methods.

Listing 7-34. Python Datetime Constructor Methods

```
>>> import datetime as dt
>>>
>>> nl        = '\n'
>>> dt_tuple = (2018, 10, 24, 1, 23, 45)
>>>
>>> dt_obj   = dt.datetime(* dt_tuple[0:5])
>>> dt_now1  = dt.datetime.utcnow()
>>> dt_now2  = dt.datetime.now()
>>>
>>> print(nl, 'dt_obj Object:     '  , dt_obj,
...        nl, 'dt_obj Data Type: '  , type(dt_obj),
...        nl,
...        nl, 'dt_now1 Object:    '  , dt_now1,
...        nl, 'dt_now1 Data Type:'  , type(dt_now1),
...        nl,
...        nl, 'dt_now2 Object:    '  , dt_now2,
...        nl, 'dt_now2 Data Type:'  , type(dt_now2))

 dt_obj Object:     2018-10-24 01:23:00
 dt_obj Data Type:  <class 'datetime.datetime'>

 dt_now1 Object:    2019-01-30 18:13:15.534488
 dt_now1 Data Type: <class 'datetime.datetime'>

 dt_now2 Object:    2019-01-30 13:13:15.534488
 dt_now2 Data Type: <class 'datetime.datetime'>
```

The datetime.datetime() constructor method accepts a tuple of values conforming to the ranges described earlier. The datetime.utc() constructor method returns the current date based on the UTC time zone, while the datetime.now() returns the current date and local time. And because the call to the datetime.now() method implies the default tz=None argument, this constructor method is the equivalent of calling the datetime.today() constructor method. Each of these methods returns a datetime object.

Likewise, we can construct a Series of SAS datetime constants. Listing 7-35 is the analog to Listing 7-34. The first portion of this example creates the user-defined py_fmt. format displaying SAS datetime constants in the same manner as the default Python datetime objects.

The PROC FORMAT PICTURE formatting directives[3] mostly follow the Python formatting directives shown in Table 7-1. The parameter to the PICTURE statement

(datatype=datetime)

is required indicating the format PICTURE is applied to a datetime variable. With the exception of the %Y for the year format directive, the remaining format directives have a zero (0) as part of the directive to left-pad the value when any of the datetime values return a single digit. This is the same behavior as the default Python format directives.

Listing 7-35. Constructing SAS Datetime Constants

```
4 proc format;
5     picture py_fmt (default=20)
6        low - high = '%Y-%0m-%0d %0I:%0M:%0s' (datatype=datetime);
7
NOTE: Format PY_FMT has been output.
8 run;
9
10 data _null_;
11
12     dt_str      = '24Oct2018:01:23:45';
13     dt_obj      = input(dt_str, datetime20.);
14     dt_obj_ty   = vtype(dt_obj);
15
16     dt_now1     = datetime();
17     dt_now1_ty  = vtype(dt_now1);
18
19     dt_now2     = tzones2u(dt_now1);
20     dt_now2_ty  = vtype(dt_now2);;
```

---

[3]SAS PROC FORMAT PICTURE Directives: https://documentation.sas.com/?docsetId=proc&d
ocsetTarget=p0n990vq8gxca6n1vnsracr6jp2c.htm&docsetVersion=1.0&locale=en#p0eubpiv9
ngaocn1uatbigc5swi2

```
21
22 put 'dt_obj Variable: '   dt_obj py_fmt.  /
23    'dt_obj Data Type: '  dt_obj_ty         //
24    'dt_now1 Variable: '  dt_now1 py_fmt. /
25    'dt_now1 Data Type: ' dt_now1_ty        //
26    'dt_now2 Variable: '  dt_now2 py_fmt. /
27    'dt_now2 Data Type: ' dt_now2_ty;
28 run;
```

OUTPUT:
```
dt_obj Variable:   2018-10-24 01:23:45
dt_obj Data Type: N

dt_now1 Variable:   2019-01-30 07:57:27
dt_now1 Data Type: N

dt_now2 Variable:   2019-01-31 12:57:27
dt_now2 Data Type: N
```

The DATETIME function is analogous to the Python datetime.datetime.now()
function returning the current datetime from the processor clock. In order to display
today's datetime based on UTC time zone, call the TZONES2U function to convert a SAS
datetime to UTC. We cover time zone further in the "Time zone Object" section later in
this chapter.

Combining Times and Dates

There are times when a dataset to be analyzed has columns consisting of separate values
for dates and times, with the analysis requiring a single datetime column. To combine
the date and time columns, use the combine() function to form a single datetime object.
This feature is shown in Listing 7-36.

Listing 7-36. combine() Method for Python Dates and Times

```
>>> from datetime import datetime, date, time
>>>
>>> nl      = '\n'
>>> fmt     = '%b %d, %Y at: %I:%M %p'
```

```
>>>
>>> d1       = date(2019, 5, 31)
>>> t1       = time(12,  34, 56)
>>> dt_comb = datetime.combine(d1,t1)
>>>
>>> print(nl, 'd1 Object:'         , d1,
...        nl, 't1 Object:'         , t1,
...        nl,
...        nl, 'dt_comb Object:'    , dt_comb.strftime(fmt),
...        nl, 'dt_comb Data Type:' , type(dt_comb))

 d1 Object: 2019-05-31
 t1 Object: 12:34:56

 dt_comb Object: May 31, 2019 at: 12:34 PM
 dt_comb Data Type: <class 'datetime.datetime'>
```

And as one would expect, the data type returned for the dt_comb object is datetime.

With SAS, use the DHMS function to combine a date and time variable. This logic is illustrated in Listing 7-37.

Listing 7-37. Combining SAS Date and Time Constants

```
4 data _null_;
5     time      = '12:34:56't;
6     date      = '31May2019'd;
7     new_dt    = dhms(date,12,34,56);
8
9     new_dt_ty = vtype(new_dt);
10
11    put 'new_dt Variable:  ' new_dt py_fmt. /
12        'new_dt Data Type: ' new_dt_ty;
13 run;

new_dt Variable:    2019-05-31 12:34:56
new_dt Data Type: N
```

Calling the DHMS function returns a numeric value that represents a SAS datetime value. The py_fmt. format is created in Listing 7-35.

Now let's turn our attention to extracting constituent components from a datetime object. Both Python and SAS provide methods to extract datetime components to returning these values as integers and strings.

Returning Datetime Components

We begin by calling Python datetime attributes to return date and time components as integers. See Listing 7-38. In this example, the date() and time() methods are attached to the dt_obj object returning date and time objects, respectively. Python datetime objects have the year, month, day, hour, minute, and second attributes to return integer values.

Listing 7-38. Python Attributes Returning Datetime Components

```
>>> import datetime as dt
>>>
>>> nl = '\n'
>>> in_fmt = '%Y-%m-%d %I:%M%S'
>>>
>>> dt_obj = dt.datetime(2019, 1, 9, 19, 34, 56)
>>> date   = dt_obj.date()
>>> time   = dt_obj.time()
>>>
>>> print(nl, 'Date:     ' , date          ,
...       nl, 'Time:     ' , time          ,
...       nl, 'Year:     ' , dt_obj.year   ,
...       nl, 'Month:    ' , dt_obj.month  ,
...       nl, 'Day:      ' , dt_obj.day    ,
...       nl, 'Hour:     ' , dt_obj.hour   ,
...       nl, 'Minute:   ' , dt_obj.minute ,
...       nl, 'Seconds:  ' , dt_obj.second)

 Date:      2019-01-09
 Time:      19:34:56
 Year:      2019
 Month:     1
 Day:       9
```

```
Hour:      19
Minute:    34
Seconds:   56
```

Not shown in this example are the microsecond and tzinfo attributes which in this case return None.

Listing 7-39 performs the same operation as Listing 7-38. The DATEPART and TIMEPART functions return the date and time as date and time constants, respectively.

Listing 7-39. SAS Functions Returning Datetime Components

```
4 data _null_;
5
6 dt_obj = '09Jan2019:19:34:56'dt;
7
8     date    = datepart(dt_obj);
9     time    = timepart(dt_obj);
10
11    year    = year(datepart(dt_obj));
12    month   = month(datepart(dt_obj));
13    day     =   day(datepart(dt_obj));
14
15    hour    = hour(dt_obj);
16    minute  = minute(dt_obj);
17    second  = second(dt_obj);
18
19 put 'Date:     ' date yymmdd10.  /
20     'Time:     ' time time8.     /
21     'Year:     ' year            /
22     'Month:    ' month           /
23     'Day:      ' day             /
24     'Hour:     ' hour            /
25     'Minute:   ' minute          /
26     'Seconds:  ' second;
27 run;
```

OUTPUT:

```
Date:      2019-01-09
Time:      19:34:56
Year:      2019
Month:     1
Day:       9
Hour:      19
Minute:    34
Seconds:   56
```

All of the variables in this example are numeric.

Strings to Datetimes

The next two examples illustrate converting Python and SAS strings to datetimes. Converting a Python string representing a datetime value to a datetime object follows the same pattern we saw earlier for converting date and time string objects by calling the strptime() function. Start with Listing 7-40. The strptime() function accepts two parameters: the first is the input string representing a datetime value followed by the second parameter, the format directive matching the input string.

Listing 7-40. Python Strings to Datetime Objects

```
>>> import datetime as dt
>>>
>>> nl = '\n'
>>>
>>> str = 'August 4th, 2001 1:23PM'
>>> dt_obj = dt.datetime.strptime(str, '%B %dth, %Y %I:%M%p')
>>>
>>> tm = dt_obj.time()
>>>
>>> print(nl, 'str Object:'        , str,
...         nl, 'str Data Type:'    , type(str),
...         nl,
...         nl, 'tm_obj Object:'    , dt_obj,
...         nl, 'tm_obj Data Type:' , type(dt_obj),
```

```
...        nl,
...        nl, 'tm Object:'         , tm,
...        nl, 'tm Data Type:'      , type(tm))

 str Object: August 4th, 2001 1:23PM
 str Data Type: <class 'str'>

 tm_obj Object: 2001-08-04 13:23:00
 tm_obj Data Type: <class 'datetime.datetime'>

 tm Object: 13:23:00
 tm Data Type: <class 'datetime.time'>
```

Converting a SAS character variable to a datetime constant is similar to the earlier examples in this chapter for converting character variables to date and time constants. Consider Listing 7-41 which illustrates this conversion. In this case, if the SAS variable value of 'August 4, 2001 1:23PM' had a delimiter between the date and time value, we can use the ANYDTDTM. informat.

Another approach is to create a user-defined format to match the value's form. The steps in this process are

1. Create a user-defined informat with PROC FORMAT.

2. Generate the CNTLIN= SAS dataset for PROC FORMAT and designate the TYPE variable in this dataset as I to indicate building an INFORMAT.

3. Call PROC FORMAT to build the user-defined informat by loading the CNTLIN= input dataset.

4. Call the INPUT function paired with the user-defined informat to create a datetime variable from the character variable value representing the datetime value.

Listing 7-41. Converting SAS Character Variable to Datetime Variable

```
4 proc format;
5    picture py_infmt (default=20)
6    low - high = '%B %d, %Y %I:%OM%p' (datatype=datetime);
NOTE: Format PY_INFMT has been output.
7 run;
```

```
8 data py_infmt;
9    retain fmtname "py_infmt"
10           type "I";
11    do label = '04Aug2001:00:00'dt to
12                 '05Aug2001:00:00'dt by 60;
13      start = put(label, py_infmt32.);
14      start = trim(left (start));
15    output;
16 end;
17 run;
```

NOTE: The dataset WORK.PY_INFMT has 1441 observations and 4 variables.

```
18 proc format cntlin = py_infmt;
NOTE: Informat PY_INFMT has been output.
19 run;
```

NOTE: There were 1441 observations read from the dataset WORK.PY_INFMT.

```
20 data _null_;
21    str        = 'August 4, 2001 1:23PM';
22    dt_obj     = input(str, py_infmt32.);
23    dt_obj_ty  = vtype(dt_obj);
24    tm         = timepart(dt_obj);
25    tm_ty      = vtype(tm);
26    yr         = year(datepart(dt_obj));
27    yr_ty      = vtype(yr);
28
29    put  'dt_obj Variable: '   dt_obj py_infmt32. /
30          'dt_obj Data Type: '  dt_obj_ty          //
31          'yr Variable: '       yr                 /
32          'yr Data Type: '      yr_ty              //
33          'tm Variable: '       tm time8.          /
34          'tm Data Type: '      tm_ty;
35    run;
```

OUTPUT:
```
dt_obj Variable: August 4, 2001 1:23PM
dt_obj Data Type: N

yr Variable: 2001
yr Data Type: N

tm Variable: 13:23:00
tm Data Type: N
```

The format directive '%B %d, %Y %I:%0M%p' on the PICTURE statement matches the input character variable value 'August 4, 2001 1:23PM'. The SAS Data Step creating the py_infmt dataset contains the minimum variables for defining a CNTLIN= dataset needed by PROC FORMAT, with the type, label, and start variables. In order to be recognized as a cntlin= dataset, these names for variables are required. SAS datetime values have a 1-second level of granularity, and since the user-defined informat deals with a minute interval, the DO loop to generate the datetime labels is divided by 60.

In the _NULL_ Data Step, the syntax

```
dt_obj = input(str, py_infmt32.);
```

assigns the SAS datetime constant to the dt_obj variable by calling the INPUT function with the user-defined py_infmt32. informat.

Datetimes to Strings

Now let's illustrate conversions going the opposite direction: datetime objects to strings. Like the examples for time and date objects, converting datetime objects to strings calls the strptime() function. Listing 7-42 illustrates the use of the Python formatted string literals, or f-string for short. An f-string contains replacement fields designated by curly braces {} and is composed of expressions evaluated at runtime.

Listing 7-42. Python Datetime Object to Strings

```
>>> import datetime as dt
>>>
>>> nl      = '\n'
>>> fmt     = '%Y-%m-%d %I:%M%S'
>>>
```

```
>>> dt_obj = dt.datetime(2019, 7, 15, 2, 34, 56)
>>> dt_str = dt_obj.strftime(fmt)
>>>
>>> wkdy_str    = f"{dt_obj:%A}"
>>> mname_str   = f"{dt_obj:%B}"
>>> day_str     = f"{dt_obj:%d}"
>>> yr_str      = f"{dt_obj:%Y}"
>>> hr_str      = f"{dt_obj:%I}"
>>> mn_str      = f"{dt_obj:%M}"
>>> sec_str     = f"{dt_obj:%S}"
>>>
>>> print(nl                      ,
...         'Weekday: ' ,wkdy_str ,
...         nl                    ,
...         'Month:    ' , mname_str,
...         nl                    ,
...         'Day:      ' , day_str ,
...         nl                    ,
...         'Year:     ' , yr_str  ,
...         nl                    ,
...         'Hours:    ' , hr_str  ,
...         nl                    ,
...         'Minutes: ' , mn_str   ,
...         nl,
...         'Seconds: ' , sec_str)
Weekday:  Monday
Month:    July
Day:      15
Year:     2019
Hours:    02
Minutes:  34
Seconds:  56
```

A format specifier is appended following the colon (:) and while the format specifiers can be a range of valid format specifiers, since we are dealing with datetime, we illustrate those in Table 7-1.

In the case of SAS, extracting the datetime components uses the same functions illustrated in Listing 7-43 along with the PUT function to convert the returned numeric values into character variables.

Listing 7-43. SAS Datetime to Character Variables

```
4 data _null_;
5
6 dt_obj      = '15Jul2019:02:34:56'dt;
7
8  wkdy_str   = put(datepart(dt_obj), downname9.);
9  mnname_str = put(datepart(dt_obj), monname.);
10
11  day_str    = put(day(datepart(dt_obj)), 8.);
12  yr_str     = put(year(datepart(dt_obj)), 8.);
13
14  hr_str     = cat('0',left(put(hour(dt_obj), 8.)));
15  mn_str     = put(minute(dt_obj), 8.);
16  sec_str    = put(second(dt_obj), 8.);
17
18  put 'Weekday: ' wkdy_str   /
19        'Month:    ' mnname_str /
20        'Day:      ' day_str    /
21        'Year:     ' yr_str     /
22        'Hours:    ' hr_str     /
23        'Minutes: ' mn_str     /
24        'Seconds: ' sec_str    /;
25  run;
```

OUTPUT:

```
Weekday: Monday
Month:    July
Day:      15
Year:     2019
Hours:    02
Minutes: 34
Seconds: 56
```

In order to render the output identical to the Python example in Listing 7-42, the CAT function is called to left-pad the value for the hr_str variable with a zero (0).

Timedelta Object

The Python Timedelta object, as the name suggests, represents a duration between two date or time objects with a granularity of 1 microsecond. A rough corollary in SAS is the INTCK and INTNX functions. The SAS INTCK returns the number of datetime intervals that lie between two dates, times, or datetimes. The INTNX function increments or decrements a date, time, or datetime value by a given interval and returns a date, time, or datetime value.

The Timedelta object has the signature

```
datetime.timedelta(days=0, seconds=0, microseconds=0, milliseconds=0,
minutes=0, hours=0, weeks=0)
```

where all arguments are options and argument values may be integers or floats either positive or negative. Timedelta objects support certain addition and subtraction operations using date and datetime objects.

Let's see some examples starting with Listing 7-44. It begins by assigning the now object the current local datetime. The timedelta() method is called to shift backward in time the datetime value held by the now object by subtracting a Timedelta interval. Similarly, a datetime value is shifted forward in time by adding a Timedelta interval to the now object.

Listing 7-44. Basic Timedelta Arithmetic

```
>>> import datetime as dt
>>>
>>> nl        = '\n'
>>> fmt       = '%b %d %Y %I:%M %p'
>>> now       = dt.datetime.now()
>>>
>>> dy_ago1   = now - dt.timedelta(days = 1)
>>> dy_ago2   = now - dt.timedelta(days = 1001)
>>>
>>> wk_ago    = now - dt.timedelta(weeks = 1)
```

```
>>> yr_fm_now = now + dt.timedelta(weeks = 52)
>>>
>>> new_td    = dt.timedelta(days = 730, weeks = 52, minutes = 60)
>>>
>>> print (nl, 'Today is:          ' , now.strftime(fmt),
...            nl, 'Day ago:           ' , dy_ago1.strftime(fmt),
...            nl, '1001 Days ago:     ' , dy_ago2.strftime(fmt),
...            nl, '1 Week ago:        ' , wk_ago.strftime(fmt),
...            nl, 'In 1 Year:         ' , yr_fm_now.strftime(fmt),
...            nl, 'In 3 Yrs, 1 Hour:' , new_td)

Today is:          Feb 04 2019 03:51 PM
Day ago:           Feb 03 2019 03:51 PM
1001 Days ago:     May 09 2016 03:51 PM
1 Week ago:        Jan 28 2019 03:51 PM
In 1 Year:         Feb 03 2020 03:51 PM
In 3 Yrs, 1 Hour: 1094 days, 1:00:00
```

The objects dy_ago1, dy_ago2, wk_ago, and yr_fm_now are datetime objects shifted in time by the different Timedelta arguments. new_td is simply a Timedelta object.

A common challenge for datetime arithmetic is finding the first and last day of the month. Here, the Timedelta object can be used for finding these dates using the following approach:

1. Obtain the target date.

2. Find the first day of the month by replacing the day ordinal with the value one (1).

3. Find the last day of the current month by finding the first day of the succeeding month and subtracting one (1) day.

This approach is illustrated in Listing 7-45.

Listing 7-45. Python First and Last Day of Month

```
>>> import datetime as dt
>>>
>>> nl    = '\n'
>>> fmt   = '%A, %b %d %Y'
```

```
>>>
>>> date   = dt.date(2016, 2, 2)
>>> fd_mn = date.replace(day=1)
>>>
>>> nxt_mn = date.replace(day=28) + dt.timedelta(days=4)
>>> ld_mn  = nxt_mn - dt.timedelta(nxt_mn.day)
>>>
>>> print(nl, 'date Object:'        , date,
...          nl, 'nxt_mn date:'      , nxt_mn,
...          nl, 'Decrement value:'  , nxt_mn.day,
...          nl,
...          nl, '1st Day of Month:' , fd_mn.strftime(fmt),
...          nl, 'Lst Day of Month:' , ld_mn.strftime(fmt))
 date Object: 2016-02-02
 nxt_mn date: 2016-03-03
 Decrement value: 3

 1st Day of Month: Monday, Feb 01 2016
 Lst Day of Month: Monday, Feb 29 2016
```

The fd_mn object is defined as the first day of the month by replacing the current day date ordinal with the value of one (1) using the replace() function. Finding the last day of the month involves two steps: first, finding the first day of the succeeding month of the input date and, second, subtracting one day from this date. For step 1, we find the "next" month using the 28th as the logical last day of every month in order to handle the month of February. The syntax

```
nxt_mn = date.replace(day=28) + datetime.timedelta(days=4)
```

replaces the actual day date ordinal with 28 and adds a Timedelta of 4 days ensuring the nxt_mn datetime object will always contain a date value for the "next" month. In step 2, we return the day date ordinal from the "next" month using the nxt_nm.day() attribute. This returned ordinal is the number of days we decrement from the nxt_nm datetime object using the syntax

```
ld_mn = nxt_mn - datetime.timedelta(nxt_mn.day)
```

creating the ld_mn datetime object holding the last day of the "current" month.

The SAS INTNX function is analogous to the Python timedelta() function able to use a datetime constant and shift values by incrementing or decrementing by date or datetime intervals. This feature is illustrated in Listing 7-46. A DO/END loop is used to generate the date constants using a BY value of 31. It simply generates 12 date constants with each value falling into a separate month of the year.

Listing 7-46. SAS First and Last Day of Month

```
4 data _null_;
5
6 put 'First Day of the Month    Last Day of the Month' /
7    '============================================' /;
8 do date_idx = '01Jan2019'd to '31Dec2019'd by 31;
9    f_day_mo = intnx("month", date_idx, 0, 'Beginning');
10   l_day_mo = intnx("month", date_idx, 0, 'End');
11   put f_day_mo weekdate22.  l_day_mo weekdate22.;
12 end;
13
14 run;

First Day of the Month    Last Day of the Month
==================================================

         Tue, Jan 1, 2019      Thu, Jan 31, 2019
         Fri, Feb 1, 2019      Thu, Feb 28, 2019
         Fri, Mar 1, 2019      Sun, Mar 31, 2019
         Mon, Apr 1, 2019      Tue, Apr 30, 2019
         Wed, May 1, 2019      Fri, May 31, 2019
         Sat, Jun 1, 2019      Sun, Jun 30, 2019
         Mon, Jul 1, 2019      Wed, Jul 31, 2019
         Thu, Aug 1, 2019      Sat, Aug 31, 2019
         Sun, Sep 1, 2019      Mon, Sep 30, 2019
         Tue, Oct 1, 2019      Thu, Oct 31, 2019
         Fri, Nov 1, 2019      Sat, Nov 30, 2019
         Sun, Dec 1, 2019      Tue, Dec 31, 2019
```

The statement

```
f_day_mo = intnx("month", date_idx, 0, 'Beginning');
```

returns the first day of the month assigning this date constant to the f_day_mo variable by calling the INTNX function with four parameters where

- "month" is a keyword to indicate the interval to be shifted between the start and end dates.

- date_idx indicates the start-from date or datetime constant to be shifted.

- 0 to indicate how many intervals to shift the start-from date or datetime constant. In this case, we are not shifting the date_idx date constant and instead finding the 'Beginning' of the interval, which is the beginning of the month.

- 'Beginning' is an optional parameter used to control the position of the date or datetime constant within the interval, in this case, the beginning or first day of the month.

Similarly, the l_day_mo variable behaves in the same manner as the f_day_mo variable when calling the INTNX function with the exception of the last parameter being 'End' to find the last day of the month.

Of course, we can easily extend the logic for finding the first and last day of the month to finding the first and last business day of the month. This is illustrated in Listing 7-47 and Listing 7-49. Each of the four functions, when called, accepts two positional parameters, year and month.

We begin with the Python functions. Because we already have the Python program to find the first and last day of the month, they are easily converted into functions named first_day_of_month and last_day_of_month. See Listing 7-47.

Next, we create the functions first_biz_day_of_month returning the first business day of the month and last_biz_day_of_month returning the last business day of the month. All four functions use a datetime object named any_date, whose scope is local to each function definition. Its role inside the function is twofold. First, it receives the year and month input parameters when these functions are called setting an "anchor" date as the first day of the inputs for month and year and second is to manipulate the "anchor" date with datetime arithmetic to return the appropriate date.

Listing 7-47. Python Functions for First, Last, First Biz, and Last Biz Day of Month

```python
import datetime as dt

def first_day_of_month(year, month):
    any_date = dt.date(year, month, 1)
    return any_date

def last_day_of_month(year, month):
    any_date = dt.date(year, month, 1)
    nxt_mn = any_date.replace(day = 28) + dt.timedelta(days=4)
    return nxt_mn - dt.timedelta(days = nxt_mn.day)

def first_biz_day_of_month(year, month):
    any_date=dt.date(year, month, 1)

    #If Saturday then increment 2 days
    if any_date.weekday() == 5:
        return any_date + dt.timedelta(days = 2)

    #If Sunday increment 1 day
    elif any_date.weekday() == 6:
        return any_date + dt.timedelta(days = 1)

    else:
        return any_date

def last_biz_day_of_month(year, month):
    any_date = dt.date(year, month, 1)

    #If Saturday then decrement 3 days
    if any_date.weekday() == 5:
        nxt_mn = any_date.replace(day = 28) + dt.timedelta(days = 4)
        return nxt_mn - dt.timedelta(days = nxt_mn.day) \
            - abs((dt.timedelta(days = 1)))

    #If Sunday then decrement 3 days
    elif any_date.weekday() == 6:
        return nxt_mn - dt.timedelta(days = nxt_mn.day) \
            - abs((dt.timedelta(days = 2)))
```

```
    else:
        nxt_mn = any_date.replace(day = 28) + dt.timedelta(days = 4)
        return nxt_mn - dt.timedelta(days = nxt_mn.day)
```

For the first_biz_day_of_month and last_biz_day_of_month functions, the weekday() function tests whether the ordinal day of the week returned is five (5) representing Saturday or six (6) representing Sunday.

When the weekday() function returns five, the local any_date datetime object is shifted forward to the following Monday by adding a Timedelta of 2 days. The same logic applies for Sunday, that is, when the ordinal 6 is returned from the weekday() function, the any_date object is shifted to the following Monday by adding a Timedelta of 1 day.

In the case of the last_biz_day_of_month() function, we can find the last day using the two-step process described in Listing 7-45.

The last_biz_day_of_month() function needs to be able to detect if the local any_date datetime object falls on a Saturday or Sunday and decrement accordingly. Finding the last business day of the month involves handling three conditions, the default condition, the Saturday condition, and the Sunday condition.

1. Default condition

    a. Create the local nxt_mn datetime object as the logical last day of the month as the 28th to handle the month of February using the replace() function.

    b. Add a Timedelta of 4 days to the local nxt_mn datetime object ensuring the month for this date value is the month succeeding the month of the "anchor" date. By replacing this day ordinal with 28 and adding 4 days, you now have the first day of the succeeding month. Subtracting 1 day returns the last day of the "anchor" month.

2. The Saturday condition uses the same logic as the default condition and includes

    a. Use of the weekday() function to test if the returned ordinal is 5. When True, decrement the local nxt_mn datetime object by 1 day to the preceding Friday.

3. The Sunday condition uses the same logic as the default condition
    and includes

    a. Use of the weekday() function to test if the returned ordinal is
        6. When True, decrement the local nxt_mn datetime object by 2
        days to the preceding Friday.

With these four functions defined, they can be called as illustrated in Listing 7-48.
This example only works if the code defining these functions, in Listing 7-47, has already
been executed in the current Python execution environment.

Listing 7-48. Calling Functions for First, Last, Day of Month and Biz Day of Month

```
>>> nl    = '\n'
>>> fmt   = '%A, %b %d %Y'
>>> year  = 2020
>>> month = 2
>>>
>>> print(nl, '1st Day    :' , first_day_of_month(year, month).
strftime(fmt),
...        nl, '1st Biz Day:' , first_biz_day_of_month(year, month).
strftime(fmt),
...        nl,
...        nl, 'Lst Day    :' , last_day_of_month(year, month).
strftime(fmt),
...        nl, 'Lst Biz Day:' , last_biz_day_of_month(year, month).
strftime(fmt))

 1st Day    : Saturday, Feb 01 2020
 1st Biz Day: Monday, Feb 03 2020

 Lst Day    : Saturday, Feb 29 2020
 Lst Biz Day: Friday, Feb 28 2020
```

These four functions are each called with a year and month parameter, in this case,
February 2020. These functions illustrate basic concepts but have no error handling logic
for malformed input nor do they take into account instances where a business day falls
on a holiday, for example, New Year's Day.

Listing 7-49 extends the logic for Listing 7-46. In this case, we use the WEEKDAY function to return the ordinal day of the week. Recall the WEEKDAY function returns 1 for Sunday, 2 for Monday, and so on.

Listing 7-49. SAS First and Last Business Day of Month

```
4 data _null_;
5 put 'First Biz Day of Month    Last Biz Day of Month' /
6      '=============================================' /;
7 do date_idx  = '01Jan2019'd to '31Dec2019'd by 31;
8    bf_day_mo = intnx("month", date_idx, 0, 'Beginning');
9    bl_day_mo = intnx("month", date_idx, 0, 'End');
10
11   beg_day  = weekday(bf_day_mo);
12   end_day  = weekday(bl_day_mo);
13
14   /* If Sunday increment 1 day */
15   if beg_day = 1 then bf_day_mo + 1;
16      /* if Saturday increment 2 days */
17      else if beg_day = 7 then bf_day_mo + 2;
18
19   /* if Sunday decrement 2 days */
20   if end_day = 1 then bl_day_mo + (-2);
21      /* if Saturday decrement 1 */
22      else if end_day = 7 then bl_day_mo + (-1);
23
24   put bf_day_mo weekdate22.  bl_day_mo weekdate22. ;
25 end;
26 run;
```

OUTPUT:
```
First Biz Day of Month    Last Biz Day of Month
=============================================

     Tue, Jan 1, 2019    Thu, Jan 31, 2019
     Fri, Feb 1, 2019    Thu, Feb 28, 2019
     Fri, Mar 1, 2019    Fri, Mar 29, 2019
```

```
Mon, Apr 1, 2019      Tue, Apr 30, 2019
Wed, May 1, 2019      Fri, May 31, 2019
Mon, Jun 3, 2019      Fri, Jun 28, 2019
Mon, Jul 1, 2019      Wed, Jul 31, 2019
Thu, Aug 1, 2019      Fri, Aug 30, 2019
Mon, Sep 2, 2019      Mon, Sep 30, 2019
Tue, Oct 1, 2019      Thu, Oct 31, 2019
Fri, Nov 1, 2019      Fri, Nov 29, 2019
Mon, Dec 2, 2019      Tue, Dec 31, 2019
```

The beg_day variable returns the ordinal for week day representing the first of the month, and the end_day variable returns the ordinal for week day representing the last of the month.

The IF-THEN/ELSE block uses the beg_day and end_day variables to determine if the date falls on a Saturday. In the case where it is the beginning of the month, we add two (2) days to shift to the following Monday. And in the case where it is month end, we decrement by one (1) day to shift to the preceding Friday.

Similarly we need logic for detecting if a date falls on a Sunday. In the case where it is the beginning of the month, we add one (1) day to shift to the following Monday. And in the case where it is the month end, we decrement by two (2) days to shift to the preceding Friday.

Time zone Object

It turns out we can write an entire chapter or even an entire book on time zone related to time and datetime objects. Consider this challenge related to working with any datetime object; on November 4, 2018, clocks in the United States returned to Standard Time. In the US/Eastern time zone, the following events happened:

- 01:00 EDT occurs.

- One hour later, at what would have been 02:00 EDT, clocks are turned back to 01:00 EST.

As a result, every instant between 01:00 and 02:00 occurred twice that day. In that case, if you created a time object in the US/Eastern time zone using the standard datetime library, you were unable to distinguish between the time before and after this transition.

And this is just the beginning of the timeless challenges facing data analysis tasks having datetime values. Generally, time zone offsets occur at 1-hour boundaries from UTC, which is often true, except in cases like India Standard Time which is +5:30 hours UTC. In contrast, New York, in the United States, is -5:00 hours UTC, but only until March 10, 2019, when EST transitions to DST.

As the world around us becomes more instrumented with billions of devices emitting timestamped data needing to be analyzed, the requirement for handling datetime in a time zone "aware" manner becomes more acute.

Naïve and Aware Datetimes

The Python Standard Library for datetime has two types of `date` and `datetime` objects: "naïve" and "aware". Up to this point, the Python `date` and `datetime` examples used in our examples are "naïve", meaning it is up to the program logic to determine the context for what the date and datetime values represent. This is much the same way a calculated linear distance value can be rendered in miles, meters, or kilometers. The benefit of using "naïve" `datetime` types is the simplicity for manipulation and ease of understanding. The downside is they do not have enough information to deal with civil adjustments to times or other shifts in time like those described previously.

In this section we will touch on the Python `timezone` object as means for representing time and datetime objects with an offset from UTC. We also introduce the `pytz` module to provide consistent cross-time zone time and datetime handling. The `pytz` module augments working with "aware" time and `datetime` objects by exposing an interface to the tz database[4] managed by the Internet Corporation for Assigned Names and Numbers, or ICANN. The tz database is a collection of rules for civil time adjustments around the world.

As a general practice, datetime functions and arithmetic should be conducted using the UTC time zone and then converting to the local time zone for human-readable output. No Daylight Savings time occurs in UTC making it a useful time zone for performing datetime arithmetic, not to mention that nearly all scientific datetime measurements use UTC and not the local time zone.

A `datetime` object is "naïve" if its `.tzinfo` attribute returns None. The following examples illustrate the distinctions between "naïve" and "aware" `datetime` objects.

---

[4]https://en.wikipedia.org/wiki/Tz_database

Begin by considering Listing 7-50. Even the simple request for time through a function call needs consideration. As a best practice, an application needing the current time should request the current UTC time. In today's virtualized and cloud-based server environments, requesting the local time is sometimes determined by the physical location of the servers, which themselves are often located in different locations around the world. Calling the datetime utcnow() function to return the current datetime eliminates this uncertainty.

Listing 7-50. Python Naïve and Aware Datetime Objects

```
>>> import datetime as dt
>>>
>>> nl          = '\n'
>>> fmt         = "%Y-%m-%d %H:%M:%S (%Z)"
>>>
>>> dt_local    = dt.datetime.now()
>>> dt_naive    = dt.datetime.utcnow()
>>> dt_aware    = dt.datetime.now(dt.timezone.utc)
>>>
>>> print(nl, 'naive dt_local:    ' , dt_local.strftime(fmt),
...       nl, 'tzinfo for dt_local:' , dt_local.tzinfo,
...       nl,
...       nl, 'naive  dt_naive:   ' , dt_naive.strftime(fmt),
...       nl, 'tzinfo for dt_naive:' , dt_naive.tzinfo,
...       nl,
...       nl, 'aware  dt_aware:   ' , dt_aware.strftime(fmt),
...       nl, 'tzinfo for dt_aware:' , dt_aware.tzinfo)

 naive dt_local:    2019-02-02 18:02:29 ()
 tzinfo for dt_local: None

 naive  dt_naive:   2019-02-02 23:02:30 ()
 tzinfo for dt_naive: None

 aware  dt_aware:   2019-02-02 23:02:30 (UTC)
 tzinfo for dt_aware: UTC
```

In this example, using the Python Standard Library, we make three requests for the current time assigning returned values to datetime objects. The first request calls the datetime.now() method returning the current local time to the "naïve" datetime object dt_local. In this case, the current local time comes from the US Eastern time zone, although the time zone is inferred, since we do not provide one when making the call. The tzinfo attribute value returned from the dt_local object confirms this is a "naïve" datetime by returning None.

The second request uses the datetime.utcnow() method call to return the current time from the UTC time zone and assign it to the dt_naive object. Interestingly, when we request the current time from the UTC time zone, we are returned a "naïve" datetime object. And because both the dt_local and dt_naive objects are "naïve" datetimes, this explains why the request for the time zone value using the (%Z) format directive returns an empty value when printing.

The third request illustrates returning the current UTC time zone and assigning the value to the "aware" dt_aware datetime object calling the datetime.now(dt.timezone.utc) method. In this case, the .tzinfo attribute returns UTC to indicate this datetime object is "aware".

Using the Standard Library, we can convert a "naïve" datetime object to an "aware" datetime object, but only to the UTC time zone by calling the replace() method using the timezone.utc argument. The conversion of a "naïve" to an an "aware" datetime object is illustrated in Listing 7-51.

This example begins by converting the dt_str object to the dt_naive datetime object calling the strptime() method. Next, we call the replace() method to, in effect, replace the None value for the tzinfo attribute of the dt_obj_naive object to UTC and keep the remainder of the datetime object values and assigning results to the dt_obj_aware object.

Listing 7-51. Converting Naïve to Aware Datetime Object

```
>>> from datetime import datetime, timezone
>>>
>>> nl       = '\n'
>>> fmt      = "%Y-%m-%d %H:%M:%S (%Z)"
>>> infmt    = "%Y-%m-%d %H:%M:%S"
>>>
>>> dt_str   = '2019-01-24 12:34:56'
```

```
>>> dt_naive = datetime.strptime(dt_str, infmt )
>>> dt_aware = dt_naive.replace(tzinfo=timezone.utc)
>>>
>>> print(nl, 'dt_naive:              '  , dt_naive.strftime(fmt),
...      nl, 'tzinfo for dt_naive:'  , dt_naive.tzinfo,
...      nl,
...      nl, 'dt_aware:              '  , dt_aware.strftime(fmt),
...      nl, 'tzinfo for dt_aware:'  , dt_aware.tzinfo)
 dt_naive:              2019-01-24 12:34:56 ()
 tzinfo for dt_naive: None

 dt_aware:              2019-01-24 12:34:56 (UTC)
 tzinfo for dt_aware: UTC
```

As a result, the `tzinfo` attribute for the `dt_aware` object returns UTC.

pytz Library

Clearly there are cases where we need to convert "naïve" objects to "aware" objects with time zone attributes other than UTC. And in order to do so, we need to utilize a third-party library such as the widely used pytz library.[5] In Listing 7-52, we convert the datetime string `2019-01-24 12:34:56` having no time zone attribute to an "aware" datetime object for the US Eastern time zone. The pytz library provisions the `timezone()` function which is a method modifying the `tzinfo` attribute of a datetime object with a supplied time zone designation.

Listing 7-52. Python Aware Datetime Object with timezone.localize

```
>>> from datetime import datetime
>>> from pytz import timezone
>>>
>>> nl        = '\n'
>>> in_fmt    = "%Y-%m-%d %H:%M:%S"
>>> fmt       = '%b %d %Y %H:%M:%S (%Z) %z'
```

---

[5]pytz, World Time zone Definitions for Python at http://pytz.sourceforge.net/

```
>>>
>>> dt_str   = '2019-01-24 12:34:56'
>>> dt_naive = datetime.strptime(dt_str, in_fmt)
>>> dt_est   = timezone('US/Eastern').localize(dt_naive)
>>>
>>> print(nl, 'dt_naive:              ' , dt_naive.strftime(fmt),
...        nl, 'tzino for dt_naive:' , dt_naive.tzinfo,
...        nl,
...        nl, 'datetime dt_est:   ' , dt_est.strftime(fmt),
...        nl, 'tzinfo for dt_est: ' , dt_est.tzinfo)
 dt_naive:           Jan 24 2019 12:34:56 ()
 tzino for dt_naive: None

 datetime dt_est:    Jan 24 2019 12:34:56 (EST) -0500
 tzinfo for dt_est:  US/Eastern
```

In this example, we create the "aware" datetime object from a datetime string. The syntax

```
dt_est = timezone('US/Eastern').localize(dt_naive)
```

creates the dt_est "aware" datetime object by calling the pytz timezone() function which has the effect of setting this object's tzinfo attribute to "US/Eastern". The localize() method is chained to this call to convert the "naïve" dt_naive datetime object to an "aware" object. The localize() method takes into account the transition to Daylight Savings time.

Before we go further, the question naturally arising is where to find the list of valid time zone values. Fortunately, the pytz library provides data structures to return this information. One structure is the common_timezones which is returned as a Python list, illustrated in Listing 7-53. At the time of this writing, it returns 439 valid time zone values available to the timezone() function.

Listing 7-53. Random pytz Common Time zone

```
>>> import random
>>> from pytz import common_timezones
>>> print('\n', len(common_timezones), 'entries in the common_timezone
list', '\n')
```

439 entries in the common_timezone list

```
>>> print('\n'.join(random.sample(common_timezones, 10)))
America/Martinique
America/Costa_Rica
Asia/Ust-Nera
Asia/Dhaka
Africa/Mogadishu
America/Maceio
America/St_Barthelemy
Pacific/Bougainville
America/Blanc-Sablon
America/New_York
```

In this example, we return a random sample of ten time zone values from the common_timezones list. Another source of time zone values is the all_timezones list which is an exhaustive list of time zone available to the pytz timezone() function.

Yet another useful list is the country_timezones. By supplying an ISO 3166[6] two-letter country code, the time zone in use by the country is returned. Listing 7-54 illustrates returning the Swiss time zone from this list.

Listing 7-54. pytz country_timezones List

```
>>> import pytz
>>> print('\n'.join(pytz.country_timezones['ch']))
Europe/Zurich
```

Even better is the country_timezones() function which accepts the ISO 3166 two-letter country code and returns the time zone in use by the country as illustrated in Listing 7-55.

Listing 7-55. pytz country_timezones() Function

```
>>> from pytz import country_timezones
>>>
>>> print('\n'.join(country_timezones('ru')))
```

---

[6]https://en.wikipedia.org/wiki/List_of_ISO_3166_country_codes

```
Europe/Kaliningrad
Europe/Moscow
Europe/Simferopol
Europe/Volgograd
Europe/Kirov
Europe/Astrakhan
Europe/Saratov
Europe/Ulyanovsk
Europe/Samara
Asia/Yekaterinburg
Asia/Omsk
Asia/Novosibirsk
Asia/Barnaul
Asia/Tomsk
Asia/Novokuznetsk
Asia/Krasnoyarsk
Asia/Irkutsk
Asia/Chita
Asia/Yakutsk
Asia/Khandyga
Asia/Vladivostok
Asia/Ust-Nera
Asia/Magadan
Asia/Sakhalin
Asia/Srednekolymsk
Asia/Kamchatka
Asia/Anadyr
```

Returning to the pytz `timezone()` function, let's look at additional examples and pitfalls to avoid.

In Listing 7-51, we used the datetime `replace()` method to replace the `tzinfo` attribute with UTC returning a `datetime` "aware" object. So what happens when you use this approach with the pytz library? Listing 7-56 illustrates the pitfall of using the datetime `replace()` method with a time zone from the pytz library. Unfortunately, calling the datetime `replace()` function with a tzinfo argument from the pytz library does not work.

Listing 7-56. pytz Interaction with tzinfo Attribute

```
>>> from datetime import datetime, timedelta
>>> from pytz import timezone
>>> import pytz
>>>
>>> nl        = '\n'
>>> fmt       = "%Y-%m-%d %H:%M:%S (%Z) %z"
>>>
>>> new_york = timezone('US/Eastern')
>>> shanghai = timezone('Asia/Shanghai')
>>>
>>> dt_loc    = new_york.localize(datetime(2018, 12, 23, 13, 0, 0))
>>> dt_sha    = dt_loc.replace(tzinfo=shanghai)
>>> tm_diff   = dt_loc - dt_sha
>>> tm_bool   = dt_loc == dt_sha
>>>
>>> print(nl, 'dt_loc datetime: ' , dt_loc.strftime(fmt),
...       nl, 'dt_loc tzinfo:   ' , dt_loc.tzinfo,
...       nl,
...       nl, 'dt_sha datetime: ' , dt_sha.strftime(fmt),
...       nl, 'dt_sha tzinfo:   ' , dt_sha.tzinfo,
...       nl,
...       nl, 'Time Difference: ' ,tm_diff)
...       nl, 'dt_loc == dt_sha:' , tm_bool)
dt_loc datetime: 2018-12-23 13:00:00 (EST) -0500
dt_loc tzinfo:   US/Eastern

dt_sha datetime: 2018-12-23 13:00:00 (LMT) +0806
dt_sha tzinfo:   Asia/Shanghai

Time Difference: 13:06:00
dt_loc == dt_sha: False
```

In this case, the dt_sha object is an "aware" object, but returns the Local Mean Time (LMT) with a time difference between New York and Shanghai of 13 hours and 6 minutes. Obviously, if both times are the same times represented by different time zone, there is no time difference.

In order to properly convert a time from one time zone to another, use the datetime astimezone() method instead. The astimezone() method returns an "aware" datetime object adjusting date and time to UTC time and reporting it in the local time zone. Consider Listing 7-57.

Listing 7-57. Datetime astimezone() Conversion Function

```
>>> from datetime import datetime, timedelta
>>> from pytz import timezone
>>> import pytz
>>>
>>> nl        = '\n'
>>> fmt       = "%Y-%m-%d %H:%M:%S (%Z) %z"
>>> new_york = timezone('US/Eastern')
>>> shanghai = timezone('Asia/Shanghai')
>>>
>>> dt_loc   = new_york.localize(datetime(2018, 12, 23, 13, 0, 0))
>>>
>>> dt_sha2  = dt_loc.astimezone(shanghai)
>>> tm_diff  = dt_loc - dt_sha2
>>> tm_bool  = dt_loc == dt_sha2
>>>
>>> print(nl, 'dt_loc datetime: '  , dt_loc.strftime(fmt),
...        nl, 'dt_sha2 datetime:' , dt_sha2.strftime(fmt),
...        nl,
...        nl, 'Time Difference: ' , tm_diff,
...        nl, 'dt_loc == dt_sha2:' , tm_bool)

 dt_loc datetime:  2018-12-23 13:00:00 (EST) -0500
 dt_sha2 datetime: 2018-12-24 02:00:00 (CST) +0800

 Time Difference:  0:00:00
 dt_loc == dt_sha2: True
```

If you need to do datetime manipulation using local datetimes, you must use the normalize() method in order to properly handle Daylight Savings and Standard Time transitions. Consider Listing 7-58 where the object dt_loc calls the localize() method to create a datetime object for 1:00 am, November 4, 2018, which is the US transition date and time from Daylight Savings to Standard Time.

Listing 7-58. Handling DST Transition

```
>>> from datetime import datetime, timedelta
>>> from pytz import timezone
>>> import pytz
>>>
>>> nl        = '\n'
>>> fmt       = "%Y-%m-%d %H:%M:%S (%Z) %z"
>>> new_york  = timezone('US/Eastern')
>>>
>>> dt_loc    = new_york.localize(datetime(2018, 11, 4, 1, 0, 0))
>>> minus_ten = dt_loc - timedelta(minutes=10)
>>>
>>> before    = new_york.normalize(minus_ten)
>>> after     = new_york.normalize(before + timedelta(minutes=20))
>>>
>>> print(nl, 'before:' , before.strftime(fmt),
...        nl, 'after: ' , after.strftime(fmt))

 before: 2018-11-04 01:50:00 (EDT) -0400
 after:  2018-11-04 01:10:00 (EST) -0500
```

The before datetime object is created using the normalize() method to subtract a Timedelta of 10 minutes from the dt_loc datetime object returning a datetime for Eastern Daylight Time. And by adding a Timedelta of 20 minutes to the before datetime object, it returns a datetime for Eastern Standard Time.

Nonetheless, the preferred way of handling datetime manipulation is to first convert datetimes to the UTC time zone, perform the manipulation, and then convert back to the local time zone for publishing results. This recommendation is illustrated in Listing 7-59. This example illustrates the problem of finding a duration between two datetimes when the duration includes the transition date from Daylight Savings to Standard Time.

We start by calling the localize() method to create the tm_end datetime object and subtract a Timedelta of one (1) week to create the tm_start_est datetime object. The datetime manipulation logic is straightforward and yet, notice, however, the tzinfo attribute for the tm_start_est object returns Eastern Standard Time, instead of correctly returning Eastern Daylight Time. This is displayed calling the first print() function in the program.

Listing 7-59. Convert to UTC for Datetime Arithmetic

```
>>> nl            = '\n'
>>> fmt           = "%Y-%m-%d %H:%M:%S (%Z) %z"
>>> new_york      = timezone('US/Eastern')
>>>
>>> tm_end        = new_york.localize(datetime(2018, 11, 8, 0, 0, 0))
>>>
>>> tm_start_est = tm_end - timedelta(weeks=1)
>>>
>>> print(nl, 'Datetime arithmetic using local time zone',
...       nl, 'tm_start_est: ' , tm_start_est.strftime(fmt),
...       nl, 'tm_end:       ' , tm_end.strftime(fmt))

 Datetime arithmetic using local time zone
 tm_start_est:  2018-11-01 00:00:00 (EST) -0500
 tm_end:        2018-11-08 00:00:00 (EST) -0500
>>>
... tm_end_utc    = tm_end.astimezone(pytz.utc)
>>>
>>> tm_delta_utc = tm_end_utc - timedelta(weeks=1)
>>>
>>> tm_start_edt = tm_delta_utc.astimezone(new_york)
>>>
>>> print(nl, 'Datetime arithmetic using UTC time zone',
...       nl, 'tm_start_edt: ' , tm_start_edt.strftime(fmt),
...       nl, 'tm_end :      ' , tm_end.strftime(fmt))

 Datetime arithmetic using UTC time zone
 tm_start_edt:  2018-11-01 01:00:00 (EDT) -0400
 tm_end :       2018-11-08 00:00:00 (EST) -0500
```

The preferred approach to solving this problem is to convert the tm_end datetime object to the UTC time zone, subtract a Timedelta of one (1) week, and then convert the new datetime object back to the US Eastern time zone. These steps are accomplished with the syntax

```
tm_end_utc = tm_end.astimezone(pytz.utc)

tm_delta_utc = tm_end_utc - timedelta(weeks=1)

tm_start_edt = tm_delta_utc.astimezone(new_york)
```

Now the correct start datetime is returned from the tm_start_edt object as shown by calling the second print() function in the program.

SAS Time zone

As we have seen, Python handles time zone for datetime objects by assigning values to the tzinfo attribute, which is a component of the datetime object itself. The SAS implementation for time zone is handled by setting options for the execution environment using the SAS System option TIMEZONE. Unless otherwise set, the default value is blank (ASCII 32) indicating that SAS uses the time zone value called from the underlying operating system. In this case, a PC running Windows 10 with the time zone set to US Eastern.

Listing 7-60 illustrates calling PROC OPTIONS to return the current value for the TIMEZONE options. Beginning with release 9.4, SAS implemented a Series of time zone options and functions, one of which is the TZONENAME function returning the local time zone in effect for the SAS execution environment. In this example, it returns a blank indicating the SAS TIMEZONE option is not set. Some SAS environment may have this option set as a restricted option and cannot be overridden.

Listing 7-60. SAS Time Zone Option

```
4   proc options option=timezone;
5   run;

    SAS (r) Proprietary Software Release 9.4   TS1M5

 TIMEZONE=          Specifies a time zone.

6
7  data _null_;
8     local_dt = datetime();
9     tz_name  = tzonename();
10     put 'Default Local Datetime: ' local_dt e8601LX. /
11          'Default Timezone:       ' tz_name;
12  run;
```

OUTPUT:
```
Default Local Datetime:   2019-02-04T10:54:52-05:00
Default Timezone:
```

Despite the fact an explicit SAS TIMEZONE option is not in effect, calling the DATETIME function returns a datetime representing the local time for the Eastern US. This is indicated by using the SAS-supplied, ISO 8601 e8601LX. datetime format which writes the datetime and appends the time zone difference between the local time and UTC. ISO 8601 is an international standard for representing dates, time, and interval values. SAS supports basic and extended ISO 8601 date, time, datetime, and interval values.

Setting the SAS TIMEZONE option impacts the behaviors of these datetime functions:

- DATE
- DATETIME
- TIME
- TODAY

Also impacted by the SAS TIMEZONE options are these SAS time zone functions:

- TZONEOFF
- TZONEID
- TZONENAME
- TZONES2U
- TZONEU2S

And the following time zone related formats are impacted:

- B8601DXw.
- E8601DXw.
- B8601LXw.
- E8601LXw.
- B8601TXw.
- E8601TXw.

- NLDATMZw.

- NLDATMTZw.

- NLDATMWZw.

We need to understand the behavior of the TIMEZONE option and its interactions with the aforementioned functions and formats since datetime values can be altered in unforeseen ways. Let's begin by considering Listing 7-61 covering the TIMEZONE-related functions.[7] The TZONEID, TZONENAME, TZONEDSTNAME, and TZONESTTNAME functions return strings representing the time zone ID, Name, time zone Daylight Savings Name, and time zone Standard Time name. The TZONEOFF, TZONESTTOFF, and TZONEDSTOFF functions return numerics representing the local time zone offset from UTC, the local UTC offset when standard time is in effect, and the UTC offset when Daylight Savings is in effect. In cases where Daylight Savings is not observed, for example, China, the TZONEDTNAME function returns a blank and the TZONEDSTOFF returns missing (.).

Listing 7-61. SAS Time zone Functions

```
4   options tz='America/New_York';
5
6   data _null_;
7       tz_ny_id        = tzoneid();
8       tz_ny_name      = tzonename();
9       tz_ny_dst_name  = tzonedstname();
10      tz_ny_st_name   = tzonesttname();
11      tz_ny_off       = tzoneoff();
12      tz_ny_off_dst   = tzonesttoff();
13      tz_ny_off_st    = tzonedstoff();
14
15  put 'TZ ID:                  ' tz_ny_id        /
16      'TZ Name:                ' tz_ny_name      /
17      'Daylight Savings Name:  ' tz_ny_dst_name  /
18      'Standard Time Name:     ' tz_ny_st_name   //
```

---

[7]SAS 9.4 National Language Support (NLS): Reference Guide, 5th Edition at https://documentation.sas.com/?docsetId=nlsref&docsetTarget=n1tj735aocxmw7n1kfoz1q pdvb91.htm&docsetVersion=9.4&locale=en

```
19      'TZ Offset from UTC:     ' tz_ny_off      /
20      'TZ DST Offset from UTC ' tz_ny_off_st    /
21      'TZ STD Offset from UTC ' tz_ny_off_dst   /;
22 run;
```

OUTPUT:

```
TZ ID:                  AMERICA/NEW_YORK
TZ Name:                EST
Daylight Savings Name: EDT
Standard Time Name:     EST

TZ Offset from UTC:     -18000
TZ DST Offset from UTC -14400
TZ STD Offset from UTC -18000
```

We can use the TZONEOFF function to find the time difference between time zone, which is illustrated in Listing 7-62. Since time zone offsets west of the prime meridian (the location for UTC) are negative and those east are positive, we take the difference between the UTC offsets and take the absolute value.

Listing 7-62. SAS Time Zone Differences

```
4 options tz=";
5
6 data _null_;
7
8   local_utc_offset = tzoneoff();
9   dn_frm_utc       = tzoneoff('America/Denver');
10  mo_frm_utc       = tzoneoff('Africa/Mogadishu');
11
12  diff_tz_hr       = abs((dn_frm_utc) - (mo_frm_utc)) / 3600;
13
14  put 'Denver UTC Offset:    ' dn_frm_utc    /
15      'Mogadishu UTC Offset: ' mo_frm_utc    /
16      'Timezone Difference:  ' diff_tz_hr ' Hours' //
17      'Local UTC Offset:     ' local_utc_offset;
18  run;
```

OUTPUT:
```
Denver UTC Offset:  -25200
Mogadishu UTC Offset: 10800
Timezone Difference:  10  Hours

Local UTC Offset:     -18000
```

And regardless of whether an instance of SAS has the TIMEZONE option explicitly set, or is implied, the TZONEOFF function always returns the number of seconds between the local time zone (which is obtained from the OS when not explicitly set) and UTC. In this case, the local UTC offset is for the Eastern US. As we shall see subsequently, the TZONEOFF function automatically takes into account transitions from Daylight Savings and Standard Time.

Consider Listing 7-63 to understand how datetimes are written and subsequently read with different TIMEZONE options in effect. This example creates a SAS datetime with the TIMEZONE option set for the US Eastern time zone and subsequently changed to create another datetime in the Shanghai, Asia time zone. The SAS TIMEZONE option, alias TZ, is set by supplying either a time zone ID or time zone name. This program executes three Data Steps. The first Data Step does the following:

- Sets the TIMEZONE option to 'America/New_York'

- Creates the NY dataset with two variables:

  - ny_dt initialized by calling the DATETIME function returning the local time for this time zone

  - ny_tz created by calling the TZONENAME function returning the time zone id in effect, in this example, EST, for Eastern Standard Time

- Uses the PUT statement to write these values to the log.

The second Data Step performs similar logic:

- Sets the TIMEZONE option set to 'Asia/Shanghai'

- Creates the sha dataset with two variables:

  - sha_dt initialized by calling the DATETIME function returning the local time for this time zone

  - sha_tz created by calling the TZONENAME function returning the time zone id in effect, in this example, CST, for China Standard Time

- Uses the PUT statement to write these values to the log.

367

The third Data Step sets the TIMEZONE option to 'America/New_York', merges the ny and sha datasets, calculates the time difference between the time zone, and uses the PUT statement to write these datetime values to the SAS log.

Listing 7-63. Setting SAS Time zone Option

```
4 %let dt_fmt = dateampm.;
5
6 options tz='America/New_York';
7    data ny;
8    ny_dt = datetime();
9    ny_tz = tzonename();
10
11 put 'Time Zone in Effect: ' ny_tz /
12     'Local Date Time:     ' ny_dt &dt_fmt;
13 run;
```

OUTPUT:
```
Time Zone in Effect: EST
Local Date Time:      05FEB19:03:24:08 PM
```

NOTE: The dataset WORK.NY has 1 observations and 2 variables.

```
14
15 options tz='Asia/Shanghai';
16 data sha;
17    sha_dt = datetime();
18    sha_tz = tzonename();
19
20 put 'Time Zone in Effect: ' sha_tz /
21     'Local Date Time:     ' sha_dt &dt_fmt;
22 run;
```

OUTPUT:
```
Time Zone in Effect: CST
Local Date Time:      06FEB19:04:24:08 AM
```

```
NOTE: The dataset WORK.SHA has 1 observations and 2 variables.
23
24 options tz='America/New_York';
25 data both;
26    merge ny
27          sha;
diff_tz = abs(tzoneoff('America/New_york', ny_dt) -
28                  tzoneoff('Asia/Shanghai', sha_dt)) /3600;
29
30 put 'New York Datetime Read:     ' ny_dt    &dt_fmt  /
31    'Shanghai Datetime Read:     ' sha_dt  &dt_fmt / /
32 'Time Difference NY and SHANGHAI: ' diff_tz ' Hours';
33 run;
```

OUTPUT:
```
New York Datetime Read:       05FEB19:03:24:08 PM
Shanghai Datetime Read:       06FEB19:04:24:08 AM
Time Difference NY and SHANGHAI: 12   Hours
```

The first thing to notice is how values returned by the DATETIME function are a function of the TIMEZONE option in effect. Secondly, writing datetime values created with one TIMEZONE option in effect and subsequently reading them using a different TIMEZONE option does not alter the values.

Which then raises the question of converting SAS datetimes written with a TIMEZONE option in effect to datetimes for another time zone? One approach is to utilize the TZONEOFF function together with the INTNX function illustrated in Listing 7-64. The purpose of this example is to illustrate datetime conversions using the INTCK function to shift datetimes based on time zone offsets.

Listing 7-64 executes two Data Steps. The first Data Step does the following:

- Sets the TIMEZONE option to 'Asia/Shanghai'

- Creates the sha dataset with one variable:

  - sha_dt_loc initialized with a DO/END block creating two datetime values of midnight November 3 and 4 local time. The BY value 86400 is the number of seconds in a day, returning two datetimes.

The second Data Step

- Sets the TIMEZONE option set to 'Asia/Shanghai'
- Creates these variables:

  - ny_utc calling the TZONEOFF function to find the datetime's Eastern time zone offset from UTC in seconds. Dividing this value by 3600 converts to hours. This variable is for illustration and not used in a calculation.

  - sha_utc calling the TZONEOFF function to find the datetime's Shanghai time zone offset from UTC in seconds. Dividing this value by 3600 converts to hours. This variable is for illustration and not used in a calculation.

  - diff_tz calling the TZONEOFF function twice, in order to find the difference of the Eastern time zone offset and the Shanghai offset. Since returned offsets can be negative, we take the absolute value.

  - sha_2_ny_tm calling the INTNX function to convert the datetime from the Shanghai time zone to the US Eastern time zone where with these four parameters:

    1. 'seconds' indicates the interval used to shift the datetime value.

    2. sha_dt_loc is the datetime variable to be shifted. Its value was created with the TIMEZONE option set for Shanghai.

    3. diff_tz variable contains the number of seconds the sha_dt_loc variable is to be shifted.

    4. 'same' is the optional alignment parameter, in this case, aligned for midnight for each datetime value.

  - diff_tz_hr to convert is the diff_tz variable from seconds to hours. This variable is for illustration and not used in a calculation.

Listing 7-64. SAS Time zone Conversions

```
4 %let dt_fmt = dateampm.;
5
6 options tz='Asia/Shanghai';
7 data sha;
8    do sha_dt_loc = '03Nov2019:00:00'dt to
9                    '04Nov2019:00:00'dt by 86400;
10       output;
11       put 'Shanghai Datetime Local:  ' sha_dt_loc &dt_fmt;
12    end;
13 run;
```

OUTPUT:

```
Shanghai Datetime Local:   03NOV19:12:00:00 AM
Shanghai Datetime Local:   04NOV19:12:00:00 AM

NOTE: The dataset WORK.SHA has 2 observations and 1 variables.

14   options tz='America/New_York';
15   data ny;
16      set sha;
17
18   ny_utc      = tzoneoff('America/New_york',
     sha_dt_loc)/3600;
19   sha_utc     = tzoneoff('Asia/Shanghai', sha_dt_loc)/3600;
20
21 diff_tz     = abs(tzoneoff('America/New_york', sha_dt_loc) -
22              tzoneoff('Asia/Shanghai', sha_dt_loc)) ;
23
24 sha_2_ny_tm = intnx('seconds', sha_dt_loc, diff_tz, 'same');
25
26 diff_tz_hr  = diff_tz / 3600;
27
28 put 'Sha Local DT Read:   ' sha_dt_loc   &dt_fmt /
29     'Sha DT to NY DT:     ' sha_2_ny_tm  &dt_fmt /
```

```
30       'Time zone Difference: ' diff_tz_hr /
31       'New York UTC Offset:  ' ny_utc /
32       'Shanghai UTC Offset:  ' sha_utc //;
33
34 run;
```

OUTPUT:

```
Sha Local DT Read:     03NOV19:12:00:00 AM
Sha DT to NY DT:       03NOV19:12:00:00 PM
Time zone Difference: 12
New York UTC Offset:   -4
Shanghai UTC Offset:   8

Sha Local DT Read:     04NOV19:12:00:00 AM
Sha DT to NY DT:       04NOV19:01:00:00 PM
Time zone Difference: 13
New York UTC Offset:   -5
Shanghai UTC Offset:   8
```

The dates chosen for this example illustrate the behavior of the TZONEOFF function when dealing with datetime values that include transition dates from Daylight Savings to Standard Time in the Eastern time zone.

Summary

As more data comes from a highly instrumented world, analysis tasks will need to effectively deal with datetime data. In this chapter we discussed dates, times, and datetimes relevant to many data analysis tasks. Understanding how the Python Standard Library handles datetimes provides a foundation for understanding how the pandas Library processes dates. We also detailed how to effectively deal with dates and datetimes across time zone.

CHAPTER 8

SASPy Module

In this chapter we discuss the open source SASPy module contributed by SAS Institute. SASPy exposes Python APIs to the SAS System. This module allows a Python session to do the following:

- From within a Python session start and connect to a local or remote SAS session

- Enable bi-directional transfer of values between SAS variables and Python objects

- Enable bi-directional exchange of data between pandas DataFrames and SAS datasets

- Enable bi-directional exchange of SAS Macro variables and Python objects

- Integrate SAS and Python program logic within a single execution context executing interactively or in batch (scripted) mode

To get started, you need to take the following steps:

- Install the SASPy module.

- Set up the sascfg_personal.py configuration file.

- Make SAS-supplied Java .jar files available to SASPy.

Install SASPy

On Windows, to install SASPy, issue the following command in a Windows terminal session:

```
python -m pip install saspy
```

373

© Randy Betancourt, Sarah Chen 2019
R. Betancourt and S. Chen, *Python for SAS Users*, https://doi.org/10.1007/978-1-4842-5001-3_8

The installation process downloads any SASPy and any of its dependent packages. Listing 8-1 displays the output from a Windows terminal for installing SASPy.

Listing 8-1. SASPy Install on Windows

```
c:\>python -m pip install saspy
Collecting saspy
  Downloading https://files.pythonhosted.org/packages/bb/07/3fd96b969959ef0
e701e5764f6a239e7bea543b37d2d7a81acb23ed6a0c5/saspy-2.2.9.tar.gz (97kB)
      100% |                                                | 102kB 769kB/s
Successfully built saspy
distributed 1.21.8 requires msgpack, which is not installed.
Installing collected packages: saspy
Successfully installed saspy-2.2.9
```

You should see the statement

```
Successfully installed saspy-2.2.9
```

Set Up the sascfg_personal.py Configuration File

After completing installation, the next step is to modify the saspy.SAScfg file to establish which access method Python uses to connect to a SAS session.

In this example, we configure an IOM (integrated object model) connection method so that the Python session running on Windows connects to a SAS session running on the same Windows machine. If you have a different setup, for example, running Python on Windows and connecting to a SAS session executing on Linux, you use the STDIO access method. The detailed instructions are at

```
https://sassoftware.github.io/saspy/install.html#configuration
```

For this step, begin by locating the saspy.SAScfg configuration file. Listing 8-2 illustrates the Python syntax needed to locate the SASPy configuration file.

Listing 8-2. Locate saspy.SAScfg Configuration File

```
>>> import saspy
>>> saspy.SAScfg
<module 'saspy.sascfg' from 'C:\\Users\\randy\\Anaconda3\\lib\\site-
packages\\saspy\\sascfg.py'>
```

As a best practice, you should copy the `sascfg.py` configuration file to `sascfg_personal.py`. Doing so ensures that any configuration changes will not be overwritten when subsequent versions of SASPy are installed later. The `sascfg_personal.py` can be stored anywhere on the filesystem. If it is stored outside the Python repo, then you must always include the fully qualified pathname to the SASsession argument like

```
sas = SASSession(cfgfile='C:\\qualified\\path\\sascfg_personal.py)
```

Alternatively, if the `sascfg_personal.py` configuration file is found in the search path defined by the PYTHONPATH environment variable, then you can avoid having to supply this argument when invoking SASPy. Use the Python `sys.path` statement to return the search path defined by the PYTHONPATH environment variable as shown in Listing 8-3.

Listing 8-3. Finding the PYTHONPATH Search Paths

```
>>> import sys
>>> sys.path
['', 'C:\\Users\\randy\\Anaconda3\\python36.zip', 'C:\\Users\\randy\\
Anaconda3\\DLLs', 'C:\\Users\\randy\\Anaconda3\\lib', 'C:\\Users\\randy\\
Anaconda3', 'C:\\Users\\randy\\Anaconda3\\lib\\site-packages', 'C:\\
Users\\randy\\Anaconda3\\lib\\site-packages\\win32', 'C:\\Users\\randy\\
Anaconda3\\lib\\site-packages\\win32\\lib', 'C:\\Users\\randy\\Anaconda3\\
lib\\site-packages\\Pythonwin', 'C:\\Users\\randy\\Anaconda3\\lib\\site-
packages\\IPython\\extensions']
```

In our case, we select to store the `sascfg_personal.py` configuration file in the same directory as the `sascfg.py` configuration file.

Copy

```
C:/Users/randy/Anaconda3/lib/site-packages/saspy/sascfg.py
```

to

```
C:/Users/randy/Anaconda3/lib/site-packages/saspy /personal_sascfg.py
```

375

Depending on how you connect the Python environment to the SAS session determines the changes needed in the `sascfg_personal.py` configuration file.

In our case, both the Python and SAS execution environments are on the same Windows 10 machine. Accordingly, we modify the following sections of the `sascfg_personal.py` configuration file:

From the original sascfg.py configuration file

```
SAS_config_names=['default']
```

is changed in the `sascfg_personal.py` configuration file to

```
SAS_config_names=['winlocal']
```

Make SAS-Supplied .jar Files Available

The following four Java .jar files are needed by SASPy and are defined by the `classpath` variable in the `sascfg_personal.py` configuration file

```
sas.svc.connection.jar
log4j.jar
sas.security.sspi.jar
sas.core.jar
```

These four .jar files are part of the existing SAS deployment. Depending on where SAS is installed on Windows, the path will be something like

```
C:\Program Files\SASHome\SASDeploymentManager\9.4\products\
deploywiz__94498__prt__xx__sp0__1\deploywiz\<required_jar_file_names.jar>
```

A fifth .jar file which is distributed with the SASPy repo, `saspyiom.jar` needs to be defined as part of the `classpath` variable in the `sascfg_personal.py` configuration file as well. In our case this jar file is located at

```
C:/Users/randy/Anaconda3/Lib/site-packages/saspy/java
```

Once you have confirmed the location of these five .jar files, modify the `sascfg_personal.py` file similar to Listing 8-4. Be sure to modify the paths specific to your environment.

Listing 8-4. CLASSPATH Variable for Windows SAScfg_personal.py File

```
# build out a local classpath variable to use below for Windows clients

cpW  =  "C:\\Program Files\\SASHome\\SASDeploymentManager\\9.4\\products\\
deploywiz__94498__prt__xx__sp0__1\\deploywiz\\sas.svc.connection.jar"

cpW += ";C:\\Program Files\\SASHome\\SASDeploymentManager\\9.4\\products\\
deploywiz__94498__prt__xx__sp0__1\\deploywiz\\log4j.jar"

cpW += ";C:\\Program Files\\SASHome\\SASDeploymentManager\\9.4\\products\\
deploywiz__94498__prt__xx__sp0__1\\deploywiz\\sas.security.sspi.jar"

cpW += ";C:\\Program Files\\SASHome\\SASDeploymentManager\\9.4\\products\\
deploywiz__94498__prt__xx__sp0__1\\deploywiz\\sas.core.jar"

cpW += ";C:\\Users\\randy\\Anaconda3\\Lib\\site-packages\\saspy\\java\\
saspyiom.jar"
```

Update the Dictionary values for the `winlocal` object definition in the `sascfg_personal.py` configuration file similar to Listing 8-5.

Listing 8-5. winlocal Definition for sascfg_personal.py Configuration File

```
winlocal = {'java'  : 'C:\\Program Files\\SASHome\\
SASPrivateJavaRuntimeEnvironment\\9.4\\jre\\bin\\java',
            'encoding'  : 'windows-1252',
            'classpath' : cpW
            }
```

SASPy has a dependency on Java 7 which is met by relying on the SAS Private JRE distributed and installed with SAS software. The SAS Private JRE is part of the existing SAS software installation. Also notice the path filename uses double backslashes to "escape" the backslash needed by the Windows pathnames. There is one final requirement. The 'sspiauth.dll file–also included in the SAS installation–must be a part of the system PATH environment variable, java.library.path, or in the home directory of the Java client. Search for this file in your SAS deployment, though it is likely in SASHome\SASFoundation\9.4\core\sasext.

SASPy Examples

With the configuration for SASPy complete, we can begin exploring its capabilities. The goal for these examples is to illustrate the ease by which DataFrame and SAS datasets can be interchanged along with calling Python or SAS methods to act on these data assets. We start with Listing 8-6 to integrate a Python and SAS session together.

Listing 8-6. Start SASPy Session

```
>>> import pandas as pd
>>> import saspy
>>> import numpy as np
>>> from IPython.display import HTML
>>>
>>> sas = saspy.SASsession(cfgname='winlocal', results='TEXT')
SAS Connection established. Subprocess id is 5288
```

In this example, the Python sas object is created by calling the saspy.SASsession() method. The saspy.SASsession() object is the main object for connecting a Python session with a SAS sub-process. Most of the arguments to the SASsession object are set in the sascfg_personal.py configuration file discussed at the beginning of this chapter.

In this example, there are two arguments, cfgname= and results=. The cfgname= argument points to the winlocal configuration values in the sascfg_personal. py configuration file indicating both the Python and the SAS session run locally on Windows. The results= argument has three possible values to indicate how tabular output returned from the SASsession object, that is, the execution results from SAS, is rendered. They are

- pandas, the default value

- TEXT, which is useful when running SASPy in batch mode

- HTML, which is useful when running SASPy interactively from a Jupyter notebook

Another useful saspy.SASsession() argument is autoexec=. In some cases, it is useful to execute a Series of SAS statements when the saspy.SASsession() method is called and before any SAS statements are executed by the user program. This feature is illustrated in Listing 8-7.

Listing 8-7. Start SASPy with Autoexec Processing

```
>>> auto_execsas="'libname sas_data "c:\data";"'
>>>
>>> sas = saspy.SASsession(cfgname='winlocal', results='TEXT',
autoexec=auto_execsas)
SAS Connection established. Subprocess id is 15020
```

In this example, we create the `auto_execsas` object by defining a Python Docstring containing the SAS statements used as the statements for the autoexec process to execute. Similar to the behavior for the traditional SAS autoexec processing, the statements defined by the `auto_execsas` object are executed by SAS before executing any subsequent SAS input statements.

To illustrate the integration between Python and SAS using SASPy, we begin by building the `loandf` DataFrame which is sourced from the LendingClub loan statistics described at

```
https://www.lendingclub.com/info/download-data.action
```

This data consists of anonymized loan performance measures from LendingClub which offers personal loans to individuals. We begin by creating the `loandf` DataFrame illustrated in Listing 8-8.

Listing 8-8. Build loandf DataFrame

```
>>> url = "https://raw.githubusercontent.com/RandyBetancourt/
PythonForSASUsers/master/data/LC_Loan_Stats.csv"
>>>
... loandf = pd.read_csv(url,
...      low_memory=False,
...      usecols=(0, 1, 2, 3, 4, 5, 6, 7, 8, 9, 10, 12, 13, 15, 16),
...      names=('id',
...              'mem_id',
...              'ln_amt',
...              'term',
...              'rate',
...              'm_pay',
...              'grade',
...              'sub_grd',
```

```
...                'emp_len',
...                'own_rnt',
...                'income',
...                'ln_stat',
...                'purpose',
...                'state',
...                'dti'),
...         skiprows=1,
...         nrows=39786,
...         header=None)
>>> loandf.shape
(39786, 15)
```

The loandf DataFrame contains 39,786 rows and 15 columns.

Basic Data Wrangling

In order to effectively analyze the loandf DataFrame, we must do a bit of data wrangling. Listing 8-9 returns basic information about the columns and values.

Listing 8-9. loandf Initial Attributes

```
loandf.info()
loandf.describe(include=['O'])
```

The df.describe() method accepts the include=['O'] argument in order to return descriptive information for all columns whose data type is object. Output from the df. describe() method is shown in a Jupyter notebook in Figure 8-1.

```
loandf.info()
```

```
<class 'pandas.core.frame.DataFrame'>
RangeIndex: 39786 entries, 0 to 39785
Data columns (total 15 columns):
id          39786 non-null int64
mem_id      39786 non-null int64
ln_amt      39786 non-null int64
term        39786 non-null object
rate        39786 non-null object
m_pay       39786 non-null float64
grade       39786 non-null object
sub_grd     39786 non-null object
emp_len     38705 non-null object
own_rnt     39786 non-null object
income      39786 non-null float64
ln_stat     39786 non-null object
purpose     39786 non-null object
state       39786 non-null object
dti         39786 non-null float64
dtypes: float64(3), int64(3), object(9)
memory usage: 4.6+ MB
```

```
loandf.describe(include=['O'])
```

	term	rate	grade	sub_grd	emp_len	own_rnt	ln_stat	purpose	state
count	39786	39786	39786	39786	38705	39786	39786	39786	39786
unique	2	371	7	35	11	5	7	14	50
top	36 months	10.99%	B	B3	10+ years	RENT	Fully Paid	debt_consolidation	CA
freq	29088	958	12029	2918	8905	18906	33669	18684	7101

Figure 8-1. *Attributes for Character Value Columns*

The `loandf.info()` method shows the `rate` column has a data type of `object` indicating they are string values. Similarly, the `term` column has a data type of `object`.

The `loandf.describe(include=['O'])` method provides further detail revealing the values for the `rate` column having a trailing percent sign (%) and the `term` column values are followed by the string 'months.'

In order to effectively use the `rate` column in any mathematical expression, we need to modify the values by

1. Stripping the percent sign

2. Mapping or casting the data type from character to numeric

3. Dividing the values by 100 to convert from a percent value to a decimal value

In the case of the `term` column values, we need to

1. Strip the string 'months' from the value

2. Map the data type from character to numeric

Both modifications are shown in Listing 8-10.

Listing 8-10. Basic Data Wrangling

```
>>> loandf['rate'] = loandf.rate.replace('%','',regex=True).
astype('float')/100
>>> loandf['rate'].describe()
count    39786.000000
mean         0.120277
std          0.037278
min          0.054200
25%          0.092500
50%          0.118600
75%          0.145900
max          0.245900
Name: rate, dtype: float64
>>> loandf['term'] = loandf['term'].str.strip('months').astype('float64')
>>> loandf['term'].describe()
count    39786.000000
mean        42.453325
std         10.641299
min         36.000000
25%         36.000000
50%         36.000000
```

```
75%              60.000000
max              60.000000
Name: term, dtype: float64
```

The syntax

```
loandf['rate'] =
loandf.rate.replace('%',",regex=True).astype('float')/100
```

performs an in-place modification to the df['rate'] column by calling the replace() method to dynamically replace values. In this case, the first argument to the replace() method is '%', indicating the percent sign (%) is the source string to replace. The second argument is " to indicate the replacement excerpt. Notice there is no space between the quotes, in effect, stripping the percent sign from the string. The third argument regex='True' indicates the replace() argument is a string.

The astype attribute is chained to the replace() method call and maps or casts the loandf['rate'] column's data type from object (strings) to a float (decimal value). The resulting value is then divided by 100.

Next, the describe() attribute is attached to the loandf['rate'] column and returns basic statistics for the newly modified values.

The syntax

```
loandf['term'] = loandf['term'].str.strip('months').astype('float64')
```

performs a similar in-place update operation on the loandf['term'] column. The strip() method removes the string 'months' from the values. Chaining the astype attribute casts this column from an object data type to a float64 data type.

Of course, we could have applied the str.strip() method to the percent (%) sign for the df['rate'] column rather than calling the replace() method.

Write DataFrame to SAS Dataset

The pandas IO Tools library does not provide a method to export DataFrames to SAS datasets. As of this writing, the SASPy module is the only Python module providing this capability. In order to write a DataFrame to a SAS dataset, we need to define two objects in the Python session.

The first object to make known to Python is the Libref to the target SAS library where the SASdata is to be created from the exported DataFrame. This object is defined by calling the sas.saslib() method to establish a SAS Libref to the target SASdata library. This step is not needed if the target SASdata library is the WORK library or if there are Libref defined as part of the autoexec processing described in Listing 8-7. Also note your site may have Libref defined with autoexec.sas processing independent of the approach described in Listing 8-7. In any of these cases, if a Libref is already known at SASPy initialization time, then you can omit this step. The assigned_librefs method returns a list of SAS Libref available in the current SASPy session, as illustrated in Listing 8-11.

Listing 8-11. SASPy assigned_librefs() Method

```
>>> import pandas as pd
>>> import saspy
>>>
>>> sas = saspy.SASsession(cfgname='winlocal', results='HTML')
SAS Connection established. Subprocess id is 17372

>>> sas.assigned_librefs()
['WORK', 'SASHELP', 'SASUSER']
```

The second step writes the DataFrame rows and columns into the target SAS dataset by calling the dataframe2sasdataset() method. Luckily, we can use the alias df2sd().

Define the Libref to Python

With the loandf DataFrame shaped appropriately, we can write the DataFrame as a SAS dataset illustrating these two steps. Step 1 defines the target Libref by calling the sas.saslib() method. This feature is illustrated in Listing 8-12.

The sas.saslib() method accepts four parameters. They are

1. Libref, in this case, sas_data defining the SASdata library location.

2. engine, or access method. In this case, we are using the default BASE engine. If accessing an SQL Server table, we would supply SQLSRV, or ORACLE if accessing an Oracle table, and so on.

3. path, the filesystem location for the BASE data library, in this case, C:\data.

4. options, which are SAS engine or engine supervisor options. In this case, we are not supplying options. An example would be SCHEMA= option to define the schema name for SAS/Access to SQL/Server. Any valid SAS LIBNAME option can be passed here.

Listing 8-12. Define the Libref to Python

```
>>> sas.saslib('sas_data', 'BASE', 'C:\data')

26    libname sas_data BASE  'C:\data'  ;
NOTE: Libref SAS_DATA was successfully assigned as follows:
      Engine:         BASE
      Physical Name: C:\data
```

Executing this particular call to the sas.saslib() method, the SASPy module forms the SAS LIBNAME statement

```
libname sas_data BASE  'C:\data'  ;
```

and sends the statement for processing to the attached SAS sub-process on your behalf.

Write the DataFrame to a SAS Dataset

Step 2 is to export the DataFrame rows and columns into the target SAS dataset. This is accomplished by calling the sas.df2sd() method. This feature is illustrated in Listing 8-13.

The sas.df2sd() method has five parameters. They are

1. The input DataFrame to be written as the output SAS dataset, in this case, the loandf DataFrame created previously.

2. table= argument which is the name for the output SAS dataset, excluding the Libref which is specified as a separate argument.

3. libref= argument which, in our case is 'sas_data' created earlier by calling the sas.saslib() method.

4. results= argument which in our case uses the default value
    PANDAS. Alternatively, this argument accepts HTML or TEXT as
    targets.

5. keep_outer_quotes= argument which in our case uses the default
    value False to strip any quotes from delimited data. If you want to
    keep quotes as part of the delimited data values, set this argument
    to True.

Listing 8-13. Write the DataFrame to a SAS Dataset

```
>>> loansas = sas.df2sd(loandf, table='loan_ds', libref='sas_data')
>>>
>>> sas.exist(table='loan_ds', libref='sas_data')
True
>>> print(type(loansas))
<class 'saspy.sasbase.SASdata'>
```

The syntax

```
loansas = sas.df2sd(loandf, table='loan_ds', libref='sas_data')
```

defines the SASdata object named loansas to Python and exports the DataFrame
loandf created in Listing 8-8 to the SAS dataset sas_data.loan_ds. By assigning the
sas.df2sd() method call to the loansas object, we now have a way to refer to the SAS
dataset sas_data.loan_ds within the Python context.

The syntax

```
>>> sas.exist(table='loan_ds', libref='sas_data')
False
```

is a method call for truth testing returning a Boolean. This is useful for scripting more
complex Python programs using the SASPy module for branching logic based on the
presence or absence of a particular SAS dataset.

Finally, the type() method call shows that the loansas object is a SASdata object
which references a SAS dataset or SAS View.

Now that the permanent SAS dataset exists and is mapped to the Python object
loansas, we can manipulate this object in a more Pythonic fashion. The loansas SASdata
Object has several available methods. Some of these methods are displayed in Figure 8-2.

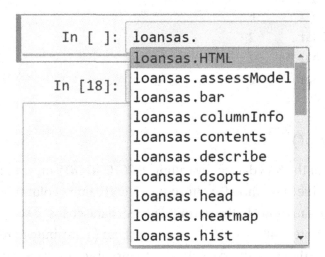

Figure 8-2. *SASdata Object Methods*

The methods for the SASdata Object are displayed by entering the syntax

`loansas.`

into the cell of a Jupyter notebook and pressing the <tab> key.

Consider Listing 8-14.

Listing 8-14. Return Column Information

```
>>> loansas.columnInfo()
```

```
                  The CONTENTS Procedure
     Alphabetic List of Variables and Attributes
#     Variable    Type     Len

15    dti         Num       8
9     emp_len     Char      9
7     grade       Char      1
1     id          Num       8
11    income      Num       8
3     ln_amt      Num       8
12    ln_stat     Char      18
6     m_pay       Num       8
2     mem_id      Num       8
10    own_rnt     Char      8
13    purpose     Char      18
```

```
5      rate        Char      6
14     state       Char      2
8      sub_grd     Char      2
4      term        Char      10
```

The syntax

```
loansas.columnInfo()
```

returns metadata for the SAS dataset by calling PROC CONTENTS on your behalf similar to the loansdf.describe() method for returning a DataFrame's column attributes. Recall the loansas object is mapped to the permanent SAS dataset sas_data.loan_ds.

Figure 8-3 illustrates calling the SASdata Object bar() attribute to render a histogram for the loan status variable, in this case, ln_stat. For this example, execute the code in Listing 8-15 in a Jupyter notebook. To start a Jupyter notebook on Windows, from a terminal session, enter the command

```
> python -m notebook
```

To start a Jupyter notebook on Linux, from a terminal session, enter the command

```
$ jupyter notebook &
```

Copy the program from Listing 8-15 into a cell and press the >|Run button.

Listing 8-15. Loan Status Histogram

```
import pandas as pd
import saspy

url = url      = "https://raw.githubusercontent.com/RandyBetancourt/
PythonForSASUsers/master/data/LC_Loan_Stats.csv"

loandf = pd.read_csv(url,
    low_memory=False,
    usecols=(0, 1, 2, 3, 4, 5, 6, 7, 8, 9, 10, 12, 13, 15, 16),
    names=('id',
                'mem_id',
                 'ln_amt',
                 'term',
                'rate',
                 'm_pay',
```

```
                'grade',
                'sub_grd',
                'emp_len',
              'own_rnt',
                'income',
                'ln_stat',
                'purpose',
                'state',
                'dti'),
        skiprows=1,
        nrows=39786,
        header=None)

sas = saspy.SASsession(cfgname='winlocal', results='HTML')
sas.saslib('sas_data', 'BASE', 'C:\data')
loansas = sas.df2sd(loandf, table='loan_ds', libref='sas_data')
loansas.bar('ln_stat')
```

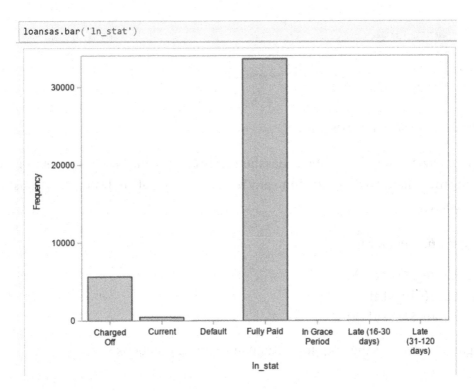

Figure 8-3. *Histogram for ln_stat Column*

We can see from the histogram that approximately 5000 loans are charged off, meaning the customer defaulted. Since there are 39,786 rows in the dataset, this represents a charge-off rate of roughly 12.6%.

During development of Python scripts used to call into the SASPy module, you will want access to the SAS log for debugging.

The syntax

```
print(sas.saslog())
```

returns the log for the entire SAS sub-process which is truncated here. Figure 8-4 shows part of the SAS log executing the statement from a Jupyter notebook.

```
In [14]:  print(sas.saslog())
167711    ! ods graphics on / outputfmt=png;
NOTE: Writing HTML5(SASPY_INTERNAL) Body file: _TOMODS1
167712        ;*';*";*/;
167713        proc sgplot data=sas_data.loan_ds;
167714            vbar ln_stat;
167715        run;

NOTE: PROCEDURE SGPLOT used (Total process time):
          real time           2.97 seconds
          cpu time            0.20 seconds

NOTE: There were 39786 observations read from the data set SAS_DATA.LOAN_DS.

167716        title;
167717
167718        ;*';*";*/;ods html5 (id=saspy_internal) close;ods listing;
167719
167720        %put E3969440A681A2408885998500000015;
E3969440A681A2408885998500000015
167721
```

Figure 8-4. *SASPy Returns Log*

The saspy.SASsession() object has the teach_me_SAS attribute when set to True, returning the generated SAS code from any method that is called. Listing 8-16 illustrates this capability.

Listing 8-16. Teach Me SAS

```
sas.teach_me_SAS(True)
loansas.bar('ln_stat')
sas.teach_me_SAS(False)
```

Figure 8-5 displays the output executed in a Jupyter notebook.

```
sas.teach_me_SAS(True)
```

```
loansas.bar('ln_stat')
```

```
proc sgplot data=sas_data.loan_ds;
        vbar ln_stat;
run;
title;
```

```
sas.teach_me_SAS(False)
```

Figure 8-5. *Teach_me_SAS Attribute*

Execute SAS Code

Another useful feature for the saspy.SASsession() object is the submit() method. This feature enables you to submit arbitrary blocks of SAS code and returns a Python Dictionary containing the SAS log and any output where 'LOG' and 'LST' are the keys respectively. Consider Listing 8-17.

Listing 8-17. SAS submit() Method

```
sas_code='''options nodate nonumber;
proc print data=sas_data.loan_ds (obs=5);
var id;
run;'''
results = sas.submit(sas_code, results='TEXT')
print(results['LST'])
```

The sas_code object is defined as a Python Docstring using three quotes ''' to mark the begin and end of the Docstring. In our case, the Docstring holds the text for a valid block of SAS code. The syntax

```
results = sas.submit(sas_code, results='TEXT')
```

calls the sas.submit() method by passing the sas_code object containing the SAS statements to be executed by the SAS sub-process. The results object receives the output, either in text or html form created by the SAS process.

In our case, we assign the output from PROC PRINT to the results Dictionary and call the print() method using the "LST" key to return the SAS output as

```
print(results['LST'])
```

The other key for the results Dictionary is 'LOG' and returns the section of the SAS log (rather than the entire log) associated with the block of submitted code. These examples are displayed in Figure 8-6 from a Jupyter notebook.

```
sas_code='''option nodate nonumber;
proc print data=sas_data.loan_ds (obs=5);
var id;
run;'''
```

```
results = sas.submit(sas_code, results='TEXT')
```

```
print(results['LST'])
```

Obs	id
1	872482
2	872482
3	878770
4	878701
5	878693

Figure 8-6. *SAS.submit() Method Output*

You can render SAS output (the listing file) with HTML as well. This capability is illustrated in Listing 8-18.

Listing 8-18. SAS.submit() method Using HTML

```
from IPython.display import HTML
results = sas.submit(sas_code, results='HTML')
HTML(results['LST'])
```

In this example, the same sas_code object created in Listing 8-17 is passed to the sas.submit() method using the argument results='HTML'.

The HTML results from a Jupyter notebook is rendered in Figure 8-7.

```
from IPython.display import HTML
results = sas.submit(sas_code, results='HTML')
HTML(results['LST'])
```

The SAS System

Obs	id
1	872482
2	872482
3	878770
4	878701
5	878693

Figure 8-7. *SAS.submit() Method with HTML Output*

Write SAS Dataset to DataFrame

SASPy provides the sas.sasdata2dataframe() method to write a SAS dataset to a pandas Dataframe. The alias is sas.sd2df(). The sas.sd2df() method portends numerous possibilities since a SAS dataset itself is a logical reference mapped to any number of physical data sources across the organization. Depending on which products you license from SAS, a SAS dataset can refer to SAS datasets on a local filesystem, on a remote filesystem, or SAS/Access Views attached to RDBMS tables, views, files, and so on.

The sas.sd2df() method has five parameters. They are

1. table: the name of the SAS dataset to export to a target DataFrame.

2. Libref: the libref for the SAS dataset.

3. dsopts: a Python Dictionary containing the following SAS dataset options:

    a. WHERE clause

    b. KEEP list

    c. DROP list

    d. OBS

e. FIRSTOBS

f. FORMAT

4. Method: The default is MEMORY. If the SAS dataset is large, you may get better performance using the CSV method.

5. Kwargs: which indicates the sas.sd2df() method can accept any number of valid parameters passed to it.

Consider Listing 8-19.

Listing 8-19. Export SAS Dataset to DataFrame

```
>>> import pandas as pd
>>> import saspy
>>> sas = saspy.SASsession(cfgname='winlocal')
SAS Connection established. Subprocess id is 17876

>>> ds_options = {'where'   : 'make = "Ford"',
...                'keep'    : ['msrp enginesize Cylinders Horsepower Make'],
...                }
>>> cars_df = sas.sd2df(table='cars', libref='sashelp', dsopts=ds_options,
method='CSV')
>>> print(cars_df.shape)
(23, 5)
>>> cars_df.head()
   Make   MSRP  EngineSize  Cylinders  Horsepower
0  Ford  41475         6.8         10         310
1  Ford  34560         4.6          8         232
2  Ford  29670         4.0          6         210
3  Ford  22515         3.0          6         201
4  Ford  13270         2.0          4         130
```

The ds_options object uses a Dictionary to pass valid SAS dataset options, in this case, a WHERE clause and a KEEP list. Notice the quoting needed for the value associated with the where key

```
'make = "Ford"'
```

The outer pair of single quotes is required since this string is a value defined for the Python Dictionary. The inner pair of double quotes are required since the SAS WHERE clause is applied to the character variable make.

The syntax

```
cars_df = sas.sd2df(table='cars', libref='sashelp', dsopts=ds_options,
method='CSV')
```

calls the sas.sd2df() method and exports the SAS dataset SASHELP.CARS to the pandas DataFrame called cars_df. Both the SAS KEEP list and the WHERE clause are applied when the call is made, thus subsetting variables and observations as part of creating the output cars_df DataFrame.

Up to this point, the examples have focused on the SASPy methods. The next example illustrates a simple pipeline to integrate SAS and Python processing logic in a single script.

The goal for this example is to illustrate the following steps:

1. Use SAS to perform an aggregation on an existing SAS dataset with the sas.submit() method, the dataset IN.LOAN_DS.

2. Export the SAS dataset to a Dataframe.

3. Call the pandas plot.bar() method to create a histogram of credit risk grades from the resulting DataFrame.

This logic is illustrated in Listing 8-20.

Listing 8-20. SAS Python Pipeline

```
>>> import pandas as pd
>>> import saspy
>>> sas = saspy.SASsession(cfgname='winlocal', results='Text')
SAS Connection established. Subprocess id is 13540

>>> sascode="'libname sas_data "c:\data";
... proc sql;
... create table grade_sum as
... select grade
...        , count(*) as grade_ct
... from sas_data.loan_ds
... group by grade;
... quit;"'
```

```
>>>
>>> run_sas = sas.submit(sascode, results='TEXT')
>>> df = sas.sd2df('grade_sum')
>>> df.head(10)
  grade  grade_ct
0    A     10086
1    B     12029
2    C      8114
3    D      5328
4    E      2857
5    F      1054
6    G       318
>>> df.plot.bar(x='grade', y='grade_ct', rot=0,
...             title='Histogram of Credit Grades')
```

In this example, the sas_code object is a Docstring containing the SAS statements

```
libname sas_data "c:\data";
proc sql;
   create table grade_sum as
   select grade
        , count(*) as grade_ct
   from in.loan_ds
group by grade;
quit;
```

These statements perform a group by aggregating the grade column in the sas_data.loan_ds SAS dataset and output the summarized result set to the SAS dataset WORK.grade_sum.

The syntax

```
df = sas.sd2df('grade_sum')
```

creates the df DataFrame by calling the sas.sd2df() method. The argument to the call is name of the SAS dataset opened on input; in this example, we specify the WORK.grade_sum dataset.

With the WORK.grade_sum dataset written as the df DataFrame, we can utilize any of the panda methods for subsequent processing.

Next the df DataFrame created from the SAS dataset WORK.grade_sum calls the plot.bar() method to produce a simple histogram. The y axis column grade_ct was created as part of the PROC SQL group by logic. The resulting histogram is displayed in Figure 8-8.

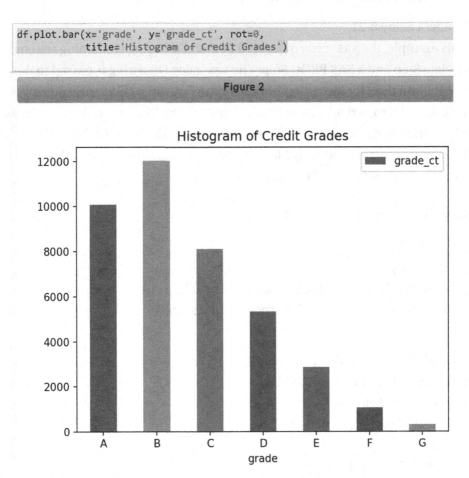

Figure 8-8. *Credit Risk Grades*

Passing SAS Macro Variables to Python Objects

Another useful feature of SASPy is the ability to pass SAS Macro variable values to and from Python objects. The SASPy SASsession object has two methods for passing values. The sas.symget() method assigns the value of a SAS Macro variable to a Python object using the syntax

```
py_obj = sas.symget(existing_sas_macro_var)
```

Use the sas.symput() method to pass the value of a Python object to a SAS Macro variable value using the syntax

```
sas.symput(sas_macro_variable, py_obj)
```

Consider Listing 8-21.

In this example, the sas_code object is a Python Docstring containing statements for a SASdata Step and a SAS PROC Step. The sas_code Docstring is passed to the sas.submit() method for execution by SAS. In the Data Step code, the value from the automatic SAS Macro variable &SYSERR is assigned to the Macro variable &STEP1_RC. Similarly, in the PROC step &SYSERR is assigned to the SAS Macro variable &STEP2_RC. &SYSERR is an automatic, read-only Macro variable containing the execution return code from the Data Step and most PROC steps.

Listing 8-21. sas.symget Method

```
>> import pandas as pd
>>> import saspy
>>> sas = saspy.SASsession(cfgname='winlocal')
SAS Connection established. Subprocess id is 16836

>>>
>>> sas_code="'data _null_;
... yes = exist('sashelp.class');
... if yes  = 1 then put
...     'Table Exists';
... else put
...     'Table Does NOT Exist';
... %let step1_rc = &syserr;
... run;
...
... proc summary data=sashelp.class;
... var weight;
... run;
... %let step2_rc = &syserr;
... "'
>>> run_sas = sas.submit(sas_code, results='TEXT')
>>>
>>> rc = []
```

398

```
>>> rc.append(sas.symget('step1_rc'))
>>> rc.append(sas.symget('step2_rc'))
>>> for i, value in enumerate(rc):
...     if value==0:
...         print ("Normal Run for Step {}.".format(i, value))
...     else:
...         print("Abnormal Run for Step {}. RC={}".format(i, value))
...
Normal Run for Step 0.
Abnormal Run for Step 1. RC=1012
>>> print(run_sas[('LOG')])
```

Passing the SAS Macro variable return codes from each SAS execution step to a Python object is accomplished calling the sas.symget() method. The syntax

```
rc = []
rc.append(sas.symget('step1_rc'))
rc.append(sas.symget('step2_rc'))
```

creates an empty list and then the append() method calls the sas.symget() method. The sas.symget() method call returns the codes and appends them to the rc list. The for loop iterates through the rc list using if/else logic to print the SAS return codes.

The statement

```
print(run_sas[('LOG')])
```

returns the SAS log fragment associated with just those statements executed by the last sas.submit() method. This is in contrast to the statement

```
print(sas.saslog())
```

which returns the SAS log for the entire session. Examining the log we can easily see the error.

```
35          proc summary data=sashelp.class;
36          var weight;
37          run;

ERROR: Neither the PRINT option nor a valid output statement has been given.
NOTE: The SAS System stopped processing this step because of errors.
```

Prompting

SASPy supports interactive prompting. The first type of prompting is done implicitly. For example, when running the SASsession() method, if any required argument to the connection method is not specified in the SAScfg_personal.py configuration file, then the connection process is halted, and the user is prompted for the missing argument(s).

The second form of prompting is explicit, meaning you as the application builder control where and how prompts are displayed and processed. Both the sas.submit() method and the sas.saslib() method accept an additional prompt argument. The prompt arguments are presented to the user at runtime and are connected to SAS Macro variables you supply either directly in your SAS code or as arguments to the method calls.

Prompt arguments are supplied as a Python Dictionary. The keys are the SAS Macro variable names, and the values are the Boolean values True or False. The user is prompted for the key values, and these entered values are assigned to the Macro variable. The Macro variable name is taken from the Dictionary key.

At SAS execution time, the Macro variables are resolved. If you specified False as the value for the key:value pair, then the user sees the input value as it is entered into the prompt area. On the SAS log, the user-entered values are rendered in clear text. If you specified True as the value for the key:value pair, then the user does not see the input values; nor is the Macro variable value rendered on the SAS log.

This feature is useful for obscuring password strings when assigning a LIBNAME statement to connect to a relational database. Figure 8-9 illustrates this feature.

```
In [44]:  sas.saslib('sqlsrvr', engine='odbc', options='user=&user pw=&pw datasrc=AdventureWorksDW',
                    prompt={'user': False, 'pw': True})

          Please enter value for macro variable user Randy
          Please enter value for macro variable pw ········
          65                                                      The SAS System
          4:37 Thursday, January 3, 2019

          732
          733          options nosource nonotes;
          736          %let user=Randy;
          737          libname sqlsrvr odbc user=&user pw=&pw datasrc=AdventureWorksDW;
          NOTE: Libref SQLSRVR was successfully assigned as follows:
                   Engine:         ODBC
                   Physical Name: AdventureWorksDW
          738          options nosource nonotes;
          741
          742
```

Figure 8-9. *SASPy Prompting*

In this example, the prompt= argument is a Python Dictionary:

```
{'user' : False, 'pw' : True}
```

Below the cell in the Jupyter notebook, you can observe the end-user prompt inputs. In this case, it defines two SAS Macro variables, &USER whose value is 'Randy' and &PW whose value is the password string needed by the SAS ODBC connection to the SQL Server Database, AdventureWorksDW. Notice also on the SAS log, the %LET assignment for &PW is not displayed.

Scripting SASPy

Up until this point, all of the examples encountered in this chapter are executed interactively, writing its output to either the Python console or in a Jupyter notebook. Once a Python script goes from development and testing into the production, we need the ability to make the script callable. In other words, execute the script in "batch" mode. SASPy provisions the set_batch() method to automate Python script execution making calls into SASPy. Consider Listing 8-22.

Combining some of the examples created previously in this chapter, this Python script executes in non-interactive mode with the following logic:

1. Creates the loandf DataFrame using the read.csv() method.

2. Performs basic Python data wrangling explained in Listing 8-10.

3. Calls the sas.saslib() method to expose the SAS Libref to the Python environment.

4. Calls the sas.df2sd() method to convert the loandf DataFrame to the SAS dataset sas_data.loan_ds.

5. Sets the SASPy execution to batch with the syntax

    ```
    sas.set_batch(True)
    ```

6. Calls the SASPy SASdata Object bar() method to generate a histogram with the syntax

    ```
    out=loansas.bar('ln_stat', title="Historgram of Loan Status",
    label='Loan Status')
    ```

The out object is a Dictionay containing two key:value pairs. The first key:value pair is the key 'LOG' whose value is the contents of the SAS log. The second pair is the key 'LST' whose value is the contents of the SAS Listing. The SAS Listing holds the HTML statements used to render the histogram. Since `sas.set_batch()` is set to True, this HTML is not rendered and instead is routed to a file. In this case, we are using

```
C:\data\saspy_batch\sas_output.html
```

as the target file location for the SAS-generated html output.

7. Assigns the SAS Listing (HTML source statements) to the object html_out object.

```
html_out = out['LST']
```

We only want the html source. Recall the out Dictionary has two key:value pairs. If both the SAS log statements and the SAS Listing output were written to the output file, our HTML output file will be invalid.

8. Uses the Python Standard Library, `open()`, `write()`, and `close()` calls to write the HTML source statements held in the html_out object to a file on the filesystem.

Listing 8-22. Automating Python Scripts Calling SASPy

```
>>> #! /usr/bin/python3.5
>>> import pandas as pd
>>> import saspy
>>> url = url = "https://raw.githubusercontent.com/RandyBetancourt/
PythonForSASUsers/master/data/LC_Loan_Stats.csv"
>>>
... loandf = pd.read_csv(url,
...      low_memory=False,
...      usecols=(0, 1, 2, 3, 4, 5, 6, 7, 8, 9, 10, 12, 13, 15, 16),
...      names=('id',
...             'mem_id',
```

```
...              'ln_amt',
...              'term',
...              'rate',
...              'm_pay',
...              'grade',
...              'sub_grd',
...              'emp_len',
...              'own_rnt',
...              'income',
...              'ln_stat',
...              'purpose',
...              'state',
...              'dti'),
...      skiprows=1,
...      nrows=39786,
...      header=None)
>>> loandf['rate'] = loandf.rate.replace('%','',regex=True).
astype('float')/100
>>> loandf['term'] = loandf['term'].str.strip('months').astype('float64')
>>>
>>> sas = saspy.SASsession(cfgname='winlocal')
SAS Connection established. Subprocess id is 1164

>>> sas.saslib('sas_data', 'BASE', 'C:\data')
25
26        libname sas_data BASE  'C:\data'  ;
NOTE: Libref SAS_DATA was successfully assigned as follows:
      Engine:        BASE
      Physical Name: C:\data
27
28
>>> loansas = sas.df2sd(loandf, table='loan_ds', libref='sas_data')
>>>
>>> sas.set_batch(True)
>>> out=loansas.bar('ln_stat', title="Historgram of Loan Status",
label='Loan Status')
```

```
>>> html_out = out['LST']
>>> f = open('C:\\data\\saspy_batch\\sas_output.html','w')
>>>
... f.write(html_out)
49354
>>> f.close()
```

This Python script is now callable using any number of methods such as a Windows shell, PowerShell, Bash shell, or being executed by a scheduler. On Windows the command to run the script is

```
> python Listing10.20_saspy_set_batch.py
```

For Linux the command to run the script is

```
$ python Listing10.20_saspy_set_batch.py
```

Datetime Handling

Recall from Chapter 7, "Date and Time," SAS and Python use different datetime offsets for their internal representation of datetime values. When data with datetime values are imported and exported between softwares, the exchange process poses a potential risk of corrupting data values. To understand the impacts of exchanging datetime values, consider Listing 8-23.

This example creates the df_dates DataFrame by using the DataFrame() constructor method to include the dates column, created by calling the date_range method, and the rnd_val column, created by calling the numpy random.randint() method, between the range of 100 and 1000 as random numbers.

Also notice we have included some elementary error handling for this script. The connection from the SASsession object checks the SASpid attribute which returns the process ID for the SAS sub-process. In the event the call to the SASsession method fails, an error message is printed and the script is exited at that point. The call to sys.exit() method is similar to the SAS ABORT statement with the ABEND argument which halts the SAS job or session. (The ABORT statement actions are influenced by how the SAS script is executed, whether it is interactive or batch.)

SASPy provisions the saslibrc() method to return the value SAS automatic Macro variable &SYSLIBRC to report whether the last LIBNAME statement executed correctly.

Here we use it as another error handler using the IF logic to exit the script if the
LIBNAME statement called by the saslib() method fails.

Listing 8-23. SASPy Datetime Handling

```
>>> import saspy
>>> import sys
>>> import pandas as pd
>>> import numpy as np
>>> from datetime import datetime, timedelta, date
>>>
>>> nl = '\n'
>>> date_today = date.today()
>>> days        = pd.date_range(date_today, date_today + timedelta(20),
freq='D')
>>>
>>> np.random.seed(seed=123456)
>>> data = np.random.randint(100, high=10000, size=len(days))
>>> df_dates = pd.DataFrame({'dates': days, 'rnd_val': data})
>>> print(df_dates.head(5))
        dates   rnd_val
0 2019-02-08      6309
1 2019-02-09      6990
2 2019-02-10      4694
3 2019-02-11      3221
4 2019-02-12      3740
>>>
>>> sas = saspy.SASsession(cfgname='winlocal', results='Text')
SAS Connection established. Subprocess id is 21024

>>> if sas.SASpid == None:
...     print('ERROR: saspy Connection Failed',
...             nl,
...   'Exiting Script')
...     sys.exit()
...
```

```
>>> print('saspy Process ID: ', sas.SASpid, nl)
saspy Process ID:   23600

>>>
>>> sas.saslib('sas_data', 'BASE', 'C:\data')

19
20            libname sas_data BASE  'C:\data'  ;
NOTE: Libref SAS_DATA was successfully assigned as follows:
      Engine:         BASE
      Physical Name: C:\data
21
22
>>> sas.assigned_librefs()
['WORK', 'SAS_DATA', 'SASHELP', 'SASUSER']
>>>
>>> if sas.SYSLIBRC() != 0:
...      print('ERROR: Invalid Libref',
...            nl,
...     'Exiting Script')
...       sys.exit()
...
>>> py_dates = sas.df2sd(df_dates, table='py_dates', libref='sas_data')
>>>
>>> py_dates.head(5)
Obs    dates                        rnd_val
1      2019-02-08T00:00:00.000000   6309
2      2019-02-09T00:00:00.000000   6990
3      2019-02-10T00:00:00.000000   4694
4      2019-02-11T00:00:00.000000   3221
5      2019-02-12T00:00:00.000000   3740
```

Calling the SASPy df2sd() method exports the df_dates DataFrame to the SAS dataset sas_data.py_dates. Displaying the first five observations of the dataset shows the datetime values from the df_dates DataFrame are correctly exported as SAS datetime values without user input. SASPy uses the E8601DT26.6 format to write the datetime values, as shown in Listing 8-24.

Listing 8-24. SASPy Default Datetime Format

```
>>> py_dates.columnInfo()
```

The CONTENTS Procedure

Alphabetic List of Variables and Attributes

#	Variable	Type	Len	Format
1	dates	Num	8	E8601DT26.6
2	rnd_val	Num	8	

Of course, we can use any valid SAS datetime format to render these values as shown in Listing 8-25.

Listing 8-25. SASPy sas.submit() Method Formatting Datetime Values

```
>>> sas_code = "'data _null_;
...              set sas_data.py_dates(obs=5);
...              put 'Datetime dates: ' dates mdyampm25.;
...              run;"'
>>> run_sas = sas.submit(sas_code, results='TEXT')
>>> print(run_sas[('LOG')])

50    data _null_;
51       set sas_data.py_dates(obs=5);
52       put 'Datetime dates: ' dates mdyampm25.;
53    run;

Datetime dates:         2/8/2019 12:00 AM
Datetime dates:         2/9/2019 12:00 AM
Datetime dates:        2/10/2019 12:00 AM
Datetime dates:        2/11/2019 12:00 AM
Datetime dates:        2/12/2019 12:00 AM
NOTE: There were 5 observations read from the dataset SAS_DATA.PY_DATES.
```

Now let's go the other direction and export the SAS dataset sas_data.py_dates to the sasdt_df2 DataFrame. Consider Listing 8-26.

Listing 8-26. Export SAS Datetimes to DataFrame

```
>>> sasdt_df2 = sas.sd2df(table='py_dates', libref='sas_data')
>>> print(sasdt_df2.head(5),
...       nl,
...       'Data type for dates:', sasdt_df2['dates'].dtype)
   dates        rnd_val
0 2019-02-08     6309
1 2019-02-09     6990
2 2019-02-10     4694
3 2019-02-11     3221
4 2019-02-12     3740
 Data type for dates: datetime64[ns]
>>>
... sasdt_df2["date_times_fmt"] = sasdt_df2["dates"].dt.strftime("%c")
>>> print(sasdt_df2["date_times_fmt"].head(5))
0    Sat Feb  8 00:00:00 2019
1    Sun Feb  9 00:00:00 2019
2    Mon Feb 10 00:00:00 2019
3    Tue Feb 11 00:00:00 2019
4    Wed Feb 12 00:00:00 2019
Name: date_times_fmt, dtype: object
```

Calling the SASPy sd2df() method exports a SAS dataset to a pandas DataFrame. Notice how the dtype attribute for the sasdt_df2['date_times'] column returns a datetime64 as the data type, indicating the SAS datetime variable date_times is exported to the pandas DataFrame as a datetime64 data type.

The syntax

```
sasdt_df2["date_times_fmt"] = sasdt_df2["date_times"].dt.strftime("%c")
```

creates the sasdt_df2["date_times_fmt"] column using the strftime method which returns the new column with a data type of object.

Summary

In this chapter we discussed the ability to integrate SAS and Python code together in a single Python execution context enabled by the SASPy module. We also presented examples on bi-directional interchange of data between a pandas DataFrame and SAS dataset as well as exchanging SAS and Python variable values. The SASPy module offers a compelling set of methods to integrate SAS and Python processing logic both interactively and through scripting methods.

APPENDIX A

Generating the Tickets DataFrame

The following Python script is associated with Listing 4-27 in Chapter 4, "Indexing and GroupBy."

The `tickets` DataFrame is generated by calling the `numpy` `randn` random number generator to create data values, defines rows and columns, and assigns both the row labels and the column labels with a MultiIndex object. The syntax

```
index = pd.MultiIndex.from_product([[2015, 2016, 2017, 2018], [1, 2, 3]],
names = ['Year', 'Month'])
```

creates the Python object `index` by calling the `MultiIndex.from_product()` constructor to form the MultiIndex structure as the Cartesian product for `Year` values by `Month` values. This structure provides row labels for the `tickets` DataFrame shown in Listing 4-27. The MultiIndex object enables the "nesting" of the `Month` levels inside the `Year` levels for the rows.

Similarly, the syntax

```
columns = pd.MultiIndex.from_product([['City', 'Suburbs', 'Rural'],
['Day', 'Night']], names = ['Area', 'When'])
```

creates the Python object columns by calling the `MultiIndex.from_product()` constructor to form the MultiIndex structure as the Cartesian product for Area levels by When levels. This structure provides the column labels nesting Area levels ('City', 'Rural', 'Suburbs') inside the When levels ('Day', 'Night').

Data values are generated with the syntax

```
data = np.round(np.random.randn(12, 6),2)
```

© Randy Betancourt, Sarah Chen 2019
R. Betancourt and S. Chen, *Python for SAS Users*, https://doi.org/10.1007/978-1-4842-5001-3

data is a 12 row by 6 column array created by calling the numpy random number generator randn. The resulting values are rounded two places to the right of the decimal.

The second call to the data = assignment

```
data = abs(np.floor_divide(data[:] * 100, 5))
```

updates values in the array using the syntax data[:] replacing them by multiplying array elements by 100 and dividing this product by 5. The abs() function returns their absolute values.

Finally, the syntax

```
tickets = pd.DataFrame(data, index=index, columns=columns).sort_index().
sort_index(axis = 1)
```

constructs the tickets DataFrame. The attribute sort_index sorts the "nested" row label values (created with the index object described previously), and the attribute sort_index(axis = 1) sorts the "nested" column values (created with the columns object described previously). Recall that axis = 0 refers to rows and axis = 1 refers to columns.

```
>>> import pandas as pd
>>> import numpy as np
>>> np.random.seed(654321)
>>> idx = pd.MultiIndex.from_product([[2015, 2016, 2017, 2018],
...                          [1, 2, 3]],
...                  names = ['Year', 'Month'])
>>> columns=pd.MultiIndex.from_product([['City' , 'Suburbs', 'Rural'],
...                          ['Day' , 'Night']],
...                  names = ['Area', 'When'])
>>>
>>> data = np.round(np.random.randn(12, 6),2)
>>> data = abs(np.floor_divide(data[:] * 100, 5))
>>>
>>> tickets = pd.DataFrame(data, index=idx, columns = columns).sort_
index().sort_index(axis=1)
>>> print(tickets)
```

Area		City		Rural		Suburbs	
When		Day	Night	Day	Night	Day	Night
Year	Month						
2015	1	15.0	18.0	9.0	3.0	3.0	3.0
	2	11.0	18.0	3.0	30.0	42.0	15.0
	3	5.0	54.0	7.0	6.0	14.0	18.0
2016	1	11.0	17.0	1.0	0.0	11.0	26.0
	2	7.0	23.0	3.0	5.0	19.0	2.0
	3	9.0	17.0	31.0	48.0	2.0	17.0
2017	1	21.0	5.0	22.0	10.0	12.0	2.0
	2	5.0	33.0	19.0	2.0	7.0	10.0
	3	31.0	12.0	19.0	17.0	14.0	2.0
2018	1	25.0	10.0	8.0	4.0	20.0	15.0
	2	35.0	14.0	9.0	14.0	10.0	1.0
	3	3.0	32.0	33.0	21.0	24.0	6.0

Many-to-Many Use Case

In Chapter 5, "Data Management," we discuss table relationships as being one-to-one, one-to-many, or many-to-many. In a one-to-one relationship, or data model, with respect to the key columns, there is exactly one row in a table that is associated with exactly one row in the other table. Said another way, the key column values in both tables must be unique.

In a one-to-many data model, with respect to the key columns, there is exactly one row that is associated with multiple rows in the other table. All the examples in Chapter 5, "Data Management," illustrate a one-to-many relationship among the tables.

And of course, there is the case where neither key column values among tables are unique, in this case, a many-to-many data model.

In this appendix, we illustrate the results of a many-to-many join with the SAS Sort/Merge logic and with PROC SQL. This is followed by the pandas merge() and corresponding join() methods.

With SAS, in cases where the table relationships are one-to-one or one-to-many, a SORT/MERGE (match-merge) and a PROC SQL outer join produce the same result set. In the case where the table relationship is many-to-many, these techniques return different result sets.

This example illustrates differences between results created by the SAS Sort/Merge operation and a PROC SQL outer join in those cases where the table relationship is many-to-many. Observe the note in the log

NOTE: MERGE statement has more than one dataset with repeats of BY values.

This indicates a many-to-many relationship exists between the tables in the match-merge operation. The default SORT/MERGE operation for tables with a many-to-many relationship is illustrated in Listing B-1.

© Randy Betancourt, Sarah Chen 2019
R. Betancourt and S. Chen, *Python for SAS Users*, https://doi.org/10.1007/978-1-4842-5001-3

Listing B-1. SORT/MERGE for Tables with Many-to-Many Relationship

```
4   data left;
5   infile datalines dlm=',';
6       input id $3.
7       value_l;
8   list;
9   datalines;
```

```
RULE:           ----+----1----+----2----+----3----+----4----+----
1064            001, 4314
1065            001, 4855
1066            001, 4761
1067            002, 4991
1068            003, 5001
1069            004, 3999
1070            004, 4175
1071            004, 4101
```
NOTE: The dataset WORK.LEFT has 8 observations and 2 variables.

```
10  ;;;;
11
12  data right;
13  infile datalines dlm=',';
14      input  id $3.
15              value_r;
16  list;
17  datalines;
```

```
RULE:           ----+----1----+----2----+----3----+----4----+----
1080            004, 1133
1081            004, 1234
1082            004, 1111
1083            002, 1921
1084            003, 2001
1085            001, 2222
```
NOTE: The dataset WORK.RIGHT has 6 observations and 2 variables.

416

```
18  ;;;;
19
20  proc sort data=left;
21      by id;
22  run;
```

NOTE: There were 8 observations read from the dataset WORK.LEFT.
NOTE: The dataset WORK.LEFT has 8 observations and 2 variables.

```
23
24  proc sort data=right;
25      by id;
26  run;
```

NOTE: There were 6 observations read from the dataset WORK.RIGHT.
NOTE: The dataset WORK.RIGHT has 6 observations and 2 variables.

```
27
28  data merge_lr;
29      merge left
30            right;
31      by id;
32  run;
```

NOTE: MERGE statement has more than one dataset with repeats of BY values.
NOTE: There were 8 observations read from the dataset WORK.LEFT.
NOTE: There were 6 observations read from the dataset WORK.RIGHT.
NOTE: The dataset WORK.MERGE_LR has 8 observations and 3 variables.

```
33
34  proc print data=left;
35      id id;
36  run;
```

NOTE: There were 8 observations read from the dataset WORK.LEFT.

```
37  proc print data=right;
38      id id;
39  run;
```

Figure B-1 displays the left dataset by calling PROC PRINT.

id	value_l
001	4314
001	4855
001	4761
002	4991
003	5001
004	3999
004	4175
004	4101

Figure B-1. *Left Dataset*

Figure B-2 displays the right dataset.

id	value_r
001	2222
002	1921
003	2001
004	1133
004	1234
004	1111

Figure B-2. *Right Dataset*

In a SORT/MERGE with tables having a many-to-many relationship, the number of observations with duplicate values returned is equal to the maximum of duplicates from both tables. Figure B-3 displays the merge_lr dataset, created by sorting and merging the input left and right dataset.

id	value_l	value_r
001	4314	2222
001	4855	2222
001	4761	2222
002	4991	1921
003	5001	2001
004	3999	1133
004	4175	1234
004	4101	1111

Figure B-3. *Results of SORT/MERGE with Tables Having a Many-to-Many Relationship*

To understand the behavior for this SORT/MERGE example carefully, observe the values for id 001 in Figure B-3. To begin, the SAS Data Step SORT/MERGE logic does not produce a Cartesian product for the left and right tables and instead uses a row-by-row merge operation. This processing logic is

1. SAS reads the descriptor portion (header) of the left and right dataset and creates a program data vector (PDV) containing all variables from both datasets for the output merge_lr dataset.

   a. ID and value_l are contributed from the left dataset.

   b. value_r is contributed from the right dataset.

2. SAS determines which BY group should appear first. In this case, observation with the value 001 for ID is the same for both input datasets.

3. SAS reads and copies the first observation from the left dataset into the PDV.

4. SAS reads and copies the first observation from the right dataset into the PDV.

5. SAS writes this observation to the output dataset, merge_lr.

6. SAS looks for the second observation in the BY group in the left
    and right dataset. The left dataset has one; the right dataset
    does not. The MERGE statement reads the second observation in
    the BY group from the left dataset. And since the right dataset
    has only one observation in the BY group, the value 001 is retained
    in the PDV for the second observation in the output dataset.

7. SAS writes the observation to the output dataset. When both input
    datasets contain no further observations for the BY group, SAS
    sets all values in PDV to missing and begins processing the next
    BY group. It continues processing observations until it exhausts all
    observations from the input datasets.

Next consider Listing B-2. In this case, we call PROC SQL to execute a full outer join on
the left and right tables. In this example, an outer join with the keywords FULL JOIN
and ON returns both matched and unmatched rows from the left and right tables.

Listing B-2. PROC SQL Outer Join

```
5  proc sql;
6     select coalesce(left.id, right.id)
7               ,value_l
8               ,value_r
9      from left
10  full join
11      right
12  on left.id = right.id;
13  quit;
```

The results are displayed in Figure B-4.

	value_l	value_r
001	4761	2222
001	4314	2222
001	4855	2222
002	4991	1921
003	5001	2001
004	4175	1111
004	4175	1133
004	4175	1234
004	3999	1111
004	3999	1133
004	3999	1234
004	4101	1111
004	4101	1133
004	4101	1234

Figure B-4. *SAS Outer Join for Left and Right Tables*

The analog to the outer join with PROC SQL is illustrated in Listing B-3.

In this example, the left and right DataFrames are created by calling the DataFrame create method. Also notice how both DataFrames are created with the default RangeIndex.

Listing B-3. pandas merge with Many-to-Many Relationship

```
>>> left = pd.DataFrame([['001', 4123],
...                      ['001', 4855],
...                      ['001', 4761],
...                      ['002', 4991],
...                      ['003', 5001],
...                      ['004', 3999],
```

421

```
...                        ['004', 4175],
...                        ['004', 4101]],
...          columns=['ID', 'Value_l'])
>>> right = pd.DataFrame([['004', 1111],
...                        ['004', 1234],
...                        ['004', 1133],
...                        ['002', 1921],
...                        ['003', 2001],
...                        ['001', 2222]],
...          columns=['ID', 'Value_r'])
>>> nl = '\n'
>>>
>>> print(nl     ,
...       left    ,
...       nl      ,
...       right)
    ID  Value_l
0  001     4123
1  001     4855
2  001     4761
3  002     4991
4  003     5001
5  004     3999
6  004     4175
7  004     4101
    ID  Value_r
0  004     1111
1  004     1234
2  004     1133
3  002     1921
4  003     2001
5  001     2222
```

```
>>> merge_lr = pd.merge(left, right, how='outer', sort=True)
>>> print(merge_lr)
     ID  Value_l  Value_r
0   001     4123     2222
1   001     4855     2222
2   001     4761     2222
3   002     4991     1921
4   003     5001     2001
5   004     3999     1111
6   004     3999     1234
7   004     3999     1133
8   004     4175     1111
9   004     4175     1234
10  004     4175     1133
11  004     4101     1111
12  004     4101     1234
13  004     4101     1133
```

The syntax

```
merge_lr = pd.merge(left, right, how='outer', sort=True)
```

creates the merge_lr DataFrame as an outer join for the left and right DataFrames, creating the same table output as the SAS PROC SQL logic from Listing B-2.

Index

© Randy Betancourt, Sarah Chen 2019
R. Betancourt and S. Chen, *Python for SAS Users*, https://doi.org/10.1007/978-1-4842-5001-3

U, V

W, X, Y

Z

Printed in the United States
By Bookmasters